**AGS**® *Reading Skills for Life*

Level B
Teacher's Guide

AGS®

American Guidance Service, Inc.
Circle Pines, Minnesota 55014-1796
1-800-328-2560   www.agsnet.com

Content Reviewers

The publisher wishes to thank the following educators for their helpful guidance and review during the development process for *Reading Skills for Life*. Their assistance has been invaluable.

Jack Cassidy, Ph.D.
Professor of Education
Texas A&M University
Corpus Christi, Texas

James Johnston
Reading Specialist
Portsmouth High School
Portsmouth, New Hampshire

Alva Webb Jones, Ed.S.
Special Education Consultant
Richmond County Board of Education
Augusta, Georgia

Robin Pence
Reading Specialist
Clay High School
Clay County Schools
Green Cove Springs, FL

Ted Stuff
School Psychologist
Special Education
    Department Chair
McLaughlin High School
Anchorage, Alaska

Development and editorial services provided by Straight Line Editorial Development, Inc.

"Pull the Next One Up" by Marc Kelly Smith used by permission.

Level B Student Worktext Photo and Illustration Credits

Page 4, Jeff Greenberg/PhotoEdit; pp. 9, 18, 24, 67, 71, 76, 89, 94, 100, 107, 125, 129, 141, 147, 158, 165, Robert Stenlake; p. 13, Jean Schalk; pp. 37, 43, Aleksandra Remezova; p. 82, Spencer Grant/PhotoEdit; p. 112, Lynn Goldsmith/CORBIS; p. 113 (top), David Young-Wolff/PhotoEdit; p. 113 (middle), Nancy Sheehan/PhotoEdit; p. 113 (bottom), Michael Newman/PhotoEdit; p. 134, Reuters New Media Inc./CORBIS; p. 170, Duomo/CORBIS; p. 171, Timothy Rue/CORBIS

Publisher's Project Staff

Director, Product Development: Karen Dahlen; Associate Director, Product Development: Teri Mathews; Editor: Jody Peterson; Development Assistant: Bev Johnson; Designer and Cover Illustrator: Denise Bunkert; Design Manager: Nancy Condon; Desktop Publishing Specialists: Jack Ross, Sandra Tennyson; Desktop Publishing Manager: Lisa Beller; Purchasing Agent: Mary Kaye Kuzma; Executive Director of Marketing: Matt Keller; Marketing Manager: Brian Holl

ISBN 0-7854-2640-X

Product Number 91712

A 0 9 8 7 6 5 4 3 2 1

Contents

Reading Skills for Life Program Overview

Level P	Level A	Level B	Level C	Level D	Level E
Prereading to 1.5	1.5 to 2.0	2.0 to 2.5	2.5 to 3.0	3.0 to 4.0	4.0 to 6.0

What is Reading Skills for Life?

Reading Skills for Life is a comprehensive reading program designed to address the specific needs of students in grades 6–12 who have been unable to achieve reading success through traditional methods of instruction. The goal of *Reading Skills for Life* is to enable these students to achieve a functional level of reading fluency. To accomplish this goal, the program utilizes research-based methods proven to be effective for below-level readers. The program is structured to build on each student's level of literacy. Multiple entry points address a range of reading abilities. *Reading Skills for Life* has six levels.

Levels A–E progress developmentally. Students enter the program at the level that matches their proficiency. New skills are introduced and practiced one at a time, giving students the opportunity to master each skill before going on to the next. Students have multiple opportunities to review and practice the skills they learn. Level A begins with a reading level of approximately 1.5; by the end of Level E, students will be reading at about the sixth grade level and may successfully transition into a mainstream reading and language arts course.

Level P is designed for nonreaders and beginning readers who have gaps in their understanding of basic letter-sound correspondences or limited phonemic awareness. Level P provides prereading instruction in phonemic awareness, the alphabet, basic concepts about print, and the 35 basic letter-sound correspondences.

Evaluation and Placement

Reading Skills for Life offers remediation for struggling readers. Two assessments are available from AGS for use in determining which level is most appropriate for your students. See page 10 of this Teacher's Guide for information about the *Reading-Level Indicator* and GRADE.

Student Worktexts

In addition to teaching students the basic skills and strategies required for reading, *Reading Skills for Life* offers students many opportunities to practice reading. High-interest, controlled-vocabulary fiction and nonfiction selections are the center of every lesson and reinforce the skills students have been taught.

Ongoing Assessment

Reading Skills for Life provides teachers and students with timely information about each student's progress. Every lesson concludes with two pages of exercises, reinforcing and extending the skills that have been learned. Summaries of skills and strategies, along with extensive Chapter Reviews offer opportunities for review and re-teaching. Reproducible chapter and end-of-level tests check students' acquisition of skills at each level.

Comprehensive Teacher's Guides

Chapter Planning Guides give teachers the tools they need to plan for each student's needs. The consistent three-step teaching plan is easy to use: **Before Reading, Reading, After Reading**. Each annotated Teacher's Guide shows the related Student Worktext pages with all answers at point of use. Reproducible chapter tests, end-of-level tests, and record forms are included for each level.

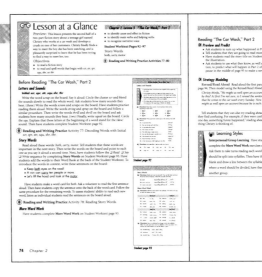

Reading Skills for Life addresses the needs of a diverse population of students. Lesson-specific activities for students with varying learning styles, learning disabilities, and limited English proficiency are included in each Teacher's Guide.

Learning Styles

Body/Kinesthetic Have groups of students role play a scene in which Jamal and one or more teammates conduct an interview with a TV talk show host. First have students choose roles and come up with questions and responses. Then have groups perform for the class.

Focus on ESL/LEP

To access prior knowledge and build vocabulary about basketball, draw or display a picture of a basketball game. Have students name things they see and describe what they know about basketball. List their responses on the board. Have students say new words after you.

Each Teacher's Guide also offers suggestions for helping students connect the content of the lessons to real-life applications at home, in the community, and the world of work.

Learning Styles

- ◆ Visual/Spatial
- ◆ Auditory/Verbal
- ◆ Body/Kinesthetic
- ◆ Logical/Mathematical
- ◆ Interpersonal/Group Learning

Focus on LD

Work with students to complete **More Word Work** on Student Worktext page 81. Write the first word, *patches*, on the board; read it aloud, and ask a volunteer to draw a line between the two syllables. Then have students write the word and divide it in the Student Worktext. Follow a similar procedure for the next four words, and have students work on their own to divide the last two words, *hatchling* and *teething*.

Application

Career Connection Students may be interested in finding out about careers that are related to sports but do not require an athlete's skill and stamina. These might include careers in sports reporting, radio or TV broadcasting, camera work, advertising, sports medicine, and administration. Students might invite a person involved with professional sports to the class to talk about career opportunities in sports.

Reading and Writing Practice

Hundreds of reproducible activities on CD-ROM give students additional practice with phonics and word study skills, automatic recognition of story vocabulary and high-frequency words, and the other skills instructed in the program.

Chapter Books

Levels A and B each include three small, easy-to-read chapter books for sustained reading and the opportunity to read for pleasure. Levels C, D, and E recommend selected books at the end of each chapter that closely match students' reading abilities and interests.

Reading Skills for Life Scope and Sequence

Phonemic Awareness	P	A	B	C	D	E
Phonemic Awareness	●	●	○	○	○	○

Phonics and Phonograms	P	A	B	C	D	E
Single Consonants (initial, final)	●	●	○	○	○	○
Double(d) Consonants (medial, final)	●	●	○	○	○	○
Consonant Blends (initial, 0al)	●	●	●	○	○	○
Consonant Digraphs (initial, final)	●	●	●	●	○	○
Consonant Digraphs (medial)		●	●	●	●	●
Silent Consonants		●	●	●	●	●
Short Vowels: CVC	●	●	●	●	●	●
Long Vowels: CVCe	●	●	●	●	●	●
Long Vowels: Digraphs		●	●	●	●	●
Long Vowels: Open Syllable		●	●	●	●	●
r-controlled Vowels		●	●	●	●	●
l-controlled Vowels		●	●	●	●	●
w-controlled Vowels			●	●	●	●
Vowel Variants			●	●	●	●
Vowel Diphthongs			●	●	●	●
Schwa			●	●	●	●

Word Study	P	A	B	C	D	E
Endings -s, -es	●	●	●	●	●	●
Ending -ies		●	●	●	●	●
Ending -ed	●	●	●	●	●	●
Ending -ing	●	●	●	●	●	●
Suffix -er (one who)		●	●	●	●	●
Suffix -or (one who)				●	●	●
Suffixes -ar, -ist (one who)						●
Prefixes un-, re-			●	●	●	●
Suffix -ly		●	●	●	●	●
Suffix -ful			●	●	●	●
Suffixes -er, -est (more, most)			●	●	●	●
Prefixes pre-, dis-				●	●	●
Suffixes -less, -ness				●	●	●
Prefixes de-, non-					●	●
Suffixes -tion, -sion, -ion					●	●
Prefixes in-, im-					●	●
Suffixes -ment, -y					●	●
Prefixes mid-, mis-						●
Prefixes sub-, trans-						●
Suffixes -able, -ible						●
Suffixes -ous, -eous, -ious						●

Reading Strategies	P	A	B	C	D	E
Make a Prediction	●	●	●	●	●	●
Summarize	●	●	●	●	●	●
Clarify	●	●	●	●	●	●
Reread/Read Ahead	●	●	●	●	●	●
Set a Purpose	●	●	●	●	●	●
Access Prior Knowledge	●	●	●	●	●	●
Use Context Clues	●	●	●	●	●	●

Reading Comprehension Skills	P	A	B	C	D	E
Topic		●	●	●	●	●
Main Idea and Supporting Details		●	●	●	●	●
Draw Conclusions	●	●	●	●	●	●
Cause and Effect	●	●	●	●	●	●
Note Sequence	●	●	●	●	●	●
Author's Purpose					●	●
Summarize		●	●	●	●	●
Compare and Contrast	●	●	●	●	●	●
Categorize	●	●	●	●	●	●
Fantasy vs. Realism		●	●	●	●	●

Critical Thinking Skills

Critical Thinking Skills	P	A	B	C	D	E
Make Judgments		●	●	●	●	●
Make Decisions		●	●	○	○	○
Problem Solving		●	●	○	○	●
Distinguish Fact from Opinion		●	●	●	●	●
Evaluate				●	●	●
Synthesize						●
Recognize Point of View and Bias						●

Spelling

Spelling	P	A	B	C	D	E
Spelling		●	●	●	●	●

Study Skills

Study Skills	P	A	B	C	D	E
Using a Dictionary		●	●	○	●	○
Using an Encyclopedia		●	●	●	○	●
Organizing Information		●	●	●	●	●
Using Graphic Aids	●	●	●	●	●	●
Following Directions	●	●	●	●	●	●
Test-Taking Strategies		●	●	●	●	●

Language

Language	P	A	B	C	D	E
Identifying Sentences		●	●	●	○	○
Subjects and Predicates		●	●	●	●	●
Common and Proper Nouns		●	●	●	●	●
Singular and Plural Nouns		●	●	●	●	●
Possessive Nouns			●	●	●	●
Action Verbs		●	●	●	●	●
Linking Verbs (including forms of *be*)		●	●	●	●	●
Subject-Verb Agreement		●	●	●	●	●
Main Verbs/Helping Verbs			●	●	●	○
Simple Tenses			●	●	●	●
Perfect Tenses					●	●
Pronouns		●	●	●	●	●
Possessive Pronouns			●	●	●	●
Adjectives		●	●	●	●	●
Adverbs			●	●	●	●
Prepositions			●	●	●	●
Prepositional Phrases				●	●	●
Compound Sentences					●	●
Complex Sentences						●
Contractions		●	●	●	●	●
Troublesome Words		●	●	●	●	○
Fixing Fragments and Run-ons				●	●	●
Capitalization		●	●	●	●	●
Punctuation		●	●	●	●	●

Writing

Writing	P	A	B	C	D	E
Persuasive		●	●	●	●	●
Narrative		●	●	●	●	●
Expository		●	●	●	●	●
Descriptive		●	●	●	●	●
Expressive		●	●	●	●	●
Functional/Real World		●	●	●	●	●

Literary Appreciation

Literary Appreciation	P	A	B	C	D	E
Story Elements		●	●	●	●	●
Theme		●	●	●	●	●
Narrative Voice		●	●	●	●	●
Appreciate Poetry		●	●	●	●	●
Literary Forms	●	●	●	●	●	●
Mood		●	●	●	●	●
Figurative Language			●	●	●	●

● Skill is instructed   ○ Skill is maintained

Building a Foundation for Reading Success

Success for Students with Special Needs

The individuals to benefit from *Reading Skills for Life* may include

- middle school or high school students who are not reading or are reading at a first or second grade level;
- students with learning disabilities;
- English language learners;
- students who are experiencing behavior problems or have experienced other risk factors that have interfered with their acquisition of basic reading skills.

Reading Skills for Life builds a foundation for reading success by addressing the needs of this varied population in a number of ways:

- Skills are introduced at a slow and steady pace, giving students an opportunity to master each skill before moving on to the next.
- Multiple opportunities for practice are presented with every skill introduced.
- Teaching methods address a variety of learning styles based on Howard Gardner's theory of multiple intelligences: visual/spatial, auditory/verbal, body/kinesthetic, logical/mathematical, and interpersonal/group learning.
- Activities are designed to help teachers capitalize on students' individual strengths and dominant learning styles. The activities reinforce each lesson by teaching or expanding upon the content in a different way.
- The content of the material is age and developmentally appropriate, high interest, and designed to motivate students to read by appealing to their interests and abilities.
- Teaching tips and activities for making the materials accessible to students with different needs appear throughout each Teacher's Guide.

Sample Teaching Tips

- ▶ Give students sufficient time to respond to questions.
- ▶ Limit the number or complexity of tasks to complete at one time.
- ▶ Narrow the focus of a question.
- ▶ Allow a student to answer orally instead of requiring a written response.
- ▶ Limit the amount of text a student encounters on a page.
- ▶ Identify phonetic elements in English that may pose difficulties for English language learners.

Phonics and Word Study

Reading Skills for Life offers a focused and comprehensive approach to reading instruction that provides explicit instruction in phonics and word attack strategies within the context of reading for meaning.

Phonemic Awareness is the ability to hear individual sounds (phonemes) in spoken words. Research has established that phonemic awareness plays a critical role in the early stages of reading acquisition (Adams 1994; Ehri 1994; Honig et al. 2000). Level P of *Reading Skills for Life* develops essential phonemic awareness skills, including recognizing phonemes and rimes and developing the ability to segment, blend, isolate, match, and manipulate sounds. Levels A–E strengthen students' basic phonemic awareness skills while developing more complex skills in the context of letter-sound relationships.

Systematic and Explicit Instruction in Phonics is central to *Reading Skills for Life*. Instruction proceeds at a slow, sequential pace and is recursive from level to level. Research has provided compelling evidence that explicit, systematic instruction in phonics can help older students who have not achieved reading mastery (Adams 1994; Chall 1996; Honig et al. 2000). The program provides instruction in the 35 basic correspondences by the end of Level P, and reinforces these skills in Levels A and B. *R*-controlled vowels, vowel variants, vowel diphthongs, other spellings for long vowel sounds, and exceptions to the rules are introduced in Level A and beyond. Students are taught the blending principle beginning with Level P, and this skill is practiced and reinforced with all the decodable words students are taught.

Phonograms are patterns of letters common to many words. Words with the same phonogram are often called *word families;* for example, the words *main, rain,* and *pain* all have the phonogram *ain*. Research has shown that nearly 500 primary-grade words can be derived from a set of just 37 phonograms (Adams 1994). *Reading Skills for Life* teaches more than 50 high-utility phonograms in the phonics lessons to which they correspond.

High-Frequency Words are drawn from Fry's *1000 Instant Words* (Fry 1997). Fry points out that just 300 words make up 65 percent of all written material. In addition, these same 300 words account for more than half the text of every newspaper article, textbook, children's story, or novel. The 1,000 words are introduced sequentially at a pace of approximately 100 words per level at Levels P, A, and B, and approximately 200 words per level at Levels C–E. Many of the words in Fry's list are in fact decodable using the basic letter-sound correspondences such as CVC, CVC*e*, CVVC, and *r*-controlled vowel patterns. Therefore, students will be able to decode many of these "sight words" at first occurrence, without introduction prior to the lesson story.

Word Recognition Strategies are taught throughout the program. Students learn a limited number (usually 3–6) of new content words before they read each story in the Student Worktext, practicing a five-step strategy for learning new words: They **hear, see, read, say**, and **write** each new word before it is encountered in a story. Students see and read each new word multiple times in the lesson and in subsequent stories.

Structural Analysis includes recognition of inflected endings, prefixes, suffixes, and certain kinds of structures such as compound words. According to Chall and Popp (1996), when students know prefixes and suffixes, they are better prepared to decode unknown multisyllabic words. Knowing prefixes and suffixes will also help in learning the meaning of a word. *Reading Skills for Life* introduces the most common prefixes, suffixes, and inflected endings, along with the generalizations that accompany them. Students practice forming, reading, and writing many words having each targeted structure.

For a list of phonics and word study skills instructed in *Reading Skills for Life*, see the Scope and Sequence of Skills on page 6 of this Teacher's Guide. On pages 12–13, you'll find the complete scope and sequence of skills instructed at this level of the program.

Integrating Skills and Strategies

Reading Skills for Life offers a comprehensive approach to teaching reading that includes direct instruction in the most useful skills and strategies:

Reading Comprehension and Critical Thinking Skills
Each lesson in the Student Worktext offers multiple opportunities for students to think literally, inferentially, and critically about the text. See the Scope and Sequence of Skills on pages 6–7 for a complete list of reading comprehension and critical thinking skills instructed in the program.

Strategic Reading Skills
Reading Skills for Life provides explicit, ongoing instruction in reading strategies. Teachers model reading strategies in the context of guiding students as they read each lesson's selection. Students are taught to make predictions about a story before reading it, to check and revise those predictions often while reading, and to use other useful reading strategies to help them get the most out of reading.

Study Skills
Functional skills that help students locate and organize information, interpret graphic data, and prepare for tests are woven across the program. At Levels A–E, *Reading Skills for Life* targets the most useful and essential skills for students attaining a basic level of literacy, and for students who are preparing to enter the working world.

Spelling Skills Research (e.g., Adams 1994) has shown that learning how to spell words (encoding) is a companion skill to learning how to read words (decoding). When students write words and word patterns they have learned to read, their visual sense of each word is reinforced kinesthetically. *Reading Skills for Life* teaches spelling patterns in conjunction with phonics skills, and provides practice with regular and irregular words most often needed for writing and words that are frequently misspelled.

Writing and Language The writing strand in *Reading Skills for Life* is developmental, cautious, and practical. Skills and expectations are linked to the reading scope and sequence. They reflect competencies students typically are required to demonstrate on state performance assessments and they emphasize real-life writing forms students will need on the job.

Literary Appreciation Skills Effective readers do not simply apply skills to comprehend text—they also enjoy what they read and appreciate literature. *Reading Skills for Life* introduces students to a variety of genres and literary forms, and helps students appreciate what the various forms have to offer.

Research References and Bibliography

Adams, M. J. 1994. *Beginning to read: Thinking and learning about print.* Cambridge, MA: MIT Press.

Anderson, R. C., E. H. Hiebert, J. A. Scott, and I. A. G. Wilkinson. 1985. *Becoming a nation of readers: The report of the Commission on Reading.* Washington, DC: National Institute of Education.

Chall, J. S. 1996. *Learning to read: The great debate.* 3rd ed. Fort Worth, TX: Harcourt Brace.

Chall, J. S., and H. M. Popp. 1996. *Teaching and assessing phonics: Why, what, when, how.* Cambridge, MA: Educator's Publishing Service.

Crawley, S. J., and K. Merritt. 2000. *Remediating reading difficulties.* 3rd ed. New York: McGraw-Hill.

Ehri, L. 1994. Development of the ability to read words: Update. In R. Ruddell, M. Ruddell, and H. Singer, eds., *Theoretical models and processes of reading.* Newark, DE: International Reading Association.

Fry, E. 1997. *1000 instant words.* Chicago: Contemporary Books.

Fry, E., J. E. Kress, and D. L. Fountoukidis. 2000. *The reading teacher's book of lists.* 4th ed. Paramus, NJ: Prentice Hall.

Honig, B. 2001. *Teaching our children to read: The components of an effective, comprehensive reading program.* 2nd ed. Thousand Oaks, CA: Corwin Press.

Honig, B., L. Diamond, L. Gutlohn, and J. Mahler. 2000. *Teaching reading: Sourcebook for kindergarten through eighth grade.* Novato, CA: Arena Press.

Miller, W. H. 1993. *Complete reading disabilities handbook.* West Nyack, NY: The Center for Applied Research in Education.

Simmons, D. C., and E. J. Kameenui, eds. 1998. *What reading research tells us about children with diverse learning needs: Bases and basics.* Mahwah, NJ: Erlbaum.

For more information on the research that supports the *Reading Skills for Life* instructional approaches outlined here, please go to **www.agsnet.com** or call Customer Service at **1-800-328-2560** to request a summary of research.

Using Reading Skills for Life

Evaluation and Placement

How do you know which level of *Reading Skills for Life* will be most appropriate for your students? Where should you begin? The evaluation and assessment methods described below will help you answer this question.

Teacher Judgment You may already know a general reading level for your students. You may have obtained this information from informal testing or by observation. If you are confident you know the level at which your students are reading, use this guide to determine where to start.

If your students are reading at this grade level	Begin here with *Reading Skills for Life:*
Less than 1.5	Level P
1.5	Level A
2.0	Level B
2.5	Level C
3.0	Level D
4.0	Level E

Reading-Level Indicator

The *Reading-Level Indicator* is a quick screening measure of reading ability available from AGS. Norm-referenced scores are reported as grade equivalents. The screener can be individually or group administered in less than 15 minutes, and it samples both vocabulary and basic comprehension skills. Use the Placement Chart on the right to identify where to place your students in *Reading Skills for Life*.

GRADE/Group Reading Assessment and Diagnostic Evaluation
The GRADE is a developmentally-based, group-administered diagnostic reading assessment also available from AGS. Developed for use with individuals ages 4–25, GRADE provides reliable diagnostic results for each student. If you need comprehensive diagnostic information about your students' reading abilities, use GRADE. The GRADE will also provide a grade-equivalent score. Use the chart below for placement in *Reading Skills for Life.*

Using Grade-Equivalent Scores for Placement

To place students in *Reading Skills for Life,* use the grade-equivalent score for the Instructional Reading Level from the *Reading-Level Indicator,* or the grade-equivalent score of the Total Test Score from the GRADE.

Placement Chart

If the grade-equivalent score is	Begin here with *Reading Skills for Life:*
1.0 or lower	Level P
1.1 to 1.9	Level A
2.0 to 2.4	Level B
2.5 to 3.0	Level C
3.1 to 4.0	Level D
4.1 to 6.0	Level E

Note: The grade-equivalent score from the Reading-Level Indicator is the median of the normative group based on two subtests, Vocabulary and Sentence Comprehension. The grade-equivalent score from the GRADE is the median of the normative group based on several subtests of items including Passage Comprehension. Therefore, there may be slight differences between the two grade equivalents. If you have given both assessments to a student, it is recommended that you use the grade-equivalent score from the GRADE.

Sequence of Instruction

Each lesson and chapter in *Reading Skills for Life* follows a predictable sequence. The easy-to-use, three-step teaching plan supports teachers in guiding students through the Student Worktext lessons. In addition to the **Before Reading, Reading,** and **After Reading** sequence, **Reinforce & Extend** at the end of each lesson in the Teacher's Guide includes spelling, study skills, language arts, writing, and literary appreciation activities, along with additional Reading and Writing Practice on CD-ROM.

The chart on the following page summarizes the sequence of instruction in *Reading Skills for Life.*

For more information about the *Reading-Level Indicator* or GRADE, please go to **www.agsnet.com** or call Customer Service at **1-800-328-2560**.

Reading Skills for Life Sequence of Instruction

STEP 1 Before Reading

Letters and Sounds
- Explicit instruction in phonics
- Introduction and practice with phonograms
- Reading and Writing Practice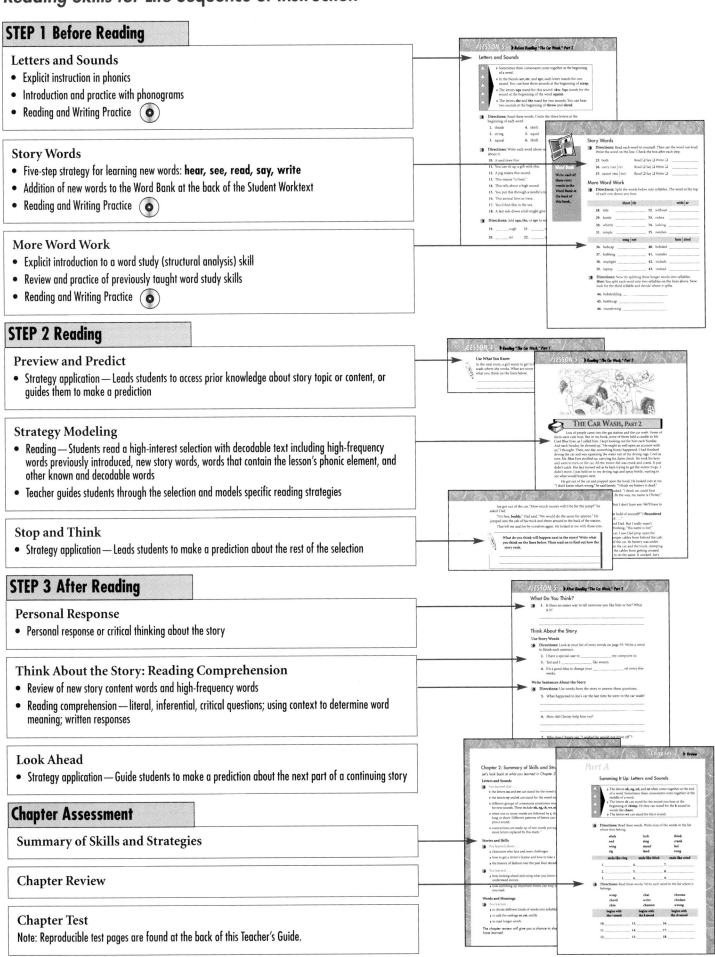

Story Words
- Five-step strategy for learning new words: **hear, see, read, say, write**
- Addition of new words to the Word Bank at the back of the Student Worktext
- Reading and Writing Practice

More Word Work
- Explicit introduction to a word study (structural analysis) skill
- Review and practice of previously taught word study skills
- Reading and Writing Practice

STEP 2 Reading

Preview and Predict
- Strategy application—Leads students to access prior knowledge about story topic or content, or guides them to make a prediction

Strategy Modeling
- Reading—Students read a high-interest selection with decodable text including high-frequency words previously introduced, new story words, words that contain the lesson's phonic element, and other known and decodable words
- Teacher guides students through the selection and models specific reading strategies

Stop and Think
- Strategy application—Leads students to make a prediction about the rest of the selection

STEP 3 After Reading

Personal Response
- Personal response or critical thinking about the story

Think About the Story: Reading Comprehension
- Review of new story content words and high-frequency words
- Reading comprehension—literal, inferential, critical questions; using context to determine word meaning; written responses

Look Ahead
- Strategy application—Guide students to make a prediction about the next part of a continuing story

Chapter Assessment

Summary of Skills and Strategies

Chapter Review

Chapter Test
Note: Reproducible test pages are found at the back of this Teacher's Guide.

Reading Skills for Life Scope and Sequence-Level B

	Lesson	Phonics and Phonograms	Word Study	Reading Strategy	Reading Comprehension Skill	Critical Thinking Skill
CHAPTER 1	Lesson 1, "A Plan for Cash"	Short Vowels *a, e, i, o, u*; Short *e* Spelled *ea (ad, int, ot, ag, it, um, ead)*	CVC Endings *-s, -es*	Make a Prediction	Note Sequence	
	Lesson 2, "The Ad"	Long Vowels *a, e, i, o, u* CVC*e (ane, ive, ope)*	CVC vs. CVC*e*; *-ed, -ing*: Drop *e*, Double Consonant	Set a Purpose (Fiction)	Cause and Effect	
	Lesson 3, "Dog Trouble"	Long *e* Spelled *ee, ea, e, y, ey (eak, eal)*	CVVC	Use Context Clues	Summarize	
	Lesson 4, "How to Read a Want Ad"	Initial *sh, th, ch, wh*; Final *th, sh, tch*	Dividing 2-Syllable Words with Digraphs	Access Prior Knowledge		Compare and Contrast
	Lesson 5, "The Video Game," Part 1"	Long *a* Spelled *ai, ay (ay)*	Possessives with *'s*	Reread/Read Ahead	Draw Conclusions	
	Lesson 6, "The Video Game," Part 2"	Long *i* Spelled *igh, y, i, ie (ied)*	Change *y* to *i*	Summarize		Make Judgments
	Lesson 7, "The Teen Net Bosses"	Long *o* Spelled *oa, ow (ow)*	Compound Words: Dividing Compound Words	Set a Purpose (Nonfiction)	Recognize Topic	
	Lesson 8, "America's Young Inventors"	Long *u* Spelled *ue, oo, u, ew*	Medial Consonants: Closed VCCV	Access Prior Knowledge	Main Idea and Supporting Details	
CHAPTER 2	Lesson 1, "The Driver's License," Part 1	Final *nk, ng, nd, nt (ung)*	Schwa (consonant plus *le*): VC/CVV; V/CCV	Clarify	Draw Conclusions	
	Lesson 2, "The Driver's License," Part 2	/ou/ Spelled *ou, ow (ow, out, ound)*	Dividing Words with Diphthongs	Summarize	Categorize	
	Lesson 3, "Getting on the Road"	Initial /k/ Spelled *ch*; Initial /r/ Spelled *wr*	Endings *-er, -est*	Set a Purpose (Real Life)	Main Idea and Supporting Details	
	Lesson 4, "The Car Wash," Part 1	Contractions with *will, not, am, have, are, is*	Dividing Words with Blends	Access Prior Knowledge	Summarize	
	Lesson 5, "The Car Wash," Part 2	Initial Digraphs and Clusters: *str, thr, squ, scr, spr, shr*		Reread/Read Ahead	Cause and Effect	
	Lesson 6, "Video Dreams"	/oi/ Spelled *oy, oi (oy)*	Ending *-ly*	Set a Purpose		Make Decisions
	Lesson 7, "Rain Dance"	/ôr/ Spelled *or, ore, our (our)*		Use Context Clues	Fantasy vs. Realism	
	Lesson 8, "Fashion Time Line"	/ûr/ Spelled *er, ur, ir (urn)*	Ending *-er* (one who)	Make a Prediction (Nonfiction)	Author's Purpose	
CHAPTER 3	Lesson 1, "Twin Trouble"	/är/ Spelled *ar, are*		Make a Prediction	Note Sequence	
	Lesson 2, "Sisters First"	/âr/ Spelled *air, are (are)*		Use Context Clues	Author's Purpose	
	Lesson 3, "A Good Trade"	/ir/ Spelled *eer, ear (ear)*		Access Prior Knowledge		Problem Solving
	Lesson 4, "The Poetry Slam"	/f/ Spelled *gh, ph*; /j/ Spelled *dge, ge, gi, gy*		Summarize	Draw Conclusions	
	Lesson 5, "Poetry Slams—Words in Action"	/aw/ Spelled *aw (aw)*		Reread/Read Ahead	Summarize (Nonfiction)	
	Lesson 6, "Stage Struck"	/s/ Spelled *ce, ci (ace)*	Open VCV vs. Closed VCV	Set a Purpose	Categorize	
	Lesson 7, "X Games!"	Prefixes *un-, re-*		Clarify	Compare/Contrast	
	Lesson 8, "X Games Stars"	Suffixes *-ly, -ful*	Dividing Words with Prefixes and Suffixes	Summarize (Nonfiction)		Distinguish Fact from Opinion

Spelling	Study Skill	Language	Writing	Literary Appreciation
Adding -s or -es to Words with Short Vowels		Recognizing Sentences		Identifying Story Elements
Adding -ed and -ing: Drop Silent e; Double Final Consonant		Four Kinds of Sentences	A List	
Words with Long e Spelled ee, ea, e, y, ey		Subject (Complete)		Recognizing Forms of Literature: Fiction
Words with sh, th, ch		Subject (Simple)	A Phone Message	
Words with Long a Spelled ai, ay		Nouns	A Realistic Fiction Story	
Words with Long i Spelled igh, y, i, ie		Common and Proper Nouns	A Paragraph of Opinion	
Words with Long o Spelled oa, ow		Singular and Plural Nouns		Recognizing Forms of Literature: Nonfiction
Words with Long u Spelled ue, oo, u, ew		Singular and Plural Possessive Nouns	A How-to Paragraph	
Words Ending with Consonant plus le		Verbs	A Dialogue	
/ou/ Spelled ou, ow		Action Verbs	A Descriptive Paragraph	
	Using a Dictionary	Linking Verbs	A Paragraph of Information	
Contractions with will, not, am, have, are, is		Subject-Verb Agreement	An Advertising Poster	
Words with thr, str		Main Verbs and Helping Verbs		Recognizing Narrative Voice
	Using an Encyclopedia	Present Tense and Past Tense Verbs	A Journal Entry	
/ôr/ Spelled or, ore, our		Pronouns		Recognizing Theme
/ûr/ Spelled er, ur, ir		Possessive Pronouns	A Summary (Paraphrase)	
/är/ Spelled ar, are		Adjectives	An Invitation	
/âr/ Spelled air, are		Adverbs	A Two-Paragraph Report	
/ir/ Spelled eer, ear		Prepositions	A Business Letter	
	Organizing Information: List, Chart, Timeline	Capitalization		Appreciating Poetry
	Using Graphic Aids: Diagram, Map	End Punctuation	A Poem	
	Following Directions	Commas	A Personal Narrative	
	Test-Taking Strategies	Troublesome Words		Recognizing Mood
Adding Suffixes: Change y to i		Writing Dates and Addresses		Recognizing Similes

CHAPTER 1

CHAPTER 2

CHAPTER 3

Chapter 1 Planning Guide

Skills and Learning Objectives

	Student Pages	Phonics and Phonograms	Word Study	Reading Strategy
Lesson 1 A Plan for Cash	10–15	Short Vowels a, e, i, o, u; Short e Spelled ea (ad, int, ot, ag, it, um, ead)	CVC Inflected Endings -s, -es	Make a Prediction
Lesson 2 The Ad	16–21	Long Vowels a, e, i, o, u (CVCe) (ane, ive, ope)	CVC vs. CVCe; -ed, -ing: Drop e, Double Consonant	Set a Purpose (Fiction)
Lesson 3 Dog Trouble	22–27	Long e Spelled ee, ea, e, y, ey (eak, eal)	CVVC	Use Context Clues
Lesson 4 How to Read a Want Ad	28–33	Initial sh, th, ch, wh; Final th, sh, tch	Dividing 2-Syllable Words with Digraphs	Access Prior Knowledge (Use What You Know)
Lesson 5 The Video Game, Part 1	34–39	Long a Spelled ai, ay (ay)	Possessives with 's	Reread/Read Ahead
Lesson 6 The Video Game, Part 2	40–45	Long i Spelled igh, y, i, ie (ied)	Change y to i	Summarize
Lesson 7 The Teen Net Bosses	46–51	Long o Spelled oa, ow (ow)	Compound Words: Dividing Compound Words	Set a Purpose (Nonfiction)
Lesson 8 America's Young Inventors	52–57	Long u Spelled ue, oo, u, ew	Medial Consonants: Closed VCCV	Access Prior Knowledge (Use What You Know)

Independent Reading

Lost in the Mountains by Corinn Codye
Lesson Plan: Teacher's Guide pages 48–51

Assessment and Review

Chapter 1 Summary of Skills and Strategies:
Student Worktext page 58

Chapter 1 Review:
Student Worktext pages 59–66

Chapter 1 Test:
Teacher's Guide pages 144–147

Reading Comprehension/ Critical Thinking	Spelling	Study Skill	Language	Writing	Literary Appreciation	Learning Styles	Focus on LEP/ESL or LD	Application	Reading and Writing Practice Activities
Note Sequence	19		19		19	17	17		1–5
Cause and Effect	23		23	23			21		6–12
Summarize	27		27		27	25		26	13–17
Compare/Contrast	31		31	31		29		30	18–24
Draw Conclusions	33		33	33		33			25–31
Make Judgments	37		37	37		37		37	32–38
Recognize Topic	43		43		43		41	41	39–43
Main Idea and Supporting Details	47		47	47		45		45	44–49

Common Reading Errors

If the Student . . .

- cannot distinguish long vowels from short vowels
- relies too heavily on the initial sounds in words
- gives up on unknown words

- fails to make appropriate inferences

- confuses the sequence of events in written text

Then . . .

- → provide extra practice with the phonics skills in Chapter 1.
- → provide additional practice reading phonograms; model the blending principle.
- → encourage the student to skip the unknown word, finish reading the sentence, and use context clues to figure out the word's meaning.
- → teach the lesson on drawing conclusions in Lesson 2; encourage the student to pause and determine why events happen.
- → suggest that the student read more slowly and note signal words such as *first* and *next*; teach the lesson on noting sequence in Lesson 1.

Lesson at a Glance

Preview: This lesson presents the first part of a three-part fiction story about Rick, a boy who comes up with a plan to walk people's dogs in order to make money for his summer vacation.

Objectives
◆ to read a fiction story
◆ to read words that contain short vowels spelled with the CVC pattern and short *e* spelled *ea*
◆ to spell plural nouns with short vowels by adding *s* or *es*

◆ to note sequence in fiction
◆ to understand what a sentence is
◆ to identify the story elements of character, plot, and setting

Student Worktext Pages 10–15

Story Words
problem, almost, nothing, mountain, walking, door

⊙ **Reading and Writing Practice Activities 1–5**

Before Reading "A Plan for Cash"

Letters and Sounds

Short Vowels *a, e, i, o, u*; Short *e* Spelled *ea*

Write the words *can, wet, rip, lock,* and *cut* on the board. Read these words aloud and have students repeat them. Point out that each of these words has a short vowel sound. Then point out the consonant-vowel-consonant, or CVC, pattern in these words. Remind students that many words with this letter pattern have a short vowel sound.

Next, write the words *head* and *thread* on the board. Read the words aloud and have students repeat them. Ask students what vowel sound they hear in these words. (short *e*) Then ask a volunteer to circle the letters in each word that stand for this sound. (the letters *ea*) Explain that the letters *ea* sometimes stand for the short *e* sound. Then ask students what other sound the letters *ea* can stand for. (long *e*) Have students complete Student Worktext page 10.

⊙ **Reading and Writing Practice** Activity 1: Decoding Words with Short Vowels

Story Words

Read aloud these words: *problem, almost, nothing, mountain, walking, door.* Tell students that these words are important in the next story. Then write the words on the board and point to each one as you say it aloud a second time. Next, have students follow the ❑ *Read* ❑ *Say* ❑ *Write* sequence by completing **Story Words** on Student Worktext page 11. Have students add the words to the Word Bank at the back of the Student Worktext. To introduce the words in context, write these sentences on the board:

◆ Can you help me with this <u>problem</u>?
◆ I have <u>almost</u> as much food as you.
◆ <u>Nothing</u> you say will change what I think.
◆ We went for a hike up the <u>mountain</u>.
◆ John is <u>walking</u> his dog around the block.
◆ Please close the <u>door</u> when you go.

Have students make a word card for *problem.* Ask a volunteer to read the first sentence aloud. Then have students copy the sentence onto the back of the word card. Follow the same procedure for the remaining words. To assess students' ability to read each new word, listen as individual students read the sentences on the board aloud.

⊙ **Reading and Writing Practice** Activity 2: Reading Story Words.

More Word Work

Have students work in pairs to complete **More Word Work** on Student Worktext page 11.

⊙ **Reading and Writing Practice** Activity 3: Reading and Writing Words with *-s* or *-es.*

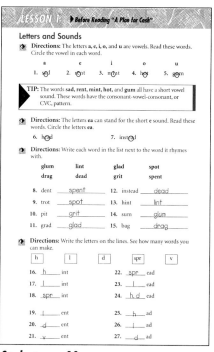

Student page 10

Student page 11

Reading "A Plan for Cash"

◆ *Preview and Predict*

- Tell students that they are about to read a story about a boy named Rick. Have a volunteer read the title of the story aloud. Point out Rick and his friend Karl in the illustration on Student Worktext page 13.
- Explain that Rick has just gotten out of school for summer vacation. He has big plans for the summer, but no money to make them happen. Ask students who have had jobs to describe some of the money-making opportunities available to young people.
- Read aloud the introductory sentences under **Use What You Know.** Have students work in small groups to make a list of other jobs kids can do.
- Have students share their responses. Then ask them to predict what Rick might do to get cash.

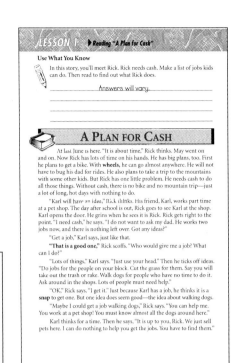

Student page 12

● Learning Styles

Visual/Spatial As students discuss money-making opportunities for the prereading discussion, display pictures showing people doing different kinds of jobs, or have students look through illustrated books or an encyclopedia and identify pictures showing jobs teens can do.

◆ *Strategy Modeling*

Make a Prediction Tell students that to make a prediction about a story is to make a guess about what might happen based on clues in the text and illustrations. Explain that making a prediction, and checking it as they read, can help readers keep track of story events. Model making a prediction. You might say:

Based on my preview, I know that Rick needs to make money. I predict that he will try to get a job. From the illustration on page 13, I see that Rick's friend works at a pet shop. Maybe Rick will try to get a job at the pet shop, too.

Invite students to make their own predictions about the story. Then have them read Student Worktext pages 12–13 to see if their predictions are correct. Point out that they will be asked to make another prediction after they have read page 12.

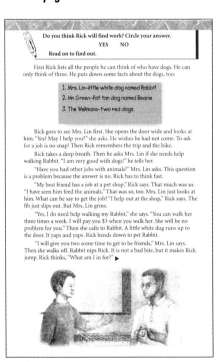

Student page 13

Focus on ESL/LEP

Explain and discuss the following terms and expressions used in the story:

- has lots of time on his hands
- to bug ("bother")
- a snap ("an easy task")
- up to you

After Reading "A Plan for Cash"

Personal Response: You Be the Judge

Discuss fibbing, or telling small lies, with students. Ask students if they think fibbing is ever a good idea, and if so, when and why. Then, as a class, discuss the questions under **You Be the Judge** on Student Worktext page 14. Have students write individual answers to the questions in their Student Worktext.

Think About the Story: Reading Comprehension

Have students complete the remaining items on Student Worktext pages 14 and 15 independently or in pairs. Check their responses to help you assess their comprehension of the story. If students' responses indicate that they did not understand the story events, reread the story in small groups.

Reading Comprehension Skill: Note Sequence

Call on volunteers to share their answers to **When Did It Happen?** on Student Worktext page 14. Write the four sentences on the board in correct order. Tell students that story events happen in a certain sequence, or order, and that thinking about the order of events can help them understand and remember stories. Explain:

- Story events happen in an order that makes sense. They happen the way events happen in real life.

- Sometimes clue words such as *first, next, then, before,* or *after* help show the order of events.

Ask students to reread the second paragraph on Student Worktext page 13 and answer these questions:

- What does Rick do when Mrs. Lin opens the door? (He doesn't say anything.)
- When does he remember the trip and the bike, before or after this? (after)
- Which words tell you the order in which these things happen? (the word *then*)

Next, ask each student to copy three sentences from the story on a sheet of paper and put them out of order. Ask students to switch papers with a partner, and write 1, 2, or 3 next to each sentence to show when it happened. Students might also add a time-order word to each sentence.

Look Ahead

Tell students that they'll read more about Rick and his dog-walking business in the next story. Ask students to form small groups and use the questions at the bottom of Student Worktext page 15 to help them predict what will happen next.

LESSON 1 ▶ *After Reading "A Plan for Cash"*

You Be the Judge

1. Rick fibbed to get the job. Do you think he should have done this? Why or why not? Write what you think on the lines below.

   _____Answers will vary._____

Think About the Story

Use Story Words

Directions: Look at your list of story words on page 11. Write a story word on each line.

2. You can open and close a ____door____ .
3. Nine out of ten people is ____almost____ all the people.
4. This means "not one thing." ____nothing____ .
5. Ten plus ten is a math ____problem____ .
6. You can hike up a ____mountain____ .
7. You use your feet for ____walking____ .

The Big Idea

8. Which sentence tells what the whole story is about? Circle it. Then write it on the line.
   a. Rick meets Mrs. Lin.
   b. Rick gets a job walking a dog.
   c. Karl finds a job at a pet shop.

   Rick gets a job walking a dog.

When Did It Happen?

9. Write a number from 1 to 4 in front of each event to show when it happened.
   __2__ Rick makes a list.
   __1__ Rick goes to see Karl at the pet shop.
   __4__ Rabbit nips Rick.
   __3__ Mrs. Lin asks Rick if he has had jobs with animals.

Student page 14

Write Sentences About the Story

Directions: Circle the word that best fits in each sentence. Then write the sentence on the line.

10. May (seem/seemed) to go on and on.
    May seemed to go on and on.
11. Rick and Karl (are/is) friends.
    Rick and Karl are friends.
12. Karl (start/starts) ticking off ideas.
    Karl starts ticking off ideas.
13. Karl (seem/seems) to think getting a job is a snap.
    Karl seems to think getting a job is a snap.

Words and Meanings

Directions: Think about how the **bold** words are used in the story. Then circle the words that show the meaning of each word or phrase.

14. In this story, a **snap** is something that is _____.
    a. not hard to do
    b. very hard to do
    c. busted

15. With **wheels,** Rick can go almost anywhere. Here, wheels are _____.
    a. a car
    b. a bike
    c. a train

16. When Rick says, **"That is a good one,"** he means _____.
    a. "What a great idea."
    b. "That is a good dog."
    c. "You must be kidding."

Look Ahead

17. How do you think Rick's job walking Rabbit will go? Why? Write what you think on the lines below.
    _____Answers will vary._____

Read on to find out how the job goes.

Student page 15

Reinforce & Extend

◈ SPELLING: Adding *s* and *es* to Words with Short Vowels

1. dogs	**3.** kids	**5.** facts	**7.** hills	**9.** buses
2. pets	**4.** plans	**6.** passes	**8.** foxes	**10.** brushes

Write *job* and *jobs* on the board. Ask students which word names one, and which word names more than one. (*Jobs* names more than one.) Explain that a noun that names more than one person, place, or thing is called a plural noun. Tell students that the plural form of most nouns is made by adding *s*. For most nouns ending in *s, sh, ch,* or *x,* the plural form is made by adding *es*. Model adding *es* to the words *mix* and *mass.* Then have students number a sheet of paper 1–10. Dictate the words above one at a time, pausing for students to write them. Finally, write the words on the board and have students check their work, making corrections as needed.

◉ **Reading and Writing Practice** Activity 4 provides additional practice spelling plural forms of nouns containing short vowels.

◈ LANGUAGE: What Is a Sentence?

Write these sentences and sentence fragments on the board:

Rick plans a trip.   *The fib slips out.*

My best friend and I.   *Works at a pet shop.*

Point to the first sentence. Ask students who or what the sentence is about. (Rick) Circle the word *Rick.* Then ask what Rick does in the sentence. (plans a trip) Underline *plans a trip.* Tell students that this is a sentence because it tells a complete thought—it names a subject, Rick, and describes an action, planning a trip. Point to the fragment *My best friend and I* and ask students if it is a complete sentence, and why or why not. (no, because it does not tell a complete thought; it is missing the action part) Explain:

- ◆ A sentence tells a complete thought.
- ◆ A sentence begins with a capital letter.
- ◆ A sentence has an end mark.

Ask pairs of students to discuss the second pair of examples and decide which one is the complete sentence. Challenge students to add words to the incomplete sentence to make it complete. Model completing the sentence in a number of ways.

◉ **Reading and Writing Practice** Activity 5 provides additional practice identifying complete sentences.

◈ LITERARY APPRECIATION: Identifying Story Elements

Explain to students that "A Plan for Cash" is a fiction story—a story that has characters and events an author has made up. Explain that most fiction stories have certain elements:

- ◆ *Characters* are the people the story is about.
- ◆ The *setting* is where and when the story takes place.
- ◆ The *events* are what happens in the story. Events make up the beginning, middle, and end of a story.
- ◆ Often a story has a *plot,* which is made up of a problem and a solution.

Have pairs of students identify the characters, setting, and plot in "A Plan for Cash." Tell them that they will learn more about how the plot develops when they read the second part of the story.

 # Lesson at a Glance

Preview: This lesson presents the second part of the three-part story begun in "A Plan for Cash," about a boy named Rick who starts a dog-walking business to make cash for the summer. In Part 2 of the story, Rick decides to expand his business and creates an ad to drum up more business.

Objectives
◆ to read a fiction story
◆ to read words that contain long *a, i, o,* and *u* spelled with the CVC*e* pattern
◆ to spell words to which *ed* or *ing* is added and the final *e* is dropped or the final consonant is doubled
◆ to understand cause and effect in a fiction story
◆ to recognize and write four kinds of sentences
◆ to write a list

Student Worktext Pages 16–21
Story Words
trouble, always, harder, pro, start

Reading and Writing Practice Activities 6–12

Before Reading "The Ad"
Letters and Sounds
Long Vowels *a, i, o, u* (CVC*e*); Phonograms *ane, ive, ope*

Write these words on the board: *rat, rip, not, cub.* Read the words aloud and point out the CVC pattern. Remind students that they have learned that words with the CVC pattern often contain a short vowel sound. Next, add the letter *e* to each word. Read the new words aloud and ask students to repeat them. Point out that these words all contain long vowel sounds. Explain that in the consonant-vowel-consonant-*e* pattern, or CVC*e* pattern, the first vowel usually has a long sound and the final *e* is usually silent.

Write the words *cane, dive,* and *hope* on the board and have students read them aloud. Change the *c* in *cane* to *l,* the *d* in *dive* to *h,* and the *h* in *hope* to r, and ask students to read the new words. Tell students that if they can read these words, they will be able to read other words with the same pattern of letters. Finally, have students complete Student Worktext page 16.

Reading and Writing Practice Activity 6: Decoding Words with Long Vowels.

Story Words

Read aloud these words: *trouble, always, harder, pro, start.* Tell students that these words are important in the next story. Then write the words on the board and point to each one as you say it aloud a second time. Next, have students follow the ❏ *Read* ❏ *Say* ❏ *Write* sequence by completing **Story Words** on Student Worktext page 17. Have students add the words to their Word Bank at the back of the Student Worktext. To introduce the words in context, write these sentences on the board. You might tell students that *pro* is a shortened form of the word *professional.*

◆ I will help you if you get into <u>trouble</u>.

◆ We <u>always</u> drive home the same way.

◆ Will this test be <u>harder</u> than the last one?

◆ I have done this job for so long that I am now a <u>pro</u>.

◆ When are you going to <u>start</u> your work?

Have students make a word card for *trouble.* Ask a volunteer to read the first sentence aloud. Then have students copy the sentence onto the back of the word card. Follow the same procedure for the remaining words. To assess students' ability to read each new word, listen as individual students read the sentences on the board aloud.

Reading and Writing Practice Activity 7: Reading Story Words.

More Word Work

Have students work in pairs to complete **More Word Work** on Student Worktext page 17.

Reading and Writing Practice Activity 8: Reading and Writing Words with -*ed* or -*ing*.

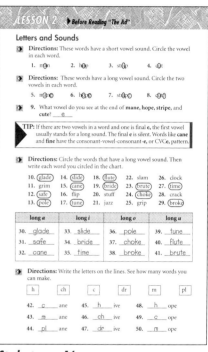

Student page 16

Student page 17

Reading "The Ad"

◆ Preview and Predict

- Tell students that they will now read the next part of the story they began reading in "A Plan for Cash." Have a volunteer read the title on Student Worktext page 18 aloud.
- Ask students to summarize what happened in "A Plan for Cash." Then invite them to recall the predictions they made at the end of that story. If necessary, remind students that at the end of "A Plan for Cash," Rick takes a job walking Rabbit, a dog who yaps and bites. Have them predict how this job will go.
- Next, have a volunteer read the first paragraph on Student Worktext page 18 aloud. Have students look at the illustration and the ads on pages 18 and 19. Invite them to predict what Rick will do, based on their preview.

◆ Strategy Modeling

Set a Purpose Tell students that people read different kinds of materials for different reasons. Explain:

- People usually read stories for fun.
- People read other kinds of materials, such as newspapers or magazines, to find out what is happening in the world.
- People read textbooks to learn facts about certain subjects.

Point out that the next story is a continuation of a story they began in Lesson 1; a good purpose, or reason, for reading it is to find out if the problem in Part 1 of the story was solved, and if so, how. Model setting a purpose. You might say:

The first part of this story ended with Rick agreeing to walk Mrs. Lin's dog, Rabbit. My purpose for reading the next part of the story is to see how it goes when Rick does this.

Have students set a purpose for reading the next part of the story. If necessary, suggest that they read Student Worktext pages 18 and 19 to find out how it goes when Rick walks Rabbit. Point out to students that they will pause in the middle of page 19 to answer a question about the story before reading on.

Focus on LD

Give students plenty of time to respond to each question you ask. Some students may need additional time to think before answering a question.

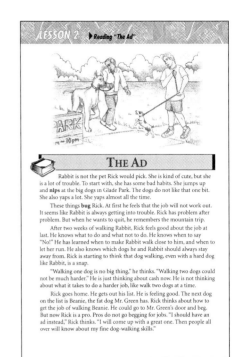

Student page 18

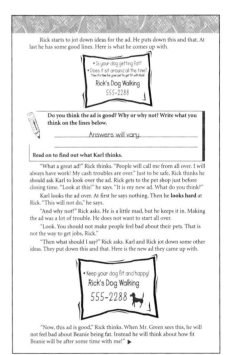

Student page 19

After Reading "The Ad"

Personal Response: You Be the Judge

Have pairs of students discuss the questions under **You Be the Judge** on Student Worktext page 20. After partners write their answers in their Student Worktexts, invite them to share their opinion with the class and identify the reasons they think as they do.

Think About the Story: Reading Comprehension

Have students complete the remaining items on Student Worktext pages 20 and 21 independently or in pairs. Check their responses to assess their comprehension of the story. If students' responses indicate that they did not understand the story, reread the story in small groups.

Reading Comprehension Skill: Recognizing Cause and Effect

Point out to students that in fiction stories, one event often causes another event to happen. Explain:

◆ A *cause* is an event that makes another event happen.

◆ An *effect* is what happens as a result.

◆ Sometimes clue words such as *because of* or *as a result* signal a cause-effect relationship. Other times readers must figure out causes and effects on their own.

◆ Thinking about what caused each thing to happen can help readers understand and keep track of story events.

Guide students to recognize causes and effects by answering these questions about "The Ad":

◆ What causes Rick to think that the job will not work out at first?

◆ Why does Rick decide to write an ad?

◆ Karl says Rick's first ad will not do. What effect does this have on Rick?

Look Ahead

Tell students that they'll find out if Rick's ad is a success in the next story. Ask them to form small groups and use the question at the bottom of Student Worktext page 21 to help them predict what will happen next.

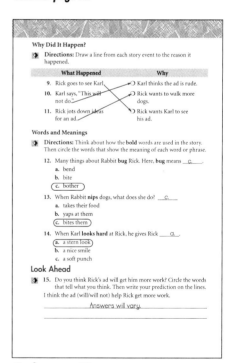

Student page 20

Student page 21

Reinforce & Extend

◆ **SPELLING: Adding *ed* and *ing* (Drop the Final *e* or Double the Final Consonant)**

1. bite	**3.** fade	**5.** liked	**7.** strut	**9.** dimmed
2. biting	**4.** faded	**6.** liking	**8.** strutted	**10.** dimming

Write *hike*, *hiked*, and *hiking* on the board. Remind students that the endings *ed* and *ing* can be added to many verbs; point out that when they add *ed* or *ing* to a word that ends in *e*, they should drop the *e* before adding the ending. Model at the board by adding *ed* and *ing* to *bake, ride,* and *rope.* Then point out that when *ed* or *ing* is added to a word like *rip* or *top*, the final consonant is doubled before the ending is added. Have students number a sheet of paper 1–10. Dictate the words above one at a time, pausing for students to write them. After that, write the words on the board and have students check their work, making corrections as needed.

Reading and Writing Practice Activity 9 provides additional practice adding the endings *-ed* and *-ing* to words with the CVC*e* pattern.

◆ **LANGUAGE: Four Kinds of Sentences**

Write these sentences on the board:

Karl looks the ad over.   *What a great ad!*

What do you think?   *Put this in the ad.*

Tell students that there are four kinds of sentences: a statement, a question, an exclamation, and a command. Use the examples on the board to explain the following:

- ◆ A statement tells something. It ends with a period.
- ◆ A question asks something. It ends with a question mark.
- ◆ An exclamation shows surprise or emotion. It ends with an exclamation point.
- ◆ A command tells someone what to do. It ends with a period or an exclamation point.

Have students suggest other examples of each kind of sentence. Write their suggestions on the board, emphasizing the appropriate end marks.

Reading and Writing Practice Activity 10 provides additional practice identifying and writing four kinds of sentences.

◆ **WRITING: A List**

Remind students that Rick made a list of all the dogs he knows in the neighborhood and their owners. Ask students why he made this list. (so he could keep track of the dogs and ask their owners if they needed help walking the dogs) Have students mention other uses for lists. Explain:

- ◆ Making a list is a good way to remember important things you need to buy, bring on a trip, or do.
- ◆ Most lists are not made up of sentences—just simple words or phrases. A list is short and easy to read.

Reading and Writing Practice Duplicate and distribute Activities 11–12. Point out the Writing Model of a list, and help students identify the title and the items in the list. Then have pairs of students write their own lists in response to one of these prompts:

- ◆ Make a list of people to buy holiday gifts for, and what to buy each person.
- ◆ Make a list of things to remember for a trip to the mountains.

Make sure students give their lists a title.

Lesson at a Glance

Preview: This lesson presents the third and final part of the story of Rick and his dog-walking business. In Part 3, Rick is successful in his quest to expand his business, but finds that he may have taken on more then he can handle. His friend Karl comes to the rescue when dog trouble erupts.

Objectives
♦ to read a fiction story
♦ to read and spell words that contain long *e* spelled *ee, ea, e, y,* and *ey*

♦ to summarize a fiction story
♦ to recognize the subject of a sentence
♦ to recognize fiction as a form of literature

Student Worktext Pages 22–27
Story Words
enough, soon, four, together, watch, phone

⊙ **Reading and Writing Practice Activities 13–17**

Before Reading "Dog Trouble"

Letters and Sounds
Long *e* Spelled *ee, ea, e, y, ey*; Phonograms *eak, eal*

Write the words *sleep, meat, he, salty,* and *monkey* on the board and read them aloud. Ask students what vowel sound they hear in all the words. (long *e*) Ask volunteers to circle the letter or letters in each word that stand for the long *e* sound. Point out that *ee, ea, e, y,* and *ey* can all stand for the long *e* sound.

Next, write the words *beak* and *meal* on the board. Have students read the words aloud. Then replace the *b* in *beak* with *sp* and the *m* in *meal* with *r*. Have students read the new words. Tell students that if they can read these words, they will be able to read other words with the same patterns of letters. Then have students complete Student Worktext page 22.

⊙ **Reading and Writing Practice** Activity 13: Decoding Words with Long *e*.

Story Words

Read aloud these words: *enough, soon, four, together, watch, phone.* Tell students that these words are important in the next story. Then write the words on the board and point to each one as you say it aloud a second time. Next, have students follow the ❑ *Read* ❑ *Say* ❑ *Write* sequence by completing **Story Words** on Student Worktext page 23. Have students add the words to the Word Bank at the back of the Student Worktext. To introduce the words in context, write these sentences on the board:

♦ Have you had <u>enough</u> to eat?
♦ I will be there <u>soon</u>.
♦ There are <u>four</u> seasons.
♦ We can go to the dance <u>together</u>.
♦ Who will <u>watch</u> your little sister?
♦ I called her on the <u>phone</u>.

Have students make a word card for *enough*. Ask a volunteer to read the first sentence aloud. Then have students copy the sentence onto the back of the word card. Follow the same procedure for the remaining words. To assess students' ability to read each new word, listen as individual students read the sentences on the board aloud.

⊙ **Reading and Writing Practice** Activity 14: Reading Story Words.

More Word Work

Have students work in pairs to complete **More Word Work** on Student Worktext page 23.

⊙ **Reading and Writing Practice** Activity 15: CVVC vs. CVC*e*

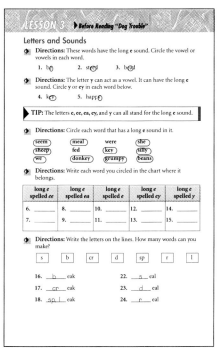
Student page 22

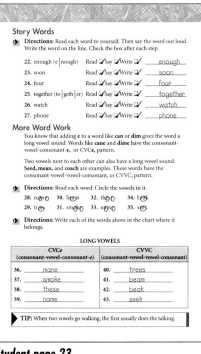
Student page 23

Reading "Dog Trouble"

◆ *Preview and Predict*

- ◆ Remind students that they have been reading about Rick, a boy who starts a dog-walking business to make money. Ask volunteers to summarize the main events in "A Plan for Cash" and "The Ad." Then tell them that "Dog Trouble" presents the final part of this story.
- ◆ Recall with students the predictions they made after reading "The Ad." Ask students whether they think Rick's ad will help him get more work. Also discuss with students whether Rick is wise to try to expand his business so soon. Ask students to speculate about what could go wrong if a person who had limited experience with dogs tried to walk more than one dog at a time.
- ◆ Next have students view the illustration on Student Worktext page 24. Based on their preview and the title "Dog Trouble," ask them to predict what will happen to Rick in this part of the story.

◆ *Strategy Modeling*

Use Context Clues   Tell students that when they come to a word that looks new, or a word that has more than one meaning, they can try using context clues to figure out the word's meaning. Explain that context clues are the words and phrases around the word in question. Draw students' attention to the last two sentences in the fourth paragraph on Student Worktext page 24. Model using context clues to figure out the meaning of the word *leash*. You might say:

> *I haven't seen this word before. I can use context clues to help me figure out its meaning. The sentence says that the leash snaps out of Rick's hand when Beanie starts to run. A leash must be a rope or strap tied to Beanie's collar that Rick holds on to in order to control him.*

Have students use context clues to help them figure out other words that look new, or words that have more than one meaning, as they continue to read.

Learning Styles

Auditory/Verbal   Have pairs of students work together to practice using story words. One partner should read aloud the word from each word card, and the other should use those words in original sentences. Then partners should switch roles.

LESSON 3 ▶ Reading "Dog Trouble"

DOG TROUBLE

Rick puts his ad up all over. He puts four ads up on four light poles. He tacks one up at the pet shop. He also slips one under Mr. Green's door. "That should be enough," he thinks. "Ads always work. Soon the phone will start to ring."

The ad works. Mr. Green does call! "Can you watch Beanie two days after school?" he asks. "I will do more than watch him," Rick thinks. "I will make him walk all that fat off." But he does not tell Mr. Green that.

"I can pick Beanie up at three," Rick says. His plan is to first get Beanie, and then pick up Rabbit. He will walk the dogs in Glade Park together. What a snap!

Beanie is a big and clumsy dog. But he is fast! Rick learns this the hard way. It is his first day walking the dogs together. Things start out OK, but Rabbit keeps nipping Beanie. Beanie is big enough to eat Rabbit in one bite. Lucky for Rick, Beanie does not do it. Then Beanie sees a cat. **In a flash**, he is off and running. The leash just snaps out of Rick's hand. Then Rabbit tugs on her leash, hard. She slips free, too.

"Rabbit, NO! Beanie, COME!" Rick yells again and again. But it is no use. The dogs race off together. Soon Rick does not see them at all. "What now?" Rick thinks. "It is all over for me. I am dead."

Student page 24

Will Rick get the dogs back? How? Write what you think on the lines below. Then read on to find out.

_____
Answers will vary.
_____
_____

Rick finds a phone. He calls Karl at the pet shop. "I lost the dogs," he says.

"You what?" Karl screams. "How could you do that?"

"Stop yelling," Rick says. "I have a plan. We can go to all the pet shops in the city. We can find two dogs that look like Beanie and Rabbit. You can help me. No one will know!"

"You must be kidding. I do not believe how **lame** that idea is," Karl says. "Do not do a thing. I get off work soon. I will meet you at Glade Park. Got it?"

Karl shows up a little bit after four. He has a bag in his hands. "Dog treats," he says with a grin. "Now I will show you a little something about dogs, Mr. Dog Pro." The boys work fast. They put the dog treats down in the grass. They make a long line of treats. The line goes from Glade Park to Rick's house. "Now watch," Karl says.

What do you know? Soon Beanie shows up, licking his lips. Then Rabbit trots up to the door. She is wet and muddy, but she is fine. Rick is so glad he does not stop grinning. But then he gets a surprise. A big black dog comes running up, and then a little fuzzy one. "Now what?" Rick asks.

"Easy. We look at the tags. Then we take all the dogs home," Karl says. And that is what they do. People are glad to get their dogs back. One man named Mr. Beck asks Rick to walk his dog, the big black one.

"I can do it," Rick answers. "But from now on, I will walk one dog at a time. One is enough for me."

Student page 25

After Reading "Dog Trouble"

Personal Response: What Do You Think?

Have students work in pairs to discuss the questions under **What Do You Think?** on Student Worktext page 26. Then have partners share their ideas with the class. Students can then write individual responses in the Student Worktext.

Think About the Story: Reading Comprehension

Have students complete the remaining items on Student Worktext pages 26 and 27 independently or in pairs. Check their responses to help you assess their comprehension of the story. If students' responses indicate that they did not understand the story events, have small groups reread and discuss the story.

Reading Comprehension Skill: Summarize

Remind students that to summarize a story is to sum up or retell the important events. Explain:

◆ A summary is short—much shorter than the story.
◆ A summary includes only the most important details.
◆ A summary does not include the reader's opinions.

Guide students in listing the main events on the first page of "Dog Trouble." The list might look like this:

1. Rick puts up ads that say he walks dogs.
2. Mr. Green calls Rick and asks him to walk his dog Beanie.
3. Rick walks two dogs at the same time—Beanie and Rabbit.
4. At first things go OK, but then things start to go wrong. Both dogs get away from Rick.

Have students work in pairs to write a four- or five-sentence summary for the second page of "Dog Trouble." Give partners a chance to read their summaries aloud.

👥 Application

In the Community Have students research pet-related services in the local area, such as grooming, boarding, veterinary, or other services. They may use a phone book or the Internet for their research. You might have pairs of students choose a local pet business and create a new ad for that business.

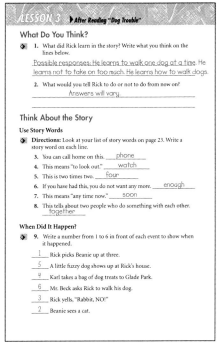

Student page 26

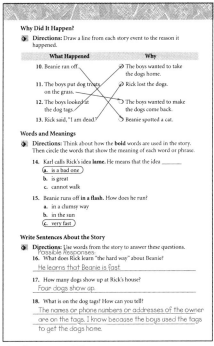

Student page 27

Reinforce & Extend

◆ SPELLING: Words with Long *e* Spelled *ee, ea, e, y,* or *ey*

1. we	**3.** city	**5.** leash	**7.** meeting	**9.** lucky
2. free	**4.** treats	**6.** donkey	**8.** key	**10.** reach

Write *me, feel, neat, happy,* and *key* on the board. Remind students that they have learned that the letters *e, ee, ea, y,* and *ey* can all stand for the long *e* sound. Then have students number a sheet of paper 1–10. Dictate the words above one at a time, pausing for students to write them. Finally, write the words on the board and have students check their work, making corrections as needed.

Reading and Writing Practice Activity 16 provides additional practice spelling words with long *e* spelled *ee, ea, e, y,* or *ey.*

◆ LANGUAGE: Subject (Complete)

Write this sentence on the board: *Rick is sick today.* Ask students who or what the sentence is about. (Rick) Circle the word *Rick* and guide students in identifying Rick as the subject of the sentence—the person the sentence tells about. Next, erase the word *Rick* and write *The boy* in its place. Read the new sentence aloud and ask students to identify the subject. If students identify *boy,* point out that this is the simple subject. Explain that the complete subject is *The boy.* To help students understand this, remind them that this phrase has taken the place of the original subject, *Rick.* Explain:

- The subject of a sentence tells who or what the sentence is about.
- The simple subject is a noun that names a person, place, or thing.
- The complete subject is made up of the simple subject plus other words that identify the subject. It does not contain the action of the sentence.

Write the following sentences on the board. Ask students to identify the complete subject of each sentence. (Answers appear in parentheses.)

A man wearing a blue shirt drove the car. (A man wearing a blue shirt)

Jake picked up his marbles. (Jake)

The dog with red hair is the one I want. (The dog with red hair)

The tired, hungry players lost the game. (The tired, hungry players)

Reading and Writing Practice Activity 17 provides additional practice recognizing the complete subject of a sentence.

◆ LITERARY APPRECIATION: Recognizing Forms of Literature: Fiction

Challenge students to name as many different kinds of writing as they can, such as stories, magazine articles, poems, and so on. List their ideas on the board in random order. Explain:

- Fiction is writing that comes from an author's imagination. In fiction stories, characters and events are made up by the author, usually for the purpose of entertaining readers.
- There are different kinds of fiction. Realistic fiction stories seem true to life. Fantasy stories could not happen in real life. Mystery stories and historical novels are other kinds of fiction.

Ask students whether "A Plan for Cash," "The Ad," and "Dog Trouble" are fiction, and what makes them so. Then ask students to name other stories that are examples of fiction.

Preview: This real-life reading lesson presents a series of classified ads as well as tips about how to read classified ads.

Objectives
- to read classified ads
- to read words that contain initial digraphs *sh, th, ch,* and *wh* and final digraphs *th, sh,* and *tch*
- to spell words that contain digraphs *sh, th, ch,* and *tch*

- to compare and contrast
- to recognize the complete predicate in a sentence
- to write a phone message

Student Worktext Pages 28–33
Story Words
hour, assistant, night, experience, full, opportunity

◎ **Reading and Writing Practice Activities 18–24**

Before Reading "How to Read a Want Ad"

Letters and Sounds

Initial Digraphs *ch, sh, th,* and *wh*; Final Digraphs *ch, sh, th,* and *tch*

Write the word *hop* on the board. Read it aloud and have students repeat it. Replace the *h* with *ch* and read the new word aloud. Explain that the letters *ch* at the beginning of a word stand for one sound. Next, write the words *shave, these, thin,* and *wheat* on the board. Circle the initial digraphs *sh, th,* and *wh.* Say each word and explain that the circled letters stand for one sound. Explain that the letters *th* can stand for either the sound at the beginning of *these* or the sound at the beginning of *thin.* Then write the words *chip, shake, those, thick,* and *white* on the board and ask volunteers to read the words.

Follow a similar procedure to teach the final digraphs *ch, sh, th,* and *tch.* Write the words *teach, fish, bath,* and *pitch* on the board. Circle the final letter combinations and have students read each word after you. Then have students complete Student Worktext page 28.

◎ **Reading and Writing Practice** Activity 18: Decoding Words with *ch, sh, th, wh,* and *tch.*

Story Words

Read aloud these words: *hour, assistant, night, experience, full, opportunity.* Tell students that these words are important in the next story. Then write the words on the board and point to each one as you say it aloud a second time. Next, have students follow the ❏ *Read* ❏ *Say* ❏ *Write* sequence by completing **Story Words** on Student Worktext page 29. Have students add the words to their Word Bank at the back of the Student Worktext. To introduce the words in context, write these sentences on the board:

- I cleaned for an <u>hour</u>.
- The baker hired an <u>assistant</u> to help her with her job.
- I could not sleep last <u>night</u>.
- Do you have any <u>experience</u> with fixing cars?
- We had a <u>full</u> tank of gas when we left home.
- That job would be a good <u>opportunity</u> for you.

Have students make a word card for *hour.* Ask a volunteer to read the first sentence aloud. Then have students copy the sentence onto the back of the word card. Follow the same procedure for the remaining words. To assess students' ability to read each new word, listen as individual students read the sentences on the board aloud.

◎ **Reading and Writing Practice** Activity 19: Reading Story Words.

More Word Work

Have students work in pairs to complete **More Word Work** on Student Worktext page 29.

◎ **Reading land Writing Practice** Activity 20: Dividing Two-Syllable Words.

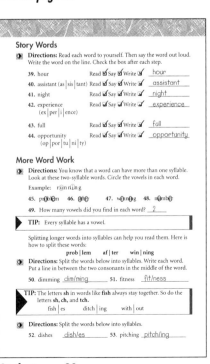

Student page 28

Student page 29

Reading "How to Read a Want Ad"

◆ *Preview and Predict*

- Have a volunteer read the title on Student Worktext page 30 aloud. Tell students that they are about to read a selection that presents several job ads similar to those found in the Classified section of a newspaper.
- If possible, display the Classified section from a local newspaper and point out the ads. Explain that there are different types of ads and ask students to mention different kinds. Be sure to include in the discussion ads in which employers list job openings, and ads placed by people looking for work.
- Next, have students view the ads on Student Worktext pages 30 and 31. Invite them to talk about what they would like to learn from this selection. You might point out some of the abbreviations used in the ads and tell students that they will learn what these abbreviations stand for as they read the selection.

◆ *Strategy Modeling*

Access Prior Knowledge Tell students that thinking about what they know about a topic before they start to read can help them focus on and understand what they read. Model using prior knowledge. You might say:

I am going to read several ads for a job opening. A job ad usually has a description of the work that needs to be done. It tells what skills people need in order to do the job. It lists the hours workers would need to be there, and sometimes it lists the pay.

Have students read the question under **Use What You Know** on Student Worktext page 30, and write their responses on the lines. Then have students read Student Worktext pages 30–31 to find out more about how to read job ads.

 Learning Styles

Interpersonal/Group Learning Have small groups of students work together to read the ads on Student Worktext page 30. As one group member reads an ad, another group member can refer to the abbreviation key on page 31 and help the reader with abbreviations as needed. After each ad is read, the group can discuss whether the job sounds appealing and why or why not. Then group members can switch roles.

Student page 30

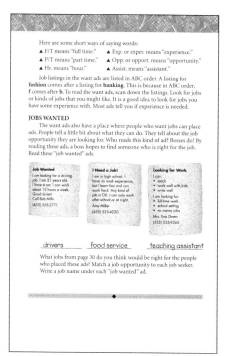

Student page 31

After Reading "How to Read a Want Ad"

Personal Response: What Do You Think?

Have students write answers to the question under **What Do You Think?** on Student Worktext page 32. Invite each student to share his or her response.

Think About the Story: Reading Comprehension

Have students complete the remaining items on Student Worktext pages 32 and 33 independently or in pairs. Check their responses to help you assess their comprehension of the selection. If students' responses indicate that they did not understand parts of the selection, have pairs of students who had difficulty with the same sections reread those sections and work together to answer the questions again.

Reading Comprehension Skill: Compare and Contrast

Tell students that thinking about how characters, events, things, or places in a story are alike and different can help them understand what they read. Explain:

- ◆ To compare two things is to tell how they are alike.
- ◆ To contrast two things is to tell how they are different.

Point out that people often compare and contrast job listings in order to help them make a decision about which jobs to apply for or to accept. Work with students to compare the first two ads on Student Worktext page 30. Record their responses in a chart.

First Ad	Both Ads	Second Ad
◆ needs full-time workers ◆ seeking experienced workers only ◆ gives phone number to call	◆ banking jobs ◆ seeking tellers	◆ needs full-time and part-time workers ◆ seeking workers with or without experience ◆ gives FAX number

Then have pairs of students create a chart that compares two jobs that are the same in some way, such as a camp counselor and a teacher's assistant, or a gardener and a park ranger.

 **Application**

Career Connection Have students create their own "job wanted" ads. They may choose to specify a job they are seeking, or simply to highlight their skills and interests. Remind them that they may use the ads on Student Worktext pages 30 and 31 as models.

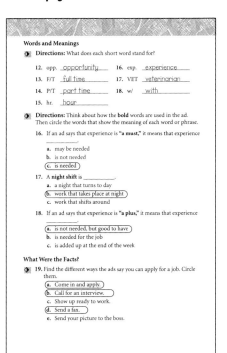

Student page 32

Student page 33

Reinforce & Extend

◈ SPELLING: Digraphs *sh, th, ch, tch*

1. shop	**3.** with	**5.** path	**7.** there	**9.** thing
2. shift	**4.** cash	**6.** champ	**8.** chime	**10.** patch

Write *ship, this, chat,* and *match* on the board. Remind students that they have learned that the letter patterns *sh, th, ch,* and *tch* each stand for one sound. Then have students number a sheet of paper 1–10. Dictate the words above one at a time, pausing for students to write them. Finally, write the words on the board and have students check their work, making corrections as needed.

(◉) **Reading and Writing Practice** Activity 21 provides additional practice spelling words with digraphs *sh, th, tch,* and *ch.*

◈ LANGUAGE: Predicate (Complete)

Write this sentence on the board: *I placed an ad in the newspaper.* Ask students to identify the subject of the sentence. (*I*) Inform students that the rest of the sentence, everything that is not part of the subject, is called the predicate. Explain:

- The predicate is the part of the sentence that tells what the subject does or is.
- The simple predicate is the verb that names the action.
- The complete predicate consists of the simple predicate plus other words that tell about the action: who or what the action is done to; how, when, or where the action happens; or other information about the action.

Write the following sentences on the board. Ask students to identify the complete predicate of each sentence. (Answers appear in parentheses.)

Mona and June went to the movies. (went to the movies)

Jen got the job! (got the job)

The kids played tennis for two hours. (played tennis for two hours)

I gave the hat to Jim. (gave the hat to Jim)

(◉) **Reading and Writing Practice** Activity 22 provides additional practice recognizing the complete predicate of a sentence.

◈ WRITING: A Phone Message

Ask students to imagine that a possible employer has called to talk to them about a job they applied for, but they are not home. Their brother answers the phone. Discuss the importance of taking a clear and complete phone message in this situation. Point out that a phone message should include who called, when he or she called, the reason for the call, including any information the person wants to give, and, if the person wants to be contacted, how he or she can be reached.

(◉) **Reading and Writing Practice** Duplicate and distribute Activities 23–24. Point out the Writing Model of a phone message, and help students identify the time, day, body of the message, caller's phone number, and name of the person who took the message. Then have students write their own phone messages in response to one of these prompts:

- A possible employer has called your brother Jesse back. She is calling from Great Vacations Travel Company. She was impressed by Jesse's résumé and would like Jesse to come in for an interview on Wednesday at 3:00 P.M. The company's phone number is (888) 555-1234.

- A man named Bob has called because he saw your sister Lila's job wanted ad. He would like to ask Lila if she would consider taking care of his three-year-old daughter on Saturday. He will call back tonight.

Tell students to make up some of the details as they write their messages, such as the time and day the call was received and the caller's phone number.

 # Lesson at a Glance

Preview: This lesson presents the first part of a two-part story about Mei-Lin, a girl whose favorite pastime is programming video games on her computer, despite her family's objection that she doesn't spend enough time with them.

Objectives
◆ to read a fiction story
◆ to read and spell words that contain long *a* spelled *ai* or *ay*

◆ to draw conclusions
◆ to recognize nouns in sentences
◆ to write a realistic fiction story

Student Worktext Pages 34–39

Story Words

computer, video, program, afternoon, family

◉ **Reading and Writing Practice Activities 25–31**

Before Reading "The Video Game," Part 1

Letters and Sounds

Long *a* Spelled *ai* and *ay*; Phonogram *ay*

Write the words *aid, nail, ray,* and *say* on the board. Read the words aloud and have students repeat them. Ask students what vowel sound all the words have. (long *a*) Explain that the letters *ai* and *ay* usually stand for the long *a* sound.

Next, replace the *s* in *say* with *d* and have students read the new word. Repeat the process, replacing *d* with *cl,* and then replacing *cl* with *st.* Tell students that many words end in *ay,* and that once they know how to read words such as *say* and *day,* they can read many other words with the same letter pattern. Finally, have students complete Student Worktext page 34 independently.

◉ **Reading and Writing Practice** Activity 25: Decoding Words with Long *a* Spelled *ai* and *ay.*

Story Words

Read aloud these words: *computer, video, program, afternoon, family.* Tell students that these words are important in the next story. Then write the words on the board and point to each one as you say it aloud a second time. Next, have students follow the ❏ *Read* ❏ *Say* ❏ *Write* sequence by completing **Story Words** on Student Worktext page 35. Have students add the words to their Word Bank at the back of the Student Worktext. To introduce the words in context, write these sentences on the board:

◆ I wrote a letter on the <u>computer</u>.
◆ Can you change the color of the <u>video</u> screen?
◆ This <u>program</u> lets you look at pictures on the screen.
◆ Jen has a basketball game this <u>afternoon</u>.
◆ Will your <u>family</u> visit you this weekend?

Have students make a word card for *computer.* Ask a volunteer to read the first sentence aloud. Then have students copy the sentence onto the back of the word card. Follow the same procedure for the remaining words. To assess students' ability to read each new word, listen as individual students read the sentences on the board aloud.

◉ **Reading and Writing Practice** Activity 26: Reading Story Words.

More Word Work

Have students work in pairs to complete **More Word Work** on Student Worktext page 35.

◉ **Reading and Writing Practice** Activity 27: Forming Possessives with *'s.*

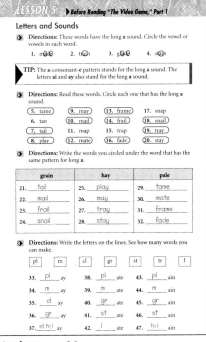

Student page 34

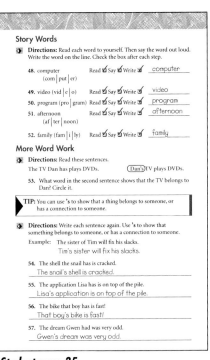

Student page 35

Reading "The Video Game," Part 1

◆ Preview and Predict

- ◆ Tell students that they are about to read the first part of a story about a girl named Mei-Lin who spends a lot of time on her computer. Write *Mei-Lin* on the board and have students pronounce it. (MAY lin). Have a volunteer read the title on Student Worktext page 36 aloud.
- ◆ Ask how many students have access to a computer at home. Then ask students with computer access how much time they spend on the computer and what they use the computer for.
- ◆ Ask a volunteer to read aloud the sentences and question under **Use What You Know.** Ask students whether any of their parents think they spend too much time doing something, and if so, have students respond to this complaint. Discuss the question with students. Then encourage each student to write an answer on the lines.
- ◆ Next, have students read the first paragraph on Student Worktext page 36 and view the illustration on page 37. Ask them to predict what happens in this part of the story.

◆ Strategy Modeling

Reread/Read Ahead Remind students that when they come across something that confuses them while reading, they can sometimes clear up confusion by rereading or by reading ahead. Read the first three sentences on Student Worktext page 36, through the words *a million miles away.* Then model the Reread/Read Ahead strategy. You might say:

I'm confused by the sentence "Mei-Lin is a million miles away." This doesn't seem to make sense. Then I read ahead and find out that Mei-Lin is playing a game on her computer. It is as though she were a million miles away because she is shooting aliens in outer space on the computer and is not paying attention to what her mom is saying.

Have students continue reading the story to find out more about Mei-Lin. Remind them to try rereading or reading ahead to clear up any confusion.

Learning Styles

Body/Kinesthetic Invite pairs of students to read Student Worktext pages 36 and 37 together and then role-play the conversation between Mei-Lin and her mother, including gestures and body language.

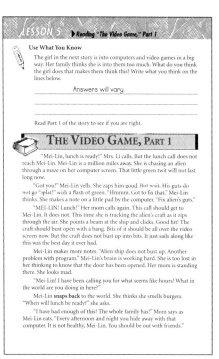

Student page 36

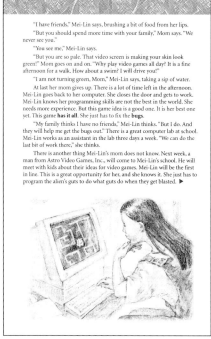

Student page 37

After Reading "The Video Game," Part 1

Personal Response: You Be the Judge

Have students read the questions under **You Be the Judge** on Student Worktext page 38. Briefly discuss students' thoughts about the questions, and then have individual students write their answers on the lines.

Think About the Story: Reading Comprehension

Have students complete the remaining items on Student Worktext pages 38 and 39 independently or in pairs. Check their responses to help you assess their comprehension of the story. If students' responses indicate that they did not understand the story, reread the story in small groups.

Reading Comprehension Skill: Draw Conclusions

Explain to students that writers do not always tell readers everything in a story; they let readers figure out some things for themselves. This is called drawing conclusions. Explain:

- Readers can use clues from the story to draw conclusions.
- Readers can use what they know from their own lives to figure out what an author doesn't say.

Guide students to draw conclusions in response to these questions:

- Does Mei-Lin's family miss spending time with her? How do you know?
- Is Mei-Lin an experienced computer user? How can you tell?
- Is Mei-Lin excited that a man from Astro Video Games is coming to her school? What makes you think this?

If necessary, model using story clues and prior knowledge to draw a conclusion. You might say:

In the story, Mei-Lin's mom says that the whole family has had enough of her hiding away with her computer all the time. She also says, "You should spend more time with your family. We never see you." If the family did not miss spending time with Mei-Lin, they would not care about her spending so much time on the computer. I can draw the conclusion that the family wants to see more of Mei-Lin.

Look Ahead

Tell students that they'll read more about Mei-Lin and her video game in the next story. Ask students to form small groups and use the questions at the bottom of Student Worktext page 39 to help them predict what will happen next.

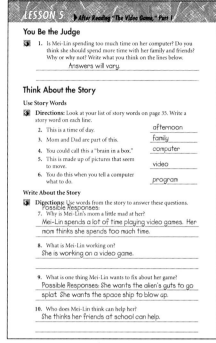

Student page 38

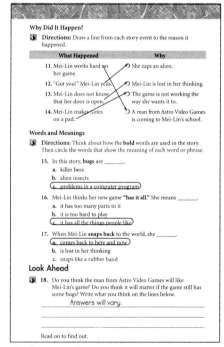

Student page 39

Reinforce & Extend

◆ SPELLING: Long *a* Spelled *ai* and *ay*

1. bait	**3.** brain	**5.** play	**7.** sails	**9.** stain
2. day	**4.** away	**6.** jail	**8.** bay	**10.** stray

Write *fail* and *pay* on the board. Remind students that they have learned that the letters *ai* and *ay* can stand for the long *a* sound. Then have students number a sheet of paper 1–10. Dictate the words above on at a time, pausing for students to write them. Finally, write the words on the board and have students check their work, making corrections as needed.

Reading and Writing Practice Activity 28 provides additional practice spelling words with long *a* spelled *ai* and *ay*.

◆ LANGUAGE: Nouns

Write these sentences on the board:

Shoot the red planets and spaceships on the screen.

I like to write letters on the computer.

Mary is working on a new game.

I will fix the program at the lab.

Tell students that a *noun* is a word that names a person, place, or thing. Point to the first sentence, read it aloud, and underline the nouns. (*planets, spaceships, screen*) Ask students if these words name people, places, or things. (things) Next, point to the second sentence and ask students which words name things. (*letters, computer*) Then guide students in finding the nouns in the third and fourth sentences. (*Mary, game, program, lab*) Classify the nouns by writing each one under the heading *person, place,* or *thing.*

Reading and Writing Practice Activity 29 provides additional practice recognizing nouns in sentences.

◆ WRITING: A Realistic Fiction Story

Remind students that they have learned that fiction stories come from a writer's imagination. Explain that there are different kinds of fiction stories. In a realistic fiction story, the characters, places, and events could exist in real life. A fantasy story contains characters, places, or events that could not exist in real life. Ask what kind of story "The Video Game" is, and why. (realistic fiction, because all the events could happen in real life) Then tell students that they will have the opportunity to write their own realistic fiction stories. Explain that realistic fiction stories usually contain these elements:

- ◆ characters who act like people in real life
- ◆ a setting, or place and time where the story takes place, that could exist in real life
- ◆ a plot, or series of events, that could happen in real life

Reading and Writing Practice Duplicate and distribute Activities 30–31, the Writing Model of a realistic fiction story, and help students identify the characters, setting, and plot. Then have students write their own short realistic stories. You might have small groups brainstorm ideas for stories before they begin writing.

Preview: This lesson presents the second part of a two-part story about Mei-Lin, a girl who programs video games on her computer. In this part of the story, Mei-Lin is surprised to learn her game idea is one of two that are selected for development by a video game company.

Objectives
♦ to read a fiction story
♦ to read and spell words that contain long *i* spelled *igh, y,* or *ie*

♦ to make judgments
♦ to identify common and proper nouns
♦ to write a paragraph of opinion

Student Worktext Pages 40–45

Story Words
develop, own, talk, action, young, begin

💿 **Reading and Writing Practice Activities 32–38**

Before Reading "The Video Game," Part 2

Letters and Sounds

Long *i* Spelled *igh, y, ie;* Phonogram *ied*

Write the words *line, like,* and *ripe* on the board. Ask volunteers to read each word aloud, identify the vowel sound (long *i*), and then underline the letters that stand for the long *i* sound. (*i* and *e*) Next, write the words *my* and *cry* on the board. Read the words aloud and ask students what vowel sound they hear in each word. (long *i*) Explain that the letter *y* often stands for the long *i* sound. Next, write the word *light* on the board. Read the word aloud and have students repeat it. Circle the letters *igh*. Explain that this combination of letters usually stands for the long *i* sound.

Write the word *cried* on the board and have students read it aloud. Underline the letters *ie* and explain that this combination of vowels can also stand for the long *i* sound. Then replace *cr* with *l* and ask students to read the new word. Repeat the process, replacing *l* with *tr*. Tell students that many words contain the letters *ied,* and that once they know how to read words such as *lied* and *cried,* they can read other words that end the same way. Then have students complete Student Worktext page 40.

💿 **Reading and Writing Practice** Activity 32: Decoding Words with Long *i* Spelled *igh, y,* or *ie*.

Story Words

Read aloud these words: *develop, own, action, young, begin, talk.* Tell students that these words are important in the next story. Then write the words on the board and point to each one as you say it aloud a second time. Next, have students follow the ❏ *Read* ❏ *Say* ❏ *Write* sequence by completing **Story Words** on Student Worktext page 41. Have students add the words to their Word Bank at the back of the Student Worktext. To introduce the words in context, write these sentences on the board:

♦ You should <u>develop</u> that idea into a story.
♦ Do you have your <u>own</u> desk?
♦ I will <u>begin</u> the class at four.
♦ I like games with lots of <u>action</u>.
♦ She is too <u>young</u> to drive.
♦ Our teacher had us <u>talk</u> about the book.

Have students make a word card for *develop*. Ask a volunteer to read the first sentence aloud. Then have students copy the sentence onto the back of the word card. Follow the same procedure for the remaining words. To assess students' ability to read each new word, listen as individual students read the sentences on the board aloud.

💿 **Reading and Writing Practice** Activity 33: Reading Story Words.

More Word Work

Have students complete **More Word Work** on Student Worktext page 40.

💿 **Reading and Writing Practice** Activity 34: Reading and Writing Words with *-es, -ed,* or *-ing* (Change *y* to *i*).

Student page 40

Student page 41

Reading "The Video Game," Part 2

◆ Preview and Predict

- Remind students that they have been reading a story about Mei-Lin, a girl who spends a lot of time programming games on her computer. Tell them that they will now read the second half of that story. Have a volunteer read the title on Student Worktext page 42 aloud.
- Ask a volunteer to summarize what happened in the first part of "The Video Game." Then ask students to recall the predictions they made at the end of the story. If necessary, remind them that a man from a video game company is coming to Mei-Lin's school, and invite them to predict whether the man will like Mei-Lin's video game.

◆ Strategy Modeling

Summarize Tell students that to summarize a story is to sum up the most important events in their own words. Explain:

- A summary includes the most important ideas or events in a piece of writing.
- A summary does not include details. It does not include opinions.
- While reading, it can help to pause at certain points and sum up what has happened so far. Summarizing while reading helps readers understand and remember what they read.

Model summarizing. You might say:

Before I start reading, I'll sum up what happened in the first part of the story: Mei-Lin's mom called her to lunch, but Mei-Lin did not hear her because she was too busy programming her computer. During lunch, Mei-Lin's mom complains that Mei-Lin is spending too much time on the computer. Then Mei-Lin goes back to her computer to work on a game she is developing. A man from a video game company is coming to her school soon, and she will show him the game. Summing up the main events so far helps me figure out what might happen next.

Have students read "The Video Game, Part 2" to find out what happens when the man from the video game company comes to Mei-Lin's school. Tell them to pause at the end of page 42 and sum up the important events before reading the ending on page 43.

Learning Styles

Interpersonal/Group Learning Have students choose the roles of Mei-Lin, Mike, Misha, and Dave and act out the important events in Part 2 after reading the story.

Student page 42

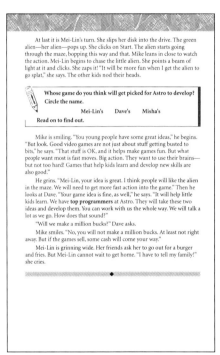

Student page 43

After Reading "The Video Game," Part 2

Personal Response: What Do You Think?

Remind students that Mei-Lin and her friends each had a different idea for a computer game. Recall those game ideas with students. Then invite students to talk about their own ideas for a great video game. You might keep track of the ideas in a list on the board. Finally, invite students to write their ideas in the space provided under **What Do You Think?** on Student Worktext page 44.

Think About the Story: Reading Comprehension

Have students complete the remaining items on Student Worktext pages 44 and 45 independently or in pairs. Check their responses to help you assess their comprehension of the story. If students' responses indicate that they did not understand the story, reread the story aloud and then answer the questions in the Student Worktext as a group.

Critical Thinking Skill: Make Judgments

Remind students that in "The Video Game, Part 2" a man from Astro Video Games comes to Mei-Lin's school and chooses which of the students' video game ideas his company will develop. Point out that to make this choice, the man must make a judgment about which game ideas are better than others. Tell students that making judgments is an important skill in real life, too. Explain:

- ◆ When we form opinions about whether something is right or wrong, or good or bad, we are making a judgment.
- ◆ When making a judgment, it is important to consider reasons in favor of an action, and reasons against it.
- ◆ People use evidence from real life, along with their own experience and beliefs, to make judgments.

Explain that readers also make judgments about what they read. Then read aloud the following scenarios and have students respond to the questions orally. Guide students in supporting their judgments with reasons.

- ◆ You saw your friend cheat on a test. Should you tell your teacher about this? Why or why not?
- ◆ Your friends have decided to enter an abandoned hotel, even though signs say, "Danger. Keep off the property." They want you to go with them. What should you do and why?

 **Application**

In the Community Invite a video game programmer or other type of computer programmer from the community to speak to the class about his or her work. You might help students prepare questions to ask the programmer before the visit takes place.

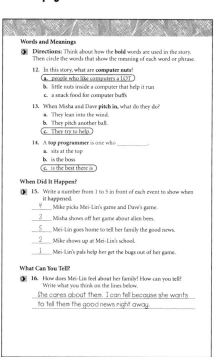

Student page 44

Student page 45

Reinforce & Extend

◆ SPELLING: Long *i* Spelled *igh, y,* or *ie*

1. by	**3.** sight	**5.** lie	**7.** cry	**9.** sly
2. why	**4.** light	**6.** high	**8.** cried	**10.** slight

Write *sigh, try,* and *pie* on the board. Remind students that they have learned that the letters *igh, y,* and *ie* can stand for the long *i* sound. Then have students number a sheet of paper 1–10. Dictate the words above one at a time, pausing for students to write them. Finally, write the words on the board and have students check their work, making corrections as needed.

◉ **Reading and Writing Practice** Activity 35 provides additional practice spelling words with long *i* spelled *igh, y,* or *ie.*

◆ LANGUAGE: Common and Proper Nouns

Write this sentence on the board:

The man from Astro asked Mei-Lin, Carlos, Dave, and Misha what games they liked.

Call on volunteers to underline the words that begin with a capital letter. (The, Astro, Mei-Lin, Carlos, Dave, Misha) Ask students if they know why these words begin with a capital letter. If necessary, explain that the word *The* begins with a capital letter because it is the first word in the sentence, and the other words begin with a capital letter because they name a specific person or company. Explain:

- ◆ A common noun names any person, place, or thing. The words *man, woman, computer,* and *idea* are common nouns.
- ◆ A proper noun names a specific person, place, or thing. Proper nouns include the names of people *(Mei-Lin, Carlos),* places *(New York City),* months *(May),* and companies *(Astro Video Games).* A proper noun begins with a capital letter.
- ◆ *Mrs.* is a title of address. Titles begin with a capital letter.

Ask pairs of students to circle three other common nouns in the story, and underline three proper nouns. Make a list of their findings in two columns on the board.

◉ **Reading and Writing Practice** Activity 36 provides additional practice with common and proper nouns.

◆ WRITING: A Paragraph of Opinion

Have students read the second paragraph on Student Worktext page 43. Point out that in this paragraph, Mike gives his opinions about the game ideas Mei-Lin and her friends presented. Explain that an opinion is a statement that tells what someone thinks or believes. An opinion is not a fact that can be proven, but it can be supported by reasons.

◉ **Reading and Writing Practice** Duplicate and distribute Activities 37–38. Point out the Writing Model of an opinion paragraph. Help students identify the topic sentence that states the writer's opinion, and the supporting sentences that give reasons why the author feels as she does. Then have students write their own paragraphs of opinion in response to one of these prompts:

- ◆ Write a paragraph about your favorite school subject. Tell why you think it is the best subject.
- ◆ Write a paragraph about something you think could be improved in your school or city. Tell why you think this change for the better is needed.

# Lesson at a Glance

Preview: This nonfiction selection profiles three teenage entrepreneurs who started their own Internet companies.

Objectives

♦ to read a nonfiction selection
♦ to read and spell words that contain long *o* spelled *oa* or *ow*
♦ to recognize the topic of a nonfiction selection
♦ to identify singular and plural nouns
♦ to recognize nonfiction as a form of literature

Student Worktext Pages 46–51

Story Words

father, group, hearing, Internet, company, music

⊙ **Reading and Writing Practice Activities 39–43**

Before Reading "The Teen Net Bosses"

Letters and Sounds

Long *o* Spelled *oa* or *ow*, Phonogram *ow*

Remind students that they have learned the word *home*. Write it on the board and ask a volunteer to underline the letters that stand for the long *o* sound. (*o* and *e*) Next, write the words *coat, soap, row,* and *low* on the board. Read these words aloud and have students repeat them. Ask students what vowel sound each word has. (long *o*) Circle the letters *oa* or *ow* in each word. Explain that these letters often stand for the long *o* sound.

Next, add *f* to the word *low* to spell *flow* and have students read the new word aloud. Repeat the process, replacing *fl* with the letters *cr*. Tell students that several words end with the letters *ow*. Now that they know how to read *low, flow,* and *crow,* they will be able to read other words with this pattern. Then have students complete Student Worktext page 46.

⊙ **Reading and Writing Practice** Activity 39: Decoding Words with Long *o* Spelled *oa* or *ow*.

Story Words

Read aloud these words: *father, group, hearing, Internet, company, music.* Tell students that these words are important in the next story. Then write the words on the board and point to each one as you say it aloud a second time. Next, have students follow the ❏ *Read* ❏ *Say* ❏ *Write* sequence by completing **Story Words** on Student Worktext page 47. Have students add the words to their Word Bank at the back of the Student Worktext. To introduce the words in context, write these sentences on the board:

♦ Where does your <u>father</u> work?
♦ Our jazz <u>group</u> is playing at a club next week.
♦ I am not <u>hearing</u> you because this phone is broken.
♦ You can find a lot of facts on the <u>Internet</u>.
♦ How many people work at your <u>company</u>?
♦ What kind of <u>music</u> do you like to listen to?

Have students make a word card for *father*. Ask a volunteer to read the first sentence aloud. Then have students copy the sentence onto the back of the word card. Follow the same procedure for the remaining words. To assess students' ability to read each new word, listen as individual students read the sentences on the board aloud.

⊙ **Reading and Writing Practice** Activity 40: Reading Story Words.

More Word Work

Have students work in pairs to complete **More Word Work** on Student Worktext page 47.

⊙ **Reading and Writing Practice** Activity 41: Reading and Writing Compound Words.

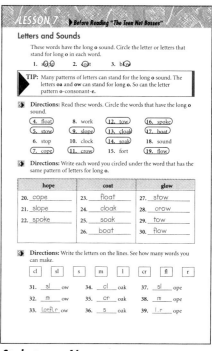

Student page 46

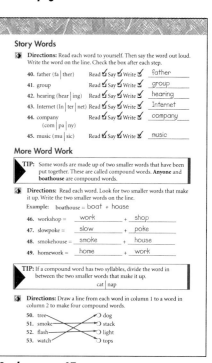

Student page 47

Reading "The Teen Net Bosses"

◆ *Preview and Predict*

- ◆ Tell students that they are about to read a selection about three real-life teenagers who started their own Internet companies. Ask students if they have downloaded music off the Internet. Then point out the section about Shawn Fanning on Student Worktext page 49. Tell students that he wrote a software program that made uploading and downloading tunes easy. Then have a volunteer read the title on page 48.
- ◆ Ask how many students use the Internet and what those students use it for. Read aloud and discuss with students the questions under **Use What You Know** on Student Worktext page 48. Have students write their answers on the lines.

◆ *Strategy Modeling*

Set a Purpose Read the first paragraph of the selection aloud and model setting a purpose for reading. You might say:

In the first paragraph, I learned that some teenagers have started their own Internet companies. I'm curious to find out about these teens and how they started their companies. I'm going to read on to learn more about what made these young people's companies successful.

Have students read the rest of pages 48 and 49 to find out about the teenagers and their companies. Encourage them to adjust their purpose for reading as appropriate.

Focus on ESL/LEP

Explain and discuss the following terms used in the story:

- ◆ fans ("enthusiasts")
- ◆ grab the opportunity
- ◆ take off ("experience success")
- ◆ full on ("completely")
- ◆ dive into something ("do something almost exclusively")
- ◆ gets sick of it ("becomes bored with or tired of it")

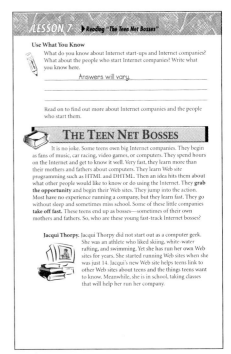

Student page 48

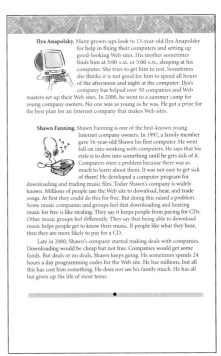

Student page 49

After Reading "The Teen Net Bosses"

Personal Response: What Do You Think?

Read aloud the sentence and question under **What Do You Think?** on Student Worktext page 50. Then have a volunteer read the choices. Have students vote for the item they think would be the hardest to give up if they owned a business that required all their time. Then have students suggest some things that might fall under the "other" category, such as playing sports or participating in other extracurricular activities. Finally, ask students to write answers to the second question, which follows these choices.

Think About the Story: Reading Comprehension

Have students complete the remaining items on Student Worktext pages 50 and 51 independently or in pairs. Check their responses to help you assess their comprehension of the story. If students' responses indicate that they did not understand the story, reread the story in small groups.

Reading Comprehension Skill: Identifying the Topic

Tell students that the *topic* of a selection is the one main subject a selection is all about. Ask students what the topic of this selection is. (teenagers who have started Internet companies) Point out that often, nonfiction selections have one or more *subtopics*, or smaller topics that are part of the larger topic. Explain that the headings and subheadings in a selection can help readers figure out what the subtopics are. Guide students in identifying the individual teenagers as subtopics in "The Teen Net Bosses."

If possible, provide students with a number of youth-oriented magazines. Have partners select one magazine, browse through it, and identify the topics of the articles they find interesting. Challenge students to find subtopics as well.

 **Application**

At Home Invite students to interview family members about their ideas for Web sites, or about any Web sites that family members maintain. Encourage students to write a summary of the interviews and include their own ideas or experiences. Students can share their summaries with the class. The class might then vote on the best Web site idea.

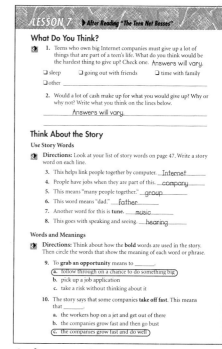

Student page 50

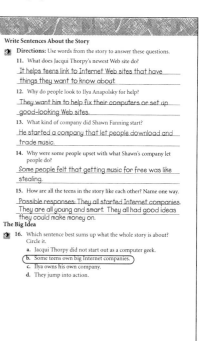

Student page 51

Reinforce & Extend

◆ SPELLING: Long *o* Spelled *oa* or *ow*

1. row	**3.** load	**5.** grow	**7.** yellow	**9.** throw
2. own	**4.** coast	**6.** roam	**8.** goal	**10.** throat

Write *boat* and *low* on the board. Remind students that they have learned that the letters *oa* and *ow* can stand for the long *o* sound. Then have students number a sheet of paper 1–10. Dictate the words above one at a time, pausing for students to write them. Finally, write the words on the board and have students check their work, making corrections as needed.

Reading and Writing Practice Activity 42 provides additional practice spelling words with long *o* spelled *oa* or *ow*.

◆ LANGUAGE: Singular and Plural Nouns

Write these sentences on the board:

One teen was developing a video game.

Three teens started a company.

Underline the words *teen* and *teens*. Ask students if they know why *teens* ends in *s*. (It tells about more than one teen.) Remind students that adding *s* to a noun makes it tell about more than one. Tell them that a noun that names one thing is called a singular noun; a noun that names more than one is a plural noun. Then write the words *crosses* and *boxes* on the board. Explain to students that they should add *es* to words that end in *s, x, z, ch,* or *sh*. Write these words on the board: *spoon, stitch, fox, boss, lash, rock, quiz, rose,* and *dish*. Ask students to work in pairs to write the plural form of each word.

Next, explain that there are some words that cannot be made plural by adding *s* or *es*. Instead, the whole word has to be changed. Write these examples on the board: *child/children, man/men*. Ask students to look up the plural form of *ox* in the dictionary. Then have a volunteer write it on the board. Remind students that if they are not sure whether a word has an irregular plural form, they can use a dictionary to check the plural form. Then have students work in pairs to write sentences using the singular and plural forms of each noun on the board.

Reading and Writing Practice Activity 43 provides additional practice with singular and plural nouns.

◆ LITERARY APPRECIATION: Recognizing Forms of Literature: Nonfiction

Ask students to name kinds of writing they can think of that give information, such as newspaper articles, history books, magazine articles, Web pages, and so on. List their ideas on the board. Explain:

- *Nonfiction* is writing that presents real information.
- Newspapers, articles in magazines, and textbooks are examples of nonfiction.
- Unlike *fiction*, the ideas in nonfiction do not come from the writer's imagination. A nonfiction selection is based on facts.

Ask students whether "The Video Game" and "The Teen Net Bosses" are fiction or nonfiction, and what makes them so. Then ask students to name other stories they have read that are examples of nonfiction.

Lesson at a Glance

Preview: This lesson presents a nonfiction selection about several young American inventors and their inventions.

Objectives
- to read a nonfiction selection
- to read and spell words that contain long *u* spelled *ue*, *oo*, *u*, or *ew*
- to note main idea and supporting details in nonfiction
- to note main idea and supporting details in nonfiction
- to identify singular and plural nouns
- to recognize and write possessive nouns
- to write instructions for how to do something

Student Worktext Pages 52–57
Story Words
began, paper, invent, invention, inventor, battery, candle

◉ **Reading and Writing Practice Activities 44–49**

Before Reading "America's Young Inventors"

Letters and Sounds

Long *u* Spelled *ue*, *oo*, *u*, or *ew*

Write the words *tube* and *rude* on the board and ask students what vowel sound they have. (long *u*) Remind students that they have learned the words *food* and *too*. Ask what vowel sound these words have. (long *u*) Write *food* and *too* on the board, and underline *oo* in both words. Explain that the letters *oo* often stand for the long *u* sound. Next, write the words *blue, unite,* and *new* on the board and read them aloud. Underline the letters that stand for the long *u* sound in each word. Explain that the letters *ue, u,* and *ew* can also stand for the long *u* sound. Then write these words on the board: *hue, crew, groom, uniform.* Have students read the words aloud. Invite volunteers to underline the letter or letters in each word that stand for the long *u* sound. Then have students complete Student Worktext page 52.

◉ **Reading and Writing Practice** Activity 44: Decoding Words with Long *u* Spelled *ue, oo, u,* or *ew*.

Story Words

Read aloud these words: *began, paper, invent, invention, inventor, battery, candle.* Tell students that these words are important in the next story. Then write the words on the board and point to each one as you say it aloud a second time. Next, have students follow the ❏ *Read* ❏ *Say* ❏ *Write* sequence by completing **Story Words** on Student Worktext page 53. Have students add the words to their Word Bank at the back of the Student Worktext. To introduce the words in context, write these sentences on the board:

- We <u>began</u> the game after lunch.
- I wrote my name on a sheet of <u>paper</u>.
- She wants to <u>invent</u> a car that needs no gas.
- The <u>inventor</u> came up with a new kind of radio.
- The <u>battery</u> in this flashlight is dead.
- Light a <u>candle</u> so we can see.
- His <u>invention</u> won a prize.

Have students make a word card for *began.* Ask a volunteer to read the first sentence aloud. Then have students copy the sentence onto the back of the word card. Follow the same procedure for the remaining words. To assess students' ability to read each new word, listen as individual students read the sentences on the board aloud.

◉ **Reading and Writing Practice** Activity 45: Reading Story Words.

More Word Work

Have students work in pairs to complete More Word Work on Student Worktext page 53.

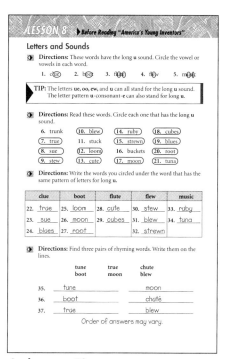

Student page 52

Student page 53

Reading "America's Young Inventors"

◆ Preview and Predict

- ◆ Tell students that they are about to read a nonfiction selection about some American young people who have come up with cool new inventions. Discuss with students what it means to invent something. Then have a volunteer read aloud the title on Student Worktext page 54.
- ◆ Read aloud and discuss with students the question under **Use What You Know** on Student Worktext page 54.
- ◆ Have a volunteer read the question below the title on page 54, as well as the bulleted items that follow. Ask students to guess what these items have in common. Then read aloud the first two sentences of the first full paragraph. Finally, ask students what they would like to learn in this selection.

◆ Strategy Modeling

Access Prior Knowledge Tell students that thinking about what they know about a topic before they start to read can help them focus on and understand what they read. Model using prior knowledge. You might say:

I am going to read a selection about young inventors. It might help to think about what I know about inventors and their inventions. I know that an invention is a new product or idea that solves a problem or fills a need. I have heard about famous inventors such as Alexander Graham Bell, Thomas Edison, and Eli Whitney. I am curious to find out what the young inventors in this selection have invented.

Have students reread the question under **Use What You Know** on Student Worktext page 54, and write their responses on the lines. Then have students read Student Worktext pages 54–55 to find out about some young American inventors.

Point out to students that after they read, they will have the opportunity to draw one of the inventions they read about or an invention of their own.

🔺 Learning Styles

Visual/Spatial Invite students to look at illustrated nonfiction books about inventors and inventions or to view the Inventions article in an encyclopedia. (The end of the article should list other articles about specific inventors and inventions; students may want to look at these articles, too.) Encourage students to look at and discuss pictures of various inventions.

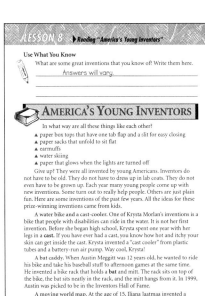

Student page 54

Student page 55

After Reading "America's Young Inventors"

Personal Response: What Do You Think?

Have pairs of students work together to answer the questions under **What Do You Think?** on Student Worktext page 56. Then invite pairs to share their ideas for inventions with the class.

Think About the Story: Reading Comprehension

Have students complete the remaining items on Student Worktext pages 56 and 57 independently or in pairs. Check their responses to help you assess their comprehension of the selection. If students' responses indicate that they did not understand the selection, reread the selection aloud, pausing after each section to have students summarize the main points about that young inventor.

Reading Comprehension Skill: Main Idea and Supporting Details

Have students reread the second to last paragraph on Student Worktext page 54. Write these sentences on the board:

- ◆ At the age of 15, Iliana Jaatmaa invented a battery-run world map.
- ◆ It shows how the world's great land masses have slowly moved over time.
- ◆ The land masses on the map begin as a group in one place and slowly move away from each other.
- ◆ Iliana got a $20,000 savings bond as a prize.
- ◆ Bet your teachers like the map, too, Iliana!

Ask students which sentence gives the main idea of the paragraph. (the first sentence) Ask them which sentences give more information, or details, about the main idea. (the second, third, fourth, and fifth sentences) Explain:

- ◆ The *main idea* of a paragraph is the most important idea in that paragraph.
- ◆ *Supporting details* are ideas and information that tell more about the main idea.

Then have students look at the paragraph beginning with **An underwater walkie-talkie** on Student Worktext page 55. Ask pairs of students to identify the main idea and find and write three details that tell more about this main idea.

🏔 Application

Career Connection Inform students that there are many organizations that help people with ideas for inventions to make their inventions a reality. These groups may help with anything from funding and development to manufacturing and legal issues such as obtaining a patent. Encourage students to use to the Internet to find out about organizations that help inventors. If necessary, guide them in conducting a key word search.

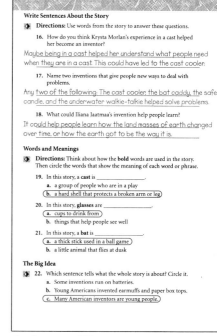

Student page 56

Student page 57

Reinforce & Extend

◆ SPELLING: Long *u* Spelled *ue, oo, u,* or *ew*

1. few **3.** boot **5.** duel **7.** mood **9.** shrewd
2. cool **4.** unite **6.** grew **8.** cruel **10.** tuba

Write *blue, room, uniform,* and *stew* on the board. Remind students that they have learned that the letters *ue, oo, u,* and *ew* can stand for the long *u* sound. Then have students number a sheet of paper 1–10. Dictate the words above one at a time, pausing for students to write them. Finally, write the words on the board and have students check their work, making corrections as needed.

Reading and Writing Practice Activity 46 provides additional practice spelling words with long u spelled *ue, oo, u,* or *ew.*

◆ LANGUAGE: Possessive Nouns

Write this sentence from the selection on the board:

Richie's family helped him develop his invention.

Ask students whose family the sentence is talking about, and how they know this. (Richie's family; the word *Richie's* tells whose family it is) Circle *'s* in *Richie's.* Explain that an apostrophe plus the letter *s* can be added to many nouns, including names, to show that something or someone belongs to, is related to, or is associated with something or someone else. Tell students that the form of a noun that shows ownership, relation, or association is called the possessive form. Explain how to make the possessive form of nouns:

- Add *'s* to most singular nouns. Examples: *girl's, Dana's*
- If a plural noun ends in *s,* just add an apostrophe. Examples: *girls', the Browns'*
- If a plural noun ends in a letter other than *s,* add *'s.* Examples: *men's, women's*

Write these phrases on the board: *the cousin of Kelly, the shirt that the woman is wearing, the dog that the brothers own, the house where the Popejoys live.* Have students rewrite each phrase using the possessive form of the second noun in each phrase. (*Kelly's cousin, the woman's shirt, the brothers' dog, the Popejoys' house*) Then write the correct responses on the board and have students check their work.

Reading and Writing Practice Activity 47 provides additional practice with possessive nouns.

◆ WRITING: How-to Instructions

Ask students to imagine that they have come up with an invention and need to tell others how to make the invention. Point out that one way to do this is to write a series of instructions. A set of instructions tells how to do something or make something. Explain:

- Any materials that are needed should be listed at the beginning of the instructions.
- The instructions should be written as a series of steps.
- The steps should be written in order. You may want to number each step.
- Be sure that each step is written clearly and that nothing is left out.

Reading and Writing Practice Duplicate and distribute Activities 48–49. Point out the Writing Model of how-to instructions, and help students identify the list of materials and the series of steps. Then have students write their own instructions in response to one of these prompts:

- Write instructions for how to make a peanut butter and jelly sandwich.
- Write instructions for how to find an article in the encyclopedia.
- Write instructions for how to log on to the Internet.

 # Lesson at a Glance

Preview: Fifteen-year-old Jessica does not like her new step-dad, Fred. When Jessica's mom and Fred plan a family camping trip to the desert, Jessica and her nine-year-old brother refuse to go. Their mother insists, although at the last minute she is unable to accompany them. Fred and the children head out into the desert in Fred's SUV. The first day out, Fred takes a turn too fast and the SUV flips, trapping him inside. While Ben waits with Fred, Jessica goes in search of help. Using maps to guide her, she finds her way to a roadside outpost, escaping snakes and a flash flood on the way. Meanwhile, with Fred's help, Ben finds the hidden car phone and is able to call for a rescue. By the time Jessica reaches the outpost, a rescue team is on the way to deliver Ben and Fred to safety.

Objectives

- to complete a chapter book successfully
- to practice the word study and phonics skills learned in Chapter 1
- to practice reading the high-frequency and content words learned in Chapter 1
- to build reading fluency

Before Reading "Lost in the Mountains"

Introduce the Small Book

Use Prior Knowledge   Display a copy of the small book for Chapter 1, *Lost in the Mountains,* and tell students that next they will have an opportunity to read a chapter book. Explain that the book uses only words and letter sounds they have learned in Chapter 1, and that they will be reading the chapter book for fun; they will not be expected to learn new words or skills. Explain:

- This book is about a girl named Jessica who goes on a camping trip to the desert. She is not looking forward to the trip.

- Although both Jessica and her brother do not want to be there, they both end up showing great courage when something unexpected occurs.

Invite students who have ever been camping or to the desert to share what that experience was like. Have them discuss the ways in which campers should prepare for wilderness excursions.

Preview and Predict

Distribute copies of *Lost in the Mountains.* Read aloud the introduction on the back cover. Have each student turn to the table of contents and read the chapter titles. Have students silently read the first three pages of the book. Guide them in making predictions about what might happen. Ask:

- Do you think Jessica will find a way to get out of the trip?
- What kinds of problems do you think the family might face out in the desert?
- Do you think Jessica and Ben will get along with Fred on the trip? Why or why not?

Read Independently

Students who have successfully read and understood the stories in Chapter 1 should be able to read *Lost in the Mountains* independently. You might periodically check their story comprehension by having them pause after completing each chapter to discuss the story. Discussion prompts for each chapter appear on the next two pages.

Read Strategically

Students who have struggled with the reading selections in Chapter 1, or who have been slow to master the phonics and word study skills presented in Chapter 1, may benefit from reading the book in groups of 3–5, pausing often to discuss events and to use reading strategies to clear up confusion. The following procedure will help ensure that all students have a successful and positive reading experience.

- Read the first three pages aloud as students follow along. Call on students to summarize the main events. Then have students read to the end of Chapter 1 silently.
- Model using a reading strategy so that students can see how the strategy helps readers clear up confusion. You might say: *At first I didn't understand why Jessica is so upset about the idea of a camping trip. When I read ahead, I learned that she does not want to go with Fred, her stepdad, because he will brag about how much he knows. She also does not want to be without TV and music.*

- Model setting a purpose for reading the next set of pages. (Example: *to find out what happens on the family camping trip*) Call on students to set their own purposes for reading. Have students read silently and pause at a designated stopping point. Each time you pause, call on students to explain how they used reading strategies as they read. Suggestions for specific questions you might ask appear on this page and the following page.

Reading "Lost in the Mountains"
◆ Comprehension Questions
Chapter 1
- Why doesn't Jessica like Fred?
- Why do Mom and Fred think a camping trip is a great idea?
- How does Jessica try to get out of the camping trip?
- Do you think Jessica will find a way out of the trip? Why or why not?

Chapter 2
- What happens that causes Jessica's mom to miss out on the trip?
- What do Fred's maps show? Why might the maps be important later in the story?
- How would you describe Fred's driving?
- What do you think will happen after the SUV goes off the cliff?

Chapter 3
- What happened to Fred? Do you think he will be OK?
- What problems do Jessica and Ben face that night in the desert?
- Do you think they should stay put, or go for help? Why?
- What do you think Jessica and Ben will do next? Why?

Read Strategically Ask students whether anything in Chapter 1, 2, or 3 confused them, and if so, what they did to clear up their confusion. Call on several students to give an oral summary of the main events in Chapters 1, 2, and 3. Ask students to predict what might happen next.

Chapter 4
- How far is Ghost Ranch Outpost? Why does Jessica want to go there?
- Why does Jessica want to take the path by the streambed?
- What things does Ben fear might happen to Jessica?
- What will Ben do while Jessica hikes to Ghost Ranch?

Chapter 5
- What surprising information does Fred give Ben?
- Does Fred feel bad about the accident? How can you tell?
- Do you think Ben will be able to find the phone?

Read Strategically Ask a volunteer to summarize the main events in Chapters 4 and 5. Call on another student to tell how he or she used the Reread/Read Ahead or the Clarify strategy to clear up confusion. Discuss students' predictions for the next part of the story, and help each student set a purpose for reading Chapters 6 and 7.

Chapter 6
- ◆ What will Jessica look for to find the streambed?
- ◆ What mistake does Jessica make?
- ◆ Why is this challenge difficult for Jessica?

Chapter 7
- ◆ What does Jessica do when she sees the snake? What happens next?
- ◆ What can Jessica do to find water?
- ◆ Do you think Jessica can trust the map to help her find the spring?
- ◆ What do you think Jessica will do next?

Read Strategically Ask each student to describe how he or she used one of these reading strategies: Use Prior Knowledge, Make a Prediction, Summarize, Clarify, Reread/Read Ahead, Use Context Clues. Then have students give an oral summary of Chapters 6 and 7, predict what might happen next, and set a purpose for reading the rest of the book.

Chapter 8
- ◆ How do Ben and Fred get the phone free?
- ◆ Why doesn't the phone work? Do you think they will be able to get the phone to work?
- ◆ What does Fred say about rain in the desert? What does he tell Ben to do?
- ◆ What happens as Ben sits on the rocks? What happens to Fred?

Chapter 9
- ◆ Do you think Jessica made a good choice in going to look for the spring?
- ◆ How does Jessica finally get some water to drink?
- ◆ What does Jessica remember about rain and the desert? What does she do after she remembers?
- ◆ Why does Jessica say Ghost Ranch has a good name?

Chapter 10
- ◆ Who does Jessica meet on the road? How did he find her?
- ◆ How does the rescue team get Fred out of the SUV?
- ◆ How have Ben's feelings about Fred changed? Why?
- ◆ Do you think Jessica's feelings about Fred will change? Why or why not?

Read Strategically Have students summarize the main events in Chapters 8, 9, and 10. Then discuss with students whether their predictions turned out to be correct. Encourage students to compare their predictions with actual story events.

After Reading "Lost in the Mountains"
Personal Response

Ask students whether they liked *Lost in the Mountains,* and why or why not. Invite several volunteers to tell what they liked about the story. If some students did not like it, encourage them to give specific reasons why.

Critical Response

Prompt students to think critically about the story by asking questions such as these:
- ◆ Did you like the characters in this book? Why or why not?
- ◆ Do you think Jessica and Ben did a good job of figuring out what to do?
- ◆ Which part of the book was most exciting? Why?
- ◆ What do you think Jessica learned as a result of her experience? Is this important?

Extension Activities

Students can work on the activities below independently, in pairs, or in small groups.

Reading

Students who are interested in learning more about deserts and campgrounds may want to do some investigating. They can start with a Web site such as www.desertusa.com, which provides information about many Southwestern deserts. Students may also request information from a group such as the Sierra Club, which leads hiking trips in the western United States.

- Sierra Club
  85 Second Street, 2nd floor
  San Francisco, CA 94105-3441

Writing

Have interested students write a short (1–3 page) sequel to *Lost in the Mountains* in which they describe what happens when Jessica and Ben tell their mom about the trip. You might prompt their ideas with questions such as:

- What parts does Jessica tell her mom? What parts does Ben tell?
- What part of the story does Fred tell?
- What does their mom think of this whole adventure?

Students who have done something they consider to be brave may want to write a personal narrative about their experience.

Students who are familiar with camping or with desert camping may want to write a how-to guide that they would give to someone going camping for the first time.

Research

Students might find answers to the following questions, using resources such as the Internet, the telephone book, or the classified section of a local newspaper:

- What are the names and locations of some campgrounds near your community?
- Where are some places you could go to learn about camping? What are some groups you could join to go on camping trips?

Chapter 1 Review

The Chapter Review on Student Worktext pages 59–66 will help students review and practice the skills presented in Chapter 1. The review is divided into four parts, A–D.

Suggestions to help students complete the Chapter Review:

- ◆ Make sure students understand that the Chapter Review is not a test. You may have students work in pairs and then compare responses, or you may work through the review as a class.
- ◆ Read the instructions for each part aloud.
- ◆ Have students complete one part of the review at a time. Pause to go over the answers and have students mark corrections using a second color.

Chapter Test

Reproducible blackline masters of the Chapter 1 Test can be found on pages 144–147 of this book. Use the test to assess students' comprehension of the skills taught in the chapter.

Additional Practice

Reading and Writing Practice Activities 1–67 can be used to reinforce the skills taught in Chapter 1.

Part A

Part A reviews the phonics skills taught in the chapter. Read aloud the summaries presented in the tip boxes before each exercise. Then have students complete the items. If students show difficulty understanding and using the new letters and sounds, review individual lessons or assign the corresponding Reading and Writing Practice Activities: 1, 6, 13, 18, 25, 32, 39, 44.

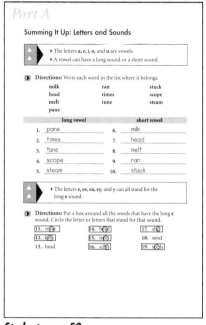

Part A

Summing It Up: Letters and Sounds

- The letters **a, e, i, o,** and **u** are vowels.
- A vowel can have a long sound or a short sound.

Directions: Write each word in the list where it belongs.

milk	ran	stuck
head	times	scope
melt	tune	steam
pane		

long vowel	short vowel
1. pane	6. milk
2. times	7. head
3. tune	8. melt
4. scope	9. ran
5. steam	10. stuck

- The letters **e, ee, ea, ey,** and **y** can all stand for the long **e** sound.

Directions: Put a box around all the words that have the long **e** sound. Circle the letter or letters that stand for that sound.

11. meat	14. bead	17. shy
12. key	15. tree	18. send
13. head	16. silly	19. seeds

Student page 59

- Words that have the CVC pattern often have a short vowel sound.
- Words that have the CVCe pattern usually have a long vowel sound.
- Words that have the CVVC pattern usually have a long vowel sound. The first vowel usually tells you what the long vowel sound is.

Directions: Write each word below in the list where it belongs.

rain	write	bench	lick
bone	beam	lame	cried
stump	crunch	room	June

CVC	CVCe	CVVC
20. stump	24. bone	28. rain
21. crunch	25. write	29. beam
22. bench	26. lame	30. room
23. lick	27. June	31. cried

- The letters **th, sh, ch,** and **wh** come at the beginning of some words. They stand for one sound.
- The letters **th, sh, ch,** and **tch** come at the end of some words. They stand for one sound.

Directions: Write each word below in the list where it belongs.

rich	path	ditch	swish	wrath
math	wish	fish	pitch	

Rhymes with *stitch*	Rhymes with *bath*	Rhymes with *dish*
32. rich	35. math	38. wish
33. ditch	36. path	39. fish
34. pitch	37. wrath	40. swish

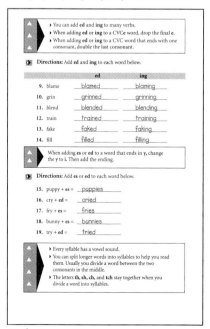

Student page 60

Part B

Part B reviews the word study and structural analysis skills taught in the chapter. Read aloud the summaries presented in the tip boxes before each exercise. Then have students complete the items. You may want to review the skills by looking back at individual lessons, presenting new examples on the board, or assigning the corresponding Reading and Writing Practice Activities: 3, 8, 15, 20, 27, 34, 41.

- Many different patterns of letters can stand for a long vowel sound.
- The letters **ai** and **ay** can stand for long **a.**
- The letters **igh, y,** and **ie** can stand for long **i.**
- The letters **oa** and **ow** can stand for long **o.**
- The letters **ue, oo, u,** and **ew** can stand for long **u.**

Directions: Write each word in the list where it belongs. Then circle the letter or letters in each word that stand for the long vowel sound.

stain	float	my	roots
stow	stay	tuba	shrewd
night	blue	crow	brain
play	pies	tight	roamed

long *a*	long *i*	long *o*	long *u*
41. stain	45. night	49. stow	53. blue
42. play	46. pies	50. float	54. tuba
43. stay	47. my	51. crow	55. roots
44. brain	48. tight	52. roamed	56. shrewd

Part B

Summing It Up: More Word Work

- Add **s** to make a word tell about more than one thing, or to make it tell about something going on now.
- If a word ends in **x, ch, sh,** or **s,** add **es** instead of **s.**

Directions: Add **s** or **es** to each word below. Write the new word on the line.

1. buzz buzzes	5. flash flashes
2. wish wishes	6. box boxes
3. pitch pitches	7. trim trims
4. bath baths	8. finish finishes

Student page 61

- You can add **ed** and **ing** to many verbs.
- When adding **ed** or **ing** to a CVCe word, drop the final **e.**
- When adding **ed** or **ing** to a CVC word that ends with one consonant, double the last consonant.

Directions: Add **ed** and **ing** to each word below.

	ed	ing
9. blame	blamed	blaming
10. grin	grinned	grinning
11. blend	blended	blending
12. train	trained	training
13. fake	faked	faking
14. fill	filled	filling

When adding **es** or **ed** to a word that ends in **y,** change the **y** to **i.** Then add the ending.

Directions: Add **es** or **ed** to each word below.

15. puppy + **es** = puppies
16. cry + **ed** = cried
17. fry + **es** = fries
18. bunny + **es** = bunnies
19. try + **ed** = tried

- Every syllable has a vowel sound.
- You can split longer words into syllables to help you read them. Usually you divide a word between the two consonants in the middle.
- The letters **th, sh, ch,** and **tch** stay together when you divide a word into syllables.

Student page 62

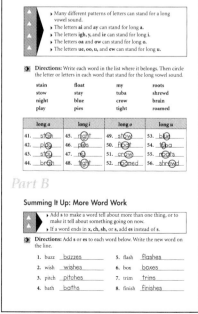

Part C

Part C reviews the story words from each story in the chapter. Students are asked to recognize story words and their meanings, and to identify the number of syllables in story words. Have students review the story words in the Word Bank at the back of their Student Worktext or refer to the stories in the chapter to help them complete the review. For additional practice with word recognition, assign the corresponding Reading and Writing Practice Activities: 2, 7, 14, 19, 26, 33, 40, 45.

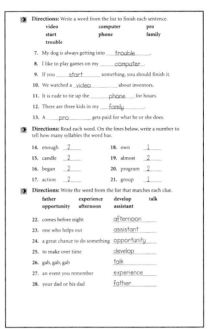

Directions: Write each word. Draw a line to divide it into syllables.

20. dinner ___din | ner___   24. pitching ___pitch | ing___
21. without ___with | out___   25. bobcat ___bob | cat___
22. sentence ___sen | tence___   26. fitness ___fit | ness___
23. only ___on | ly___   27. wishes ___wish | es___

▸ You can use 's to show that a thing belongs to someone, or has a connection to someone.

Directions: Write each sentence again. Use 's to show that something belongs to someone, or has a connection to someone.

28. The car Ron owns has stalled.
   ___Ron's car has stalled.___
29. The cat Tim has is cute.
   ___Tim's cat is cute.___
30. The song Tom wrote is great.
   ___Tom's song is great.___

Part C

Story Words

Directions: Write the word from the list that matches each clue.

| problem | paper | mountain |
| young | always | night |

1. not old ___young___
2. not day ___night___
3. made from trees ___paper___
4. something wrong ___problem___
5. something tall ___mountain___
6. all the time ___always___

Student page 63

Directions: Write a word from the list to finish each sentence.

video	computer	pro
start	phone	family
trouble		

7. My dog is always getting into ___trouble___.
8. I like to play games on my ___computer___.
9. If you ___start___ something, you should finish it.
10. We watched a ___video___ about inventors.
11. It is rude to tie up the ___phone___ for hours.
12. There are three kids in my ___family___.
13. A ___pro___ gets paid for what he or she does.

Directions: Read each word. On the lines below, write a number to tell how many syllables the word has.

14. enough ___2___   18. own ___1___
15. candle ___2___   19. almost ___2___
16. began ___2___   20. program ___2___
17. action ___2___   21. group ___1___

Directions: Write the word from the list that matches each clue.

| father | experience | develop | talk |
| opportunity | afternoon | assistant | |

22. comes before night ___afternoon___
23. one who helps out ___assistant___
24. a great chance to do something ___opportunity___
25. to make over time ___develop___
26. gab, gab, gab ___talk___
27. an event you remember ___experience___
28. your dad or his dad ___father___

Student page 64

Part D

Part D reviews the content of the stories in the chapter. Students are asked to identify story characters, settings, and events, or to recall the main ideas in nonfiction selections. If students are having difficulty remembering story details, have them reread the stories they have trouble recalling and work in pairs or as a class to complete Part D again.

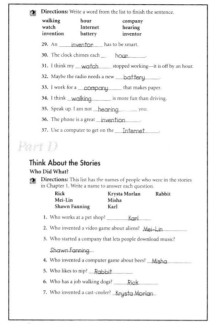

Directions: Write a word from the list to finish the sentence.

walking   hour   company
watch   Internet   hearing
invention battery   inventor

29. An ____inventor____ has to be smart.

30. The clock chimes each ____hour____.

31. I think my ____watch____ stopped working—it is off by an hour.

32. Maybe the radio needs a new ____battery____.

33. I work for a ____company____ that makes paper.

34. I think ____walking____ is more fun than driving.

35. Speak up. I am not ____hearing____ you.

36. The phone is a great ____invention____.

37. Use a computer to get on the ____Internet____.

Part D

Think About the Stories

Who Did What?

Directions: This list has the names of people who were in the stories in Chapter 1. Write a name to answer each question.

Rick   Krysta Morlan   Rabbit
Mei-Lin   Misha
Shawn Fanning Karl

1. Who works at a pet shop? ____Karl____

2. Who invented a video game about aliens? ____Mei-Lin____

3. Who started a company that lets people download music?
____Shawn Fanning____

4. Who invented a computer game about bees? ____Misha____

5. Who likes to nip? ____Rabbit____

6. Who has a job walking dogs? ____Rick____

7. Who invented a cast-cooler? ____Krysta Morlan____

Student page 65

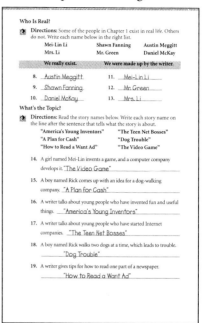

Who Is Real?

Directions: Some of the people in Chapter 1 exist in real life. Others do not. Write each name below in the right list.

Mei-Lin Li   Shawn Fanning   Austin Meggitt
Mrs. Li   Mr. Green   Daniel McKay

We really exist.	We were made up by the writer.
8. Austin Meggitt	11. Mei-Lin Li
9. Shawn Fanning	12. Mr. Green
10. Daniel McKay	13. Mrs. Li

What's the Topic?

Directions: Read the story names below. Write each story name on the line after the sentence that tells what the story is about.

"America's Young Inventors"   "The Teen Net Bosses"
"A Plan for Cash"   "Dog Trouble"
"How to Read a Want Ad"   "The Video Game"

14. A girl named Mei-Lin invents a game, and a computer company develops it. "The Video Game"

15. A boy named Rick comes up with an idea for a dog-walking company. "A Plan for Cash"

16. A writer talks about young people who have invented fun and useful things. "America's Young Inventors"

17. A writer talks about young people who have started Internet companies. "The Teen Net Bosses"

18. A boy named Rick walks two dogs at a time, which leads to trouble. "Dog Trouble"

19. A writer gives tips for how to read one part of a newspaper. "How to Read a Want Ad"

Student page 66

Chapter 2 Planning Guide

Skills and Learning Objectives

	Student Pages	Phonics and Phonograms	Word Study	Reading Strategy
Lesson 1 The Driver's License, Part 1	68–73	Final *nk, ng, nd, nt (ung)*	Schwa (consonant plus *le*): VC/CVV; V/CCV	Clarify
Lesson 2 The Driver's License, Part 2	74–79	/ou/ Spelled *ou, ow (ow, out, ound)*	Dividing Words with Diphthongs	Summarize
Lesson 3 Getting on the Road	80–85	Initial /k/ Spelled *ch*; initial /r/ Spelled *wr*	Endings *-er, -est*	Set a Purpose (Real Life)
Lesson 4 The Car Wash, Part 1	86–91	Contractions with *will, not, am, have, are, is*	Dividing Words with Blends	Access Prior Knowledge (Use What You Know)
Lesson 5 The Car Wash, Part 2	92–97	Initial Diagraphs and Clusters: *str, thr, squ, scr, spr, shr*		Reread/Read Ahead
Lesson 6 Video Dreams	98–103	/oi/ Spelled *oy, oi (oy)*	Ending *-ly*	Set a Purpose
Lesson 7 Rain Dance	104–109	/ôr/ Spelled *or, ore, our (our)*		Use Context Clues
Lesson 8 Fashion Time Line	110–115	/ûr/ Spelled *er, ur, ir (urn)*	Ending *-er* (one who)	Make a Prediction (Nonfiction)

Independent Reading

Catch a Wave by Corinn Codye
Lesson Plan: Teacher's Guide pages 90–93

Assessment and Review

Chapter 2 Summary of Skills and Strategies:
Student Worktext page 116

Chapter 2 Review:
Student Worktext pages 117–124

Chapter 2 Test:
Teacher's Guide pages 148–151

Reading Comprehension/ Critical Thinking	Spelling	Study Skill	Language	Writing	Literary Appreciation	Learning Styles	Focus on LEP/ESL or LD	Application	Reading and Writing Practice Activities
Draw Conclusions	61		61	61		59			50–56
Categorize	65		65	65		64	63	62	57–62
Main Idea and Supporting Details		69	69	69			67	67	63–69
Summarize	73		73	73		72	71		70–76
Cause and Effect	77		77		77	75		75	77–80
Make Decisions		81	81	81		79	79		81–87
Fantasy vs. Realism	85		85		85	82	83	84	88–91
Author's Purpose	89		89	89			87	88	92–98

Common Reading Errors

If the Student . . .

◆ appears to have difficulty recognizing letters and/or commonly used words

◆ reads too quickly and ignores punctuation marks so that comprehension is impacted

◆ mispronounces words without self-correcting

◆ has difficulty reading longer words or words with inflected endings

◆ fails to adjust schema when new information is presented

Then . . .

→ ◆ arrange for vision screening.

→ ◆ teach the language arts lessons on Recognizing Sentences and on the Four Kinds of Sentences.

→ ◆ have the student reread the sentence and try a different pronunciation using context clues for help; repeat process until he or she comes to a pronunciation that sounds right and makes sense.

→ ◆ reteach the lessons on inflected endings; model how to identify base words and endings; model how to divide words into syllables.

→ ◆ reteach the Make a Prediction reading strategy; encourage frequent checking of predictions and revising of predictions to match story content.

 # Lesson at a Glance

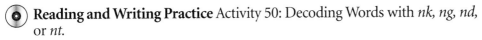 **Chapter 2, Lesson 1 "The Driver's License," Part 1**

Preview: This lesson presents the first half of a two-part realistic fiction story about a young man who overcomes his physical disability to obtain a driver's license.

Objectives

◆ to read a realistic fiction story
◆ to read words that contain the consonant pairs *nk, ng, nd, nt*, and the phonogram *ung*
◆ to spell words ending with a consonant plus *le*

◆ to draw conclusions
◆ to identify and use verbs
◆ to write dialogue

Student Worktext Pages 68–73

Story Words

don't, below, above, license, control

⊙ **Reading and Writing Practice Activities 50–56**

Before Reading "The Driver's License," Part 1

Letters and Sounds

Final *nk, ng, nd, nt*; Phonogram *ung*

Write the words *sing, sink, send,* and *sent* on the board and say them aloud. Circle the letters *nk, ng, nd* and *nt*. Tell students that these consonant pairs often come at the end of a word. Write *rung* on the board. Replace the *r* with *l* and read the new word aloud. Replace the *l* with *s* and ask students to read the new word aloud. Explain that once they can read the words *rung* and *lung*, they can read many other words that end with the same letters.

Next write the words *singing, thinking, mended,* and *rented* on the board. Circle the letters *ng, nk, nd* and *nt*. Explain that these consonant pairs can also come together in the middle of a word. Say each word and ask students how many syllables they hear in each. (two) Then have students complete Student Worktext page 68.

⊙ **Reading and Writing Practice** Activity 50: Decoding Words with *nk, ng, nd,* or *nt*.

Story Words

Read aloud these words: *don't, below, above, license, control*. Tell students that these words are important in the next story. Then write the words on the board and point to each one as you say it aloud a second time. Next, have students follow the ❑ *Read* ❑ *Say* ❑ *Write* sequence by completing **Story Words** on Student Worktext page 69. Have students add the words to their Word Bank at the back of the Student Worktext. To introduce the words in context, write these sentences on the board:

◆ <u>Don't</u> go swimming after eating a big meal!
◆ We must drive at or <u>below</u> the the speed limit.
◆ The bird flew <u>above</u> the trees.
◆ You need a <u>license</u> to drive.
◆ It is hard to <u>control</u> a car on ice.

Have students make a word card for *don't*. Ask a volunteer to read the first sentence aloud. Then have students copy the sentence onto the back of the word card. Follow the same procedure for the remaining words. To assess students' ability to read each new word, listen as individual students read the sentences on the board aloud.

⊙ **Reading and Writing Practice** Activity 51: Reading Story Words.

More Word Work

Have students work in pairs to complete **More Word Work** on Student Worktext page 69.

⊙ **Reading and Writing Practice** Activity 3: Reading and Writing Words with *le*.

LESSON 1 ▸ *Before Reading "The Driver's License," Part 1*

Letters and Sounds

These consonants often come together at the end of a word:

nk   ng   nd   nt

Directions: Read these words. Circle the two consonants at the end of each word.
1. ink   2. sung   3. land   4. went

Directions: Sometimes these consonants come together in the middle of a word. Circle each word. Circle **nk, ng, nd,** or **nt**.
5. sinking   sinking   8. dented   dented
6. ringer   ringer   9. linking   linking
7. landing   landing   10. dunked   dunked

Directions: Write the letters on the lines. See how many words you can make.

| b | m | str | k | r | th | s | l | h |

11. str ung   14. b ent
12. r ung   15. n,l ent
13. s,l,h ung   16. s ent
17. b and   20. m,k ink
18. str and   21. r ink
19. s,l,h and   22. th,s,l ink

The letters **nk, ng,** and **nd** usually stay together when you divide a word into syllables.
Examples: sink|ing   ring|ing   send|ing

Directions: Write each word. Divide it into syllables with a line.
23. inkjet   ink|jet   25. ringtail   ring|tail
24. tanker   tank|er   26. blended   blend|ed

Student page 68

Story Words

Directions: Read each word to yourself. Then say the word out loud. Write the word on the line. Check the box after each step.
27. don't   Read ☑ Say ☑ Write ☑   don't
28. below (be|low)   Read ☑ Say ☑ Write ☑   below
29. above (a|bove)   Read ☑ Say ☑ Write ☑   above
30. license (li|cense)   Read ☑ Say ☑ Write ☑   license
31. control (con|trol)   Read ☑ Say ☑ Write ☑   control

More Word Work

Directions: You know the word **little.** Many words end like **little.** Write **little** on the line. Circle the letters **le.**
32. little   lit tle

If you can read **little,** you can read many words that end with a consonant and **le.** Try reading these words.

brittle   battle   settle

The letters **le** stand for the same sound in each word. Write the words above on the lines. Circle the letter pattern **le** in each. Underline the consonant that is next to the letters **le.**
Example: little   lit tle

33. brittle   34. battle   35. settle

Directions: All these words have two syllables. The last syllable is made of a consonant plus **le.** Circle the last syllable in these words.
36. brit|tle   37. crum|ble

Directions: Draw a line to divide each word below into syllables. That last syllable is made of a consonant plus **le.**
38. bat|tle   39. set|tle   40. sim|ple   41. sam|ple

▸ **TIPS:** ▸ If the first syllable ends with a consonant, it probably has a short vowel sound.   bat|tle
▸ If the first syllable ends with a vowel, it probably has a long vowel sound.   ti|tle

Student page 69

Reading "The Driver's License," Part 1

◆ *Preview and Predict*

- Have a volunteer read the title on the Student Worktext page 70 aloud. Point to the picture of Haksu on Student Worktext page 71. Tell students they are about to read about a young man named Haksu and his two friends, Jay and Brodie. Write the names on the board for students.
- Read aloud the question under **Use What You Know.** Discuss the answer as a group. Then have students write their responses.
- Once students begin reading, have them pause at the top of page 71 to make a prediction about whether or not they think Haksu is ready for the test.
- You may also want to point out the symbol for percent (%) on Student Worktext page 71 and explain its meaning.

◆ *Strategy Modeling*

Clarify   Remind students that when they come to a word, phrase, or sentence that they do not understand while reading, it is often a good idea to pause and clear up their confusion before they continue reading. Model using the Clarify strategy. You might say:

At first, I'm confused by the phrase "being able to drive takes the 'dis' out of disability." But then I stop and think about it. I know when you "dis" someone, you do something bad to them. So taking some of the "dis" out of disability might mean taking one of the bad things out of being disabled. This phrase must mean that driving makes having a disability easier to live with.

Have students read Student Worktext pages 70 and 71 to find out if Haksu gets a driver's license. Remind them to pause to clarify if anything confuses them.

▲ Learning Styles

Auditory/Verbal   Once students have read the story through one time silently, have groups of students read the story aloud. Assign them the roles of Haksu, Jay, Brodie, the DMV examiner, and a narrator or narrators. Then have each student go through the story and highlight portions he or she will read. Finally, have students take turns reading their parts of the story aloud.

Use What You Know

How do people who cannot use their legs get around? Write what you think on the lines below.

Answers will vary.

THE DRIVER'S LICENSE, PART 1

Haksu gave a push to the control stick for his battery-run wheelchair. The chair smoothly moved up the ramp. He drove the chair up so it sat on the lift gate at the side of his friend Jay's van. He stopped, locked in, and pushed the control switch to raise the gate. Above, he rolled his chair into the van, closed up the gate, and drove into the dropped driver's space. The seat had been taken out, so Haksu could roll his wheelchair into the space. He stopped above the lock-downs and clicked the locks into place.

Haksu looked over the driving controls and put the key in the switch below. He slipped his hand through the cuff at the left of the driver's wheel. What a great invention! The cuff was part of a hand-control set for pushing the brake, and for hitting the gas. He knew how to pull back to gain speed and push to brake. A long rod led down to the brake below. When he pushed, it pushed the brake down.

He reached back and above, pulling the seat belt into place. Another click. Buckle up! He would not forget that step any more. If only he had had on a seat belt two years in the past. Then his neck would not have been broken. No risking that again. No way.

Below, Jay sat in his own wheelchair outside the van. He looked up at Haksu above. "You got it, buddy. In this thing, you bring your own driver's seat. Now, fool, don't you go crashing my van. And don't bungle your license test."

Haksu smiled back at Jay. "Don't go there, Jay! You know I have had enough of car crashes."

Haksu's legs were useless, but he had just enough use of his hands to be a driver. He was glad for it. He thanked Jay again for letting him use the van to learn to drive. Getting his license meant being free to do so many more things on his own. As Jay said, being able to drive **takes some of the "dis" out of the disability.**

Brodie, Haksu's driving coach, hopped into the van in the right-hand seat. She buckled in. "OK, Haksu," she said. "I am going to test you as if this were the true driver's license test. Are you ready?"

Student page 70

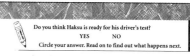

Do you think Haksu is ready for his driver's test?

YES   NO

Circle your answer. Read on to find out what happens next.

Haksu smiled weakly at Brodie and nodded. He hoped his smile hid his feelings. He had six weeks of training with Brodie. But deep down, he still did not feel **100% ready** for the driving test.

Brodie led him through the steps of the test. She asked him to show her the lights for braking and turning, and the headlights. He worked the hand brake. Then he turned the key and backed out of the driveway. Brodie talked him through a few more tasks, like backing up for 50 feet. It was not easy to keep in line. Remember to check traffic before each move. Switch lanes. Look back and check traffic. Then ease into the next lane. Remember to blink the turning lights. Then they got on and off the freeway.

"Haksu, I think you are all set," she said. "Head for the DMV."

They pulled up to the DMV and got in line for the driving test. Brodie stepped out of the van as a man walked up. He held a clipboard with papers on it. "I think you are ready," said Brodie again. **"Hang in there."**

Haksu sucked in a breath and blew it out with a sigh. Outside the van, the man asked Haksu the same questions that Brodie had asked. Then he got into the van. Haksu pulled out of the driveway. Go right. Then go left. Check for traffic. Pull over and stop. The wheels of the van got hung up at the lip at the side of the street. "Now I'm fried," Haksu thought. The man made a check on his paper. Pull out. Check for traffic. Turn around. Back

up. The back of the van swung out of line. Oops. Not in a line. The man made another check. Now it was time to get on and off the freeway. Haksu's hand got so sweaty he thought it might slip off the wheel. Then they were back at the DMV. Haksu's hands were shaking badly. He did not want to hear the news.

The man spoke to him, "Good job, young man." Haksu did not think he was hearing right. "You will be a fine driver. You might work on backing up and pulling over. I wrote you up for those things. But you passed!" ▶

Student page 71

After Reading "The Driver's License," Part 1

Personal Response: What Do You Think?

Ask students whether they think Haksu will make a good driver, and why or why not. Then invite each student to write his or her opinion under **What do You Think?** on Student Worktext page 72.

Think About the Story: Reading Comprehension

Have students complete the remaining items on Student Worktext pages 72 and 73 independently. Then ask them to compare responses with a partner to check comprehension. If responses differ, have pairs reread the story and answer the questions again.

Reading Comprehension Skill: Drawing Conclusions

Remind students that writers do not always tell readers everything directly. Readers therefore have to figure out some things they read on their own. When readers have to figure out what an author doesn't tell them, they are drawing conclusions. Explain:

- Readers can use clues in a story to draw conclusions.
- Readers can use what they know to draw a logical conclusion about how characters act or feel or why certain things happen.

Ask students the following questions and help them draw reasonable conclusions:

- Why do you think Haksu took the test in Jay's van?
- When Jay says, "Now, fool, don't you go crashing my van," is he serious? How do you know?
- At the end of the test, does Haksu think he passed? How do you know?

If necessary, model drawing a conclusion. You might say:

When Haksu gets into Jay's van and buckles his seatbelt, it says, "If only he had on a seatbelt two years in the past. Then his neck would not have been broken." I know that people can be born with disabilities or become disabled through a disease or accident. I think that Haksu lost control of his legs because he was in a car accident, and he wasn't wearing a seatbelt.

Look Ahead

Tell students that they will learn more about Haksu in the next story they read. Ask students to predict what might happen next.

LESSON 1 ▶ After Reading "The Driver's License," Part 1

What Do You Think?

1. Do you think Haksu will make a fine driver? Why or why not? Write what you think on the lines below.

Answers will vary.

Think About the Story

Use Story Words

Directions: Look at your list of story words on page 69. Write a story word for each clue.

2. This is a card that says you can drive. _license_
3. This is a short way of saying "do not." _don't_
4. This word tells where the sky is. _above_
5. This word tells where the grass is. _below_
6. When you turn or stop a car, you do this to it. _control_

Write Sentences About the Story

Directions: Use words from the story to answer these questions.

7. How did Haksu's neck get broken?
He was in a car wreck. He was not wearing his seat belt.

8. Why does Haksu need a special van?
He has no use of his legs and only some use of his arms. He needs a van that he can drive.

When Did It Happen?

9. Write a number from 1 to 6 in front of each event to show when it happened.

_5_ Haksu takes the driving test.
_2_ Brodie hops into the van next to Haksu.
_3_ Haksu drives to the DMV.
_6_ The man from the DMV says, "Good job, young man."
_1_ Haksu gets into Jay's van.
_4_ Brodie gets out of the van.

Student page 72

What Are the Facts?

Directions: Write **yes** in front of each sentence that gives a fact from the story. Write **no** in front of each sentence that does not.

10. _yes_ Jay's van has a special dropped space for the driver.
11. _no_ Jay and Haksu can drive all kinds of cars.
12. _yes_ Haksu still has some use of his hands.
13. _no_ Haksu did everything right on the driver's test.
14. _no_ Haksu has his own van, specially fitted for him.
15. _yes_ Haksu and Jay need a special lift to get them into the van.

Words and Meanings

Directions: Think about how the **bold** words are used in the story. Then circle the words that show the meaning of each word or phrase.

16. To **take the 'dis' out of disability"** means to _____.
a. help someone with a disability do more
b. add a new part to the word disability
c. help someone learn to walk

17. To be **"100% ready"** means to be _____.
a. almost as ready as you can be
b. 100 times more ready than you need
c. as ready as you can be

18. Brodie tells Haksu to **"hang in there."** She means _____.
a. keep hanging around the DMV until it is your turn
b. hang around in the van until the test is over
c. keep a cool head and try your best

Look Ahead

19. Do you think Haksu will want a van of his own?
Answers will vary.

20. How do you think he might go about getting one?
Answers will vary.

Student page 73

Reinforce & Extend

◆ SPELLING: Words Ending in a Consonant plus *le*

1. little   **3.** bottle   **5.** dimple   **7.** simple   **9.** buckle
2. cattle   **4.** bungle   **6.** kettle   **8.** puddle   **10.** sample

Write *brittle* on the board. Circle the letters *le* and underline the *t* immediately in front of them. Remind students that the letters *le* follow a consonant at the end of many words; the letters *le* stand for the /əl/ sound at the end of brittle. Then have students number a sheet of paper 1–10. Dictate the words above one at a time, pausing for students to write them. Next write the words on thc board and have students check their work, making corrections as needed.

◉ **Reading and Writing Practice** Activity 53 provides additional practice spelling words ending with a consonant plus *le*.

◆ LANGUAGE: Verbs

Write these sentences on the board:

Haksu drove to the DMV.
He got his license.

Ask students to underline the word in each sentence that tells about an action. (drove, got) Explain that these words are *verbs*. Explain:

- Each sentence has a verb.
- A verb can tell what a person or thing in the sentence does or is like.
- The verb in a sentence usually comes after the person or thing it tells about.

Write these sentences on the board and ask pairs of students to underline the verbs: *Haksu and Jay joke a lot. Brodie helped Haksu.* (joke, helped) Then have partners write two of their own sentences and underline the verb in each.

◉ **Reading and Writing Practice** Activity 54 provides additional practice identifying the verb in a sentence.

◆ WRITING: Dialogue

Write these sentences on the board and ask a volunteer to read them aloud:

"Don't bungle your license test," Jay said.
Haksu said, "Don't go there, Jay!"

Tell students that these two sentences are an example of dialogue, or conversation, between two characters. Explain:

- Writers use dialogue to tell exactly what characters in a story say.
- The words that the characters say are in quotation marks. (Circle the quotation marks in the sample sentences so students can see how they appear on each side of what is said.)
- Writers put a comma, question mark, or exclamation point at the end of what the characters say, just inside the second quotation mark. (Underline the comma and exclamation point in the dialogue and point out how they are inside the quotes.)
- Writers usually add the character's name plus a word like *said* or *asked* so that it is clear who is speaking. A comma sets off the speaker's name from the words he or she says.

◉ **Reading and Writing Practice** Duplicate and distribute Activities 55–56. Point out the Writing Model of a dialogue, and help students identify key elements of dialogue: quotation marks; the comma, question mark, or exclamation point; and the speaker's name. Then have pairs of students write a brief dialogue between two of the story characters they have read about so far in the Student Worktext.

 # Lesson at a Glance

Preview: This lesson presents the second half of a two-part story about a young man who obtains a driver's license despite his inability to use his legs. This part tells how his family, friends, and community come together to raise money for a specially-equipped van.

Objectives
- to read a realistic fiction story
- to read and spell words that contain *ou* or *ow*
- to categorize information
- to identify action verbs
- to write a paragraph of description

Student Worktext Pages 74–79

Story Words
every, once, story, money, special, account

Reading and Writing Practice Activities 57–62

Before Reading "The Driver's License," Part 2

Letters and Sounds

Vowel Sound /ou/ Spelled *ou* or *ow*

Write the word *out* on the board and say it aloud. Circle the letters *ou* and explain that they can stand for the /ou/ vowel sound. Write the words *sound, round, count,* and *ground* on the board and ask volunteers to read them aloud.

Remind students that they also know the word *now.* Write it on the board and circle the letters *ow.* Point out that these letters also can stand for the /ou/ sound. Write the words *down, town, cow,* and *plow* on the board and ask volunteers to read them aloud. Then have students complete Student Worktext page 74.

Reading and Writing Practice Activity 57: Decoding Words with /ou/ Spelled *ou* or *ow.*

Story Words

Read aloud these words: *every, once, story, money, special, account.* Tell students that these words are important in the next story. Then write the words on the board and point to each one as you say it aloud a second time. Next, have students follow the ❏ *Read* ❏ *Say* ❏ *Write* sequence by completing **Story Words** on Student Worktext page 75. Have students add the words to their Word Bank at the back of the Student Worktext. To introduce the words in context, write these sentences on the board:

- We talk on the phone <u>every</u> week.
- I walk my dog <u>once</u> a day.
- The end of the <u>story</u> was sad.
- My rent <u>money</u> is due on the first.
- Jay drives a <u>special</u> van.
- Do you have an <u>account</u> at the bank?

Have students make a word card for *every.* Ask a volunteer to read the first sentence aloud. Then have students copy the sentence onto the back of the word card. Follow the same procedure for the remaining words. To assess students' ability to read each new word, listen as individual students read the sentences on the board aloud.

Reading and Writing Practice Activity 58: Reading Story Words.

More Word Work

Have students complete **More Word Work** on Student Worktext page 75.

🏰 Application

At Home Students might enjoy learning about how physically disabled people adapt their homes to suit their needs. You might invite a disabled person to your class to speak about how entry ways, kitchens, bedrooms, and other parts of a house are altered for people with limited use of their hands, legs, or eyesight.

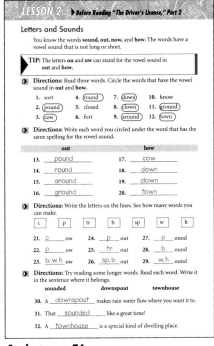
Student page 74

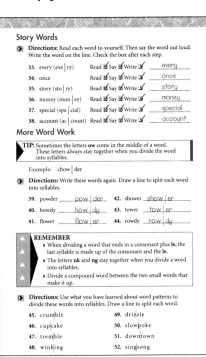
Student page 75

Reading "The Driver's License," Part 2

◈ Preview and Predict

- Tell students that they are going to read more about Haksu and Jay. Have one volunteer read the title on Student Worktext page 76. Then ask students to preview the illustration.
- Ask students to predict what might happen next in the story.
- While reading, have students stop at the top of page 77 to predict whether Haksu will get his own van.

◈ Strategy Modeling

Summarize Remind students that while reading, or when reading a story in two parts, it can help to pause and sum up what they have read so far. This can help readers understand and remember more of what they read. Explain:

- A summary includes the most important ideas or events in a piece of writing.
- A person summarizes by using his or her own words, not the original sentences from the story.
- A summary does not include details.

Have students summarize key events in Part 1 of "The Driver's License." Write their responses on the board. If necessary, model the Summarize strategy. You might say:

Before I read Part 2 of the story, I'll sum up what I know from Part 1. Haksu is a young man who has lost the use of his legs. He borrows a special van to take the driving test. He is very nervous, but he is able to pass the test. Now that I have summed up the main events so far, I am ready to find out what else Haksu will do.

Have students read "The Driver's License," Part 2 to find out what happens to Haksu next. Tell them to pause at the bottom of Student Worktext page 76 and sum up the important events before reading the ending on page 77.

Focus on ESL/LEP

Explain and discuss the following terms used in the story:

- on the loose
- booting up his computer
- not too keen on
- go nuts for
- the word got out
- knew it down deep

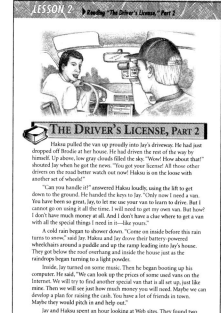

Student page 76

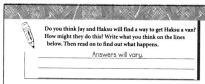

Student page 77

After Reading "The Driver's License," Part 2

Personal Response: You Be the Judge

Have students work in pairs to write answers to the question under you **You Be The Judge** on Student Worktext page 78. Then invite students to read their responses to the whole class.

Think About the Story: Reading Comprehension

Have students complete the remaining activities on Student Worktext pages 78 and 79. Then have them compare answers as a group. Assign groups to report one section to the class.

Reading Comprehension Skill: Categorize

Write these terms from the story on the board: *ramp, wheel, brake, seat belt, hand-control set, lock-downs*. Ask students which things all cars have. (wheel, brake, seat belt). Put a check next to those words, write them in a separate list, and label it "Things all cars have." Then put the remaining items in a list titled "Things special vans have." Point out that these lists show two categories, or groups, of information. Explain:

- *Categorizing,* or grouping things that are alike, helps readers keep track of similar items or ideas.
- In order to put things into categories, think about what features ideas or items share.

Have students reread the first three paragraphs on Student Worktext page 76. Then have pairs do the following:

- Circle words in paragraphs 1–3 that have to do with weather. (low gray clouds, cold rain, shower down, snow, puddle, raindrops, light powder)
- Circle words in paragraphs 1–3 that have to do with driving. (pulled up, van, driveway, driven, license, drivers, road, wheels, keys).

Then write these two categories of words on the board. Once students have practiced identifying related ideas, have them think of two categories of their own and list several things that fit into each category. You can then collect all the lists from students and play a game in which you call out items in a list and students try to name the category that the listed items belong to.

🔺 Learning Styles

Body/Kinesthetic Duplicate the eight sentences under **Why Did It Happen?** on Student Worktext page 78 and cut them apart into sentence strips. Distribute the strips to students. Have each student read his or her sentence. Then have each student look for his or her match. Once each "event" has found its matching "reason," have the partners read the paired sentences aloud.

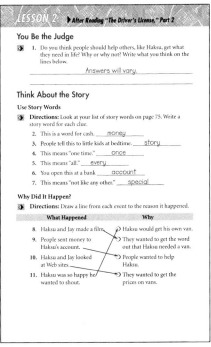

Student page 78

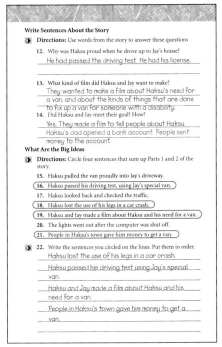

Student page 79

Reinforce & Extend

◆ SPELLING: Vowel Sound /ou/ Spelled *ou* or *ow*

1. shout   **3.** down   **5.** around   **7.** brown   **9.** ground

2. proudly   **4.** count   **6.** town   **8.** powder   **10.** about

Write the words *out* and *now* on the board. Remind students that they have learned that the letter patterns *ou* and *ow* can both stand for the /ou/ sound. Then have students number a sheet of paper 1–10. Dictate the words above one at a time, pausing for students to write them. Next write the words on the board and have students check their work, making corrections as needed.

◉ **Reading and Writing Practice** Activity 59 provides additional practice spelling words with /ou/ spelled *ou* or *ow*.

◆ LANGUAGE: Action Verbs

Write these sentences on the board:

Haksu and Jay made a video.

People sent money.

Ask volunteers to underline the verb in each sentence. (made, sent) Remind students that every sentence has a verb. Point out that the verbs *made* and *sent* are *action verbs* because they tell about something someone did. Explain:

- An action verb tells what someone or something does or did.
- Action verbs make sentences active and interesting to read.

Ask students three other things that Haksu did in the story. Write their sentences on the board. Invite volunteers to underline the action verbs. Then have students work in pairs to write two additional sentences about the story using action verbs.

◉ **Reading and Writing Practice** Activity 60 provides additional practice identifying action verbs.

◆ WRITING: A Paragraph of Description

Write this sentence on the board:

Disabled drivers need special vans.

Elicit from students the things that made Jay's van different from an ordinary van. Write their responses on the board. Then guide students to write a paragraph of description about vans adapted for disabled drivers.

◉ **Reading and Writing Practice** Duplicate and distribute Activities 61–62. Point out the Writing Model of a descriptive paragraph, and help students identify the topic sentence and supporting details. Then have pairs of students write their own descriptive paragraph in response to one of these prompts:

- Describe the vehicle (car, bus, or train) that you travel in most often.
- Describe a helpful friend of yours.

 Lesson at a Glance

Preview: This lesson presents a nonfiction selection about how to obtain a driver's license. It also presents a sample quiz from the written portion of a driver's test.

Objectives
◆ to read a nonfiction selection and take a sample driving test
◆ to read words that contain the initial /k/ sound spelled *ch* and the initial /r/ sound spelled *wr*

◆ to identify main idea and details
◆ to locate information in a dictionary
◆ to identify linking verbs
◆ to write a paragraph of information

Student Worktext Pages 80–85
Story Words
eye, chaos, sign, signal, front, behind

⊙ **Reading and Writing Practice Activities 63–69**

Before Reading "Getting on the Road"

Letters and Sounds

Initial /k/ Spelled *ch*; Initial /r/ Spelled *wr*

Write the word *chip* on the board. Say the word aloud, circle the *ch*, and remind students that these letters can stand for the /ch/ sound. Next, write the word *chord* on the board. Invite a volunteer to tell what a musical chord is, or explain it yourself if necessary. Circle the *ch* and explain that at the beginning of some words, the letters *ch* stand for the /k/ sound in the word *chord*. Write *chrome, character,* and *chaos* on the board and ask volunteers to read the words aloud, using the new rule.

Write the word *write* on the board. Say it aloud and circle the *wr*. Point out that the letters *wr* at the beginning of a word stand for the /r/ sound at the beginning of *write*. Then write *wrench, wring,* and *wrestle* on the board and invite volunteers to read them aloud. Then have students complete Student Worktext page 80.

Note: You may want to read aloud the example words on page 80 because some of them may be unfamiliar to students, and because some, such as *chaos,* have vowel patterns students have not yet learned.

⊙ **Reading and Writing Practice** Activity 63: Decoding Words with the /k/ Sound Spelled *ch*, and with the /r/ Sound Spelled *wr*.

Story Words

Read aloud the words: *eye, chaos, sign, signal, front, behind.* Tell students that these words are important in the next story. Then write the words on the board and point to each one as you say it aloud a second time. Next, have students follow the ❑ *Read* ❑ *Say* ❑ *Write* sequence by completing **Story Words** on Student Worktext page 81. Have students add the words to their Word Bank at the back of the Student Worktext. To introduce the words in context, write these sentences on the board:

◆ A bit of dust made my <u>eye</u> water.
◆ After the party, the house was in a state of <u>chaos</u>.
◆ A stop <u>sign</u> is red and white.
◆ You must <u>signal</u> before you turn.
◆ Our right <u>front</u> tire went flat.
◆ Look <u>behind</u> you when you change lanes.

Have students make a word card for *eye.* Ask a volunteer to read the first sentence aloud. Then have students copy the sentence onto the back of the word card. Follow the same procedure for the remaining words. To assess students' ability to read each new word, listen as individual students read the sentences on the board aloud.

⊙ **Reading and Writing Practice** Activity 64: Reading Story Words.

More Word Work

Have students complete **More Word Work** on Student Worktext page 65.

⊙ **Reading and Writing Practice** Activity 65: Adding Suffixes *-er* and *-est.*

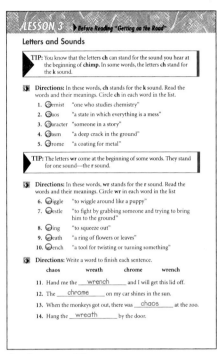
Student page 80

Student page 81

Reading "Getting on the Road"

◆ Preview and Predict

- ◆ Ask a volunteer to read the title of the passage on Student Worktext page 82 aloud. Then instruct students to silently read the other words in dark print aloud. Remind students that these are called subtitles, and they give clues to what each shorter section is about. Invite students to use what they have read to guess what the passage will be about. (how to get a driver's license)
- ◆ Then ask students if they expect to read a fiction selection or a nonfiction selection based on facts. (a nonfiction selection)
- ◆ Have students answer the questions under **Use What You Know** on Student Worktext page 82. Invite students to share their responses.
- ◆ Next, point out the sample test on page 83 and explain that it is very similar to the written part of a driver's license test, and that it will give them practice taking a written test. After students have taken the test, ask for a show of hands for each answer. Then tell students what the correct answers are and have them correct their tests as needed.

◆ Strategy Modeling

Set a Purpose Tell students that they can get more out of a reading if they have specific questions in mind as they read. Their own questions can give them a purpose for reading and help them understand and remember the information that is most important for them. Model setting a purpose for reading. You might say:

I know from previewing the selection that it will give information about how to get a driver's license. I want to know if I can practice driving before I take a written test. I'll read to see if my question will be answered.

Have students ask a question of their own. Then have them read Student Worktext page 82 to see if your question and their questions are answered. Finally, ask them to ask another question to set a new purpose for reading Student Worktext page 83.

Focus on LD

Point out the sample test on Student Worktext page 83. Tell students that they will be taking this test for practice only, not for a grade. Model how to put a check in the box next to an answer choice. Ask students to cover up all of the questions except the first one. Then have students read the question and the answer choices carefully before choosing an answer. Once they have answered number one, write the answer on the board and have students self-correct their tests. Repeat this process for the remaining items.

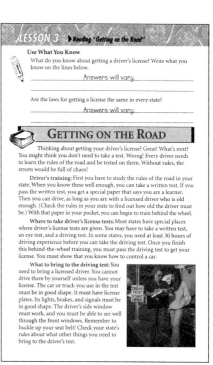

Student page 82

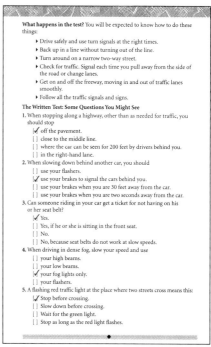

Student page 83

After Reading "Getting on the Road"

Personal Response: You Be the Judge

Ask groups of students to answer the question under **You Be The Judge** on Student Worktext page 84. Then lead a whole class discussion on whether people should have to pass three kinds of tests to get a driver's license.

Think About the Story: Reading Comprehension

Have students complete the remaining items on Student Worktext pages 84 and 85. Point out that the last activity titled **Take a Test** is not based on information found in the story. It is merely designed as an additional challenge so that students can show what they already know about driving. Once students have completed these two pages, have them compare their responses in small groups. If their responses demonstrate a lack of comprehension, you might have them reread some or all of the selection.

Reading Comprehension Skill: Main Idea and Supporting Details

Remind students that most paragraphs in a piece of nonfiction writing are made up of a main idea and supporting details. Explain:

◆ The main idea of a paragraph is the one idea the paragraph mostly tells about.

◆ Supporting details give more specific information that helps readers understand the main idea.

◆ Often the main idea is stated in one sentence, but sometimes the reader has to "add up" the details to figure out what the main idea is.

Remind students that being able to recognize the main idea and details will help them become better readers. Experienced readers do not always try to remember all the details they read, but they do try to understand and remember the main ideas. Read aloud the second paragraph on Student Worktext page 82. Ask students to identify what they think the main idea of the paragraph is. (Drivers need to train before they can get a license.) Point out that, in this case, the main idea is not stated in one sentence, but that the subtitle gives a clue to the main idea. Then ask which sentences give supporting details. (All sentences in the paragraph.) Repeat this process with paragraph four. (Possible main idea: You need to bring several things to a driving test.)

 **Application**

Career Connection   Students may be interested in finding out what kind of jobs require a valid driver's license. They may also want to find out which professions require a special license, such as a van, bus, or taxicab driver.

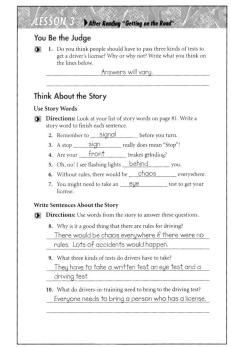

Student page 84

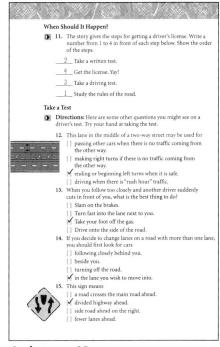

Student page 85

Reinforce & Extend

◆ STUDY SKILL: Using a Dictionary

Ask students what they can do when they come across a word they do not know. Point out that one thing they can do is look the word up in the dictionary. Ask students what information they expect to find when they look up a word. List their responses on the board. Then model looking up the word *chaos* in the dictionary. Point out these features: guide words, entry word, pronunciation, definition(s), sample sentences. Then have student pairs look up these words from the reading selection: *signal, narrow, dense.* Then ask students to use the information they learned to write three sentences using the words.

Reading and Writing Practice Activity 66 provides additional practice using a dictionary.

◆ LANGUAGE: Linking Verbs

Write these sentences on the board:

You drive well.

You are a good driver.

As a volunteer to underline the verb in the first sentence. (drive) Remind students that they can identify a verb because it usually comes after the subject. Point out that in this case, the verb shows action, so it is called an action verb. Underline *are* in the second sentence. Ask students if *are* shows an action they can see. (no) Explain that *are* is called a linking verb. Explain:

- ◆ Linking verbs do not show action. They link a subject with information about the subject.
- ◆ The verbs *am, is, are, was* and *were* can be linking verbs. The verbs *seem, become,* and *appear* are other linking verbs.

Write these sentences on the board:

The test was long.
Many questions were hard.

Ask students to underline the linking verb in each sentence. (was, were) Then have student pairs write two sentences using different linking verbs.

Reading and Writing Practice Activity 67 provides additional practice identifying linking verbs.

◆ WRITING: A Paragraph of Information

Tell students that just as readers use main ideas and details to organize and make sense of the information they read, writers also use main ideas and details to organize their writing. Explain that when writers write a paragraph of information, they often start by stating the main idea in a topic sentence. Then they write several other sentences that give supporting details about the main idea. Model the process of writing an informative paragraph. Use this as the topic sentence: *New drivers have to show that they can control a car.* Then have students suggest details that support this sentence. Help them organize and write this information in a paragraph.

Reading and Writing Practice Duplicate and distribute Activities 68–69. Point out the Writing Model of an informational paragraph, and help students identify the topic sentence and supporting details. Then have students write their own informational paragraphs in response to this prompt:

- ◆ Write a paragraph of information about a specific skill you have. Include a topic sentence and supporting details.

Before students begin writing, make sure they understand what a skill is and list some examples on the board (such as singing, drawing, playing a sport, cooking, and so on).

Lesson at a Glance

Preview: This lesson presents the first half of a two-part fiction story about a teenage girl who works at a car wash and develops a crush on one of her customers.

Objectives
◆ to read a fiction story
◆ to read and spell contractions with *am, are, is, have, will,* and *not*

◆ to summarize a fiction story
◆ to make subjects and verbs agree in a sentence
◆ to write a persuasive advertising poster

Student Worktext Pages 86–91

Story Words
saw, took, book, wash, station, stomach

🔘 **Reading and Writing Practice Activities 70–76**

Before Reading "The Car Wash," Part 1

Letters and Sounds

Contractions with *am, are, is, have, will, not*

Write this sentence on the board: *I am in class now.* Underline *I am.* Point out that when people talk, they do not usually say *I am* as two words. Instead they say one word, *I'm.* Write *I'm* under *I am.* Tell students that *I'm* and *I am* have the same meaning; *I'm* is a shortened form of *I am* called a contraction. In a contraction, one or more letters are dropped and replaced with a mark called an *apostrophe.*

Tell students that in addition to *am, is,* and *are,* there are other words that are often shortened into contractions: *will, have,* and *not.* Demonstrate how each contraction is formed by using the following sentence frames:

She is (She's) my teacher.   We are (We're) lucky to be in this class.

I will (I'll) be in class on Monday.   I have (I've) always come on time.

I will not (won't) be in class on Sunday.

Then have students complete Student Worktext page 86.

🔘 **Reading and Writing Practice** Activity 70: Reading Contractions with *am, are, is, have, will, not.*

Story Words

Read aloud the words: *saw, took, book, wash, station, stomach.* Tell students that these words are important in the next story. Then write the words on the board and point to each one as you say it aloud a second time. Next, have students follow the ❏ *Read* ❏ *Say* ❏ *Write* sequence by completing **Story Words** on Student Worktext page 87. Have students add the words to their Word Bank at the back of the Student Worktext. To introduce the words in context, write these sentences on the board:

◆ We <u>saw</u> a good show on TV.
◆ My dad <u>took</u> the car to work.
◆ What <u>book</u> do you like the most?

◆ Can you help <u>wash</u> the dishes?
◆ I sat for a long time at the bus <u>station</u>.
◆ My <u>stomach</u> was full after lunch.

Have students make a word card for *saw.* Ask a volunteer to read the first sentence aloud. Then have students copy the sentence onto the back of the word card. Follow the same procedure for the remaining words. To assess students' ability to read each new word, listen as individual students read the sentences on the board aloud.

🔘 **Reading and Writing Practice** Activity 71: Reading Story Words.

More Word Work

Have students complete **More Word Work** on Student Worktext page 87.

🔘 **Reading and Writing Practice** Activity 72: Dividing Two-Syllable Words.

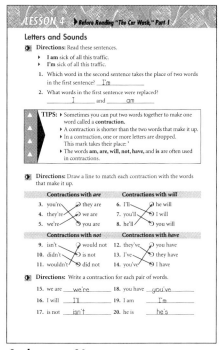

Student page 86

Student page 87

Reading "The Car Wash," Part 1

◆ Preview and Predict

- Tell students that they are going to read the first half of a two-part story about a teenage girl named Christy who has a job at her dad's car wash.
- Have a volunteer read aloud the title on Student Worktext page 88 and ask students to preview the illustration on page 89.
- Ask students to describe what they know about how a car wash operates.
- Invite students to make predictions about what might happen in the story.

◆ Strategy Modeling

Access Prior Knowledge Have students work with a partner to write a response under **Use What You Know** on Student Worktext page 88. Then invite students to share their responses. Explain to students that thinking about what they know about a topic can help them understand more of what they read. Model using prior knowledge. You might say:

I am going to read a story about a girl who wants to get to know a boy she sees at a car wash where she works. I think this might be hard to do because it takes only about 20 minutes to wash a car. If the girl is busy working, how will she have time to meet the boy and get to know him? Thinking about what I know helps me understand the challenge the girl has.

Have students read Student Worktext pages 88–89 to find out whether Christy is able to meet the boy.

Focus on ESL/LEP

Explain and discuss the following terms used in the story:

- a freak
- caked on
- dashed over
- plopped down
- snuck a peek
- cranked the car

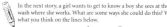

Use What You Know

In the next story, a girl wants to get to know a boy she sees at the car wash where she works. What are some ways she could do this? Write what you think on the lines below.

Answers will vary.

THE CAR WASH, PART 1

Is it such an odd thing to see a girl washing cars? At times I see people looking at me like I'm a freak or something. I know, most of the time you see boys doing this kind of work. But you see, my father owns this gas station and car wash. So, it's kind of a special family thing. At some point, I just began helping out here.

I do more than wash cars. I do other jobs, too. Dad insists that I know how to do every job at the station. That is how I got my nickname, Christy-Doo. It came from him saying, "Christy, do this," or "Christy, do that," all the time. Sometimes I work behind the desk, taking money. At other times I help Dad with the company books, writing checks or entering sales into the computer accounting program.

One Sunday I was working the drive-off area. That's where we drive cars from the front of the car wash line for drying. I got my license last year, so this is now one of my jobs. Anyway, I happened to look up. Right then, I saw this little old blue car drive into the station. This one was a real mess. The mud was caked on that thing so thick you couldn't even see the paint. No surprise—it got in the car wash line.

Then came the surprise. This tall boy stepped out of the car—black hair, shades, cool look. I was impressed! Something about him gave off an air of smooth control. Wow! Well, I couldn't wait until that car came off the line. I dashed over and plopped down in the front seat before anyone else could get there. I snuck a peek over to the waiting area. I saw him there. He was looking at me. Or maybe he was looking at his car. Whatever! My stomach went into a state of chaos.

I tried to keep my hands from shaking as I dried his car. I took time with it. I shined the windows, the signal lights, and the chrome hubcaps. I took time inside, too. The inside was just about as filthy as the outside had been. I swept off the rugs. Then I dusted above and below the dash and made it all shine. I held my breath. This was it. I wrung out my drying rags. Then I beeped once as a sign that I was finished. Before I could hold up the keys, there he was. He took off his shades and gave me a fast look.

Student page 88

His eyes were this deep, deep blue, a deeper blue than his car. He flipped me the claim check, grabbed the keys from my hand, and mumbled, "Thanks." He hopped in his car and turned the key. The car growled a bit before it got going, as if the battery were low. Mr. Cool Blue Eyes did not look up at me again. He just sped out of the driveway.

Do you think Christy will see the boy with the blue eyes again? Write what you think on the lines below. Then keep reading to find out what happens.

Answers will vary.

The next Sunday, I was sitting at the back of the car wash, having a snack and studying for my chem test. I happened to look up at the video screen that shows the cars that are pulling up to the gas pumps. I saw that same blue car in the driveway! It was just as caked with mud as the week before. I thought, "What does Mr. Cool do all week to get his car this filthy?" Anyway, I dropped the book and raced up to the front of the car wash. "Where's my spray bottle? Where're the drying rags?" I wanted to be the one to drive his car again.

It was the same story as the week before. Again, butterflies took control of my stomach. Again, he walked up and gave me a glance with those blue eyes. Again, he grabbed the keys, mumbled thanks, and cranked the car till it sputtered. Once it chugged fast enough to get going, he drove off.

I began to like Sundays. Every week he would drive up in the late afternoon. His car was always a muddy mess. I invented a way each week to be the one to drive his car off the line. I couldn't believe how much mud was on his car, but I didn't think twice about it. As long as his car got muddy, I got to see him. Soon we were trading friendly smiles. But we never really talked. ▸

Student page 89

After Reading "The Car Wash," Part 1

Personal Response: What Do You Think?

Have students write sentences in response to the two questions under **What Do You Think?** on Student Worktext page 90. Then ask them to share their responses.

Think About the Story: Reading Comprehension

Have students complete the remaining items on Student Worktext pages 90 and 91. Check their responses, and if they indicate any difficulty in comprehending key story words and events, have students reread the story in groups and answer the questions again collaboratively.

Reading Comprehension Skill: Summarize

Ask volunteers to tell you what they have learned about how and why readers summarize a story. If necessary, explain:

◆ Summarizing, or summing up, a story can help readers check whether they understand the most important story events. It also helps them remember story events.

◆ A summary of a story includes only the most important ideas and events, not details.

◆ A summary is a retelling in the reader's own words.

Ask volunteers to name the key events from "The Car Wash," Part 1. List their responses on the board. Then guide them to write the sentences in the form of a summary.

To give students the opportunity to practice summarizing, have groups of students choose another story they know or have read in class and ask them to work collaboratively to write a one-paragraph summary. Then have them read their summaries to the class.

Look Ahead

Tell students that they'll learn more about Christy in the next story. Ask students to form small groups and use the question at the bottom of Student Worktext page 91 to think about what might happen in Part 2.

 **Learning Styles**

Logical/Mathematical Help students use the sentences under **Why Did It Happen?** on Student Worktext page 91 to make a graphic organizer showing causes and effects. Then have students work in groups to add one or two pairs of causes and effects from the story to their graphic organizer.

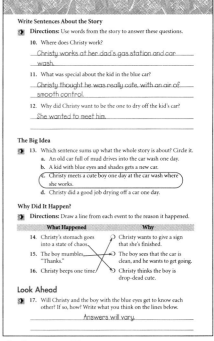

Student page 90

Student page 91

Reinforce & Extend

◆ SPELLING: Contractions with *am, are, is, have, will, not*

1. I am   **3.** could not   **5.** you've   **7.** isn't   **9.** it's

2. I'm   **4.** couldn't   **6.** we'll   **8.** he'll   **10.** we've

Write *I've* on the board. Remind students that they have learned that contractions such as *I've* can be formed from two words by dropping one or more letters and replacing them with an apostrophe ('). Then have students number a sheet of paper 1–10. Dictate the words above one at a time, pausing for students to write them. Next write the words on the board and have students check their work, making corrections as needed.

Reading and Writing Practice Activity 73 provides additional practice spelling contractions with *am, are, is, have, will, not.*

◆ LANGUAGE: Subject-Verb Agreement

Write these sentences on the board:

Christy and her dad work at the car wash.

Christy works hard.

Have a volunteer circle the subject and underline the verb in each sentence. (Christy and her dad/work, Christy/works) Ask another volunteer what is different about the two verbs (the second ends in *s*). Then ask students how the two subjects are different. (The first names two people and the second names one.) Explain:

- ◆ Verbs that describe present actions or states have to agree with their subjects.
- ◆ If the subject names one person, place, or thing, then the verb ends in *s*.
- ◆ If the subject names more than one person, place, or thing, then the verb does not end in *s*.

Give each student the name(s) of one or two classmates. Have each student write a sentence using the name(s) he or she receives. Then check the accuracy of students' subject-verb agreement.

Reading and Writing Practice Activity 74 provides additional practice with subject-verb agreement.

◆ WRITING: An Advertising Poster

Ask students what Christy's father might tell about his car wash if he wanted to draw more customers there. Write their responses on the board. Then guide students to use this information to write a persuasive poster designed to attract more people to the car wash. Have students think of a name for the car wash to use in their posters. Explain:

- ◆ A persuasive poster or ad clearly identifies an event or product and tells why people will like it.
- ◆ To persuade, or convince, people that their product is good, poster-writers or ad-writers use strong, positive, and colorful words.

Reading and Writing Practice Duplicate and distribute Activities 75–76, the Writing Model of a poster. Help students identify its key features, such as its organization and its use of persuasive language. Ask students to imagine that their school is planning a fundraiser such as a car wash or bake sale. Then have groups of students work together to make advertising posters to persuade people in the community to come to the fundraiser.

Lesson at a Glance

Preview: This lesson presents the second half of a two-part fiction story about a teenage girl named Christy who works at a car wash and develops a crush on one of her customers. Christy finally finds a way to meet the boy she has been watching, and is pleasantly surprised to learn that he has been trying to find a way to meet her, too.

Objectives
- to read a fiction story
- to read and spell words that begin with *scr, str, spr, squ, shr,* or *thr*

- to identify cause and effect in fiction
- to identify main verbs and helping verbs
- to recognize narrative voice

Student Worktext Pages 92–97
Story Words
both, carry, motor

Reading and Writing Practice Activities 77–80

Before Reading "The Car Wash," Part 2

Letters and Sounds

Initial *scr, spr, str, squ, shr, thr*

Write the word *scrap* on the board. Say it aloud. Circle the cluster *scr* and blend the sounds slowly to read the whole word. Ask students how many sounds they hear. (three) Write the words *scram* and *scrape* on the board. Have students practice reading them aloud. Write the words *string* and *spray* on the board and follow a similar procedure. Then write the words *thrill* and *shrill* on the board and ask students how many sounds they hear. (two) Finally, write *squid* on the board. Circle the *squ*. Explain that these letters at the beginning of a word stand for the /skw/ sound. Then have students complete Student Worktext page 92.

Reading and Writing Practice Activity 77: Decoding Words with Initial *scr, spr, str, squ, shr, thr.*

Story Words

Read aloud these words: *both, carry, motor.* Tell students that these words are important in the next story. Then write the words on the board and point to each one as you say it aloud a second time. Next, have students follow the ❏ *Read* ❏ *Say* ❏ *Write* sequence by completing **Story Words** on Student Worktext page 93. Have students add the words to their Word Bank at the back of the Student Worktext. To introduce the words in context, write these sentences on the board:

- Keep <u>both</u> eyes on the road!
- A van can <u>carry</u> ten people or more.
- Let's lift the hood and look at the <u>motor</u>.

Have students make a word card for *both.* Ask a volunteer to read the first sentence aloud. Then have students copy the sentence onto the back of the word card. Follow the same procedure for the remaining words. To assess students' ability to read each new word, listen as individual students read the sentences on the board aloud.

Reading and Writing Practice Activity 78: Reading Story Words.

More Word Work

Have students complete **More Word Work** on Student Worktext page 93.

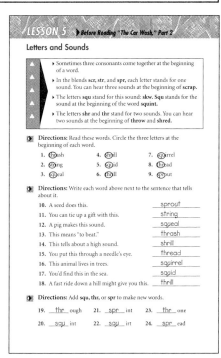

Student page 92

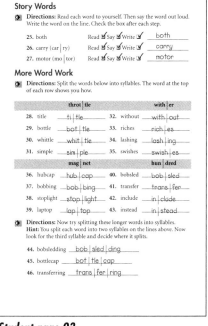

Student page 93

Reading "The Car Wash," Part 2

◆ Preview and Predict
- Ask students to sum up what happened in Part 1 of "The Car Wash."
- Tell students that they are going to read more about Christy in this story.
- Have students read the story title on Student Worktext page 94 and preview the illustration.
- Ask students to use what they know, as well as what they see in the illustration, to predict what will happen in Part 2 of the story. Remind them to pause in the middle of page 95 to make a new prediction.

◆ Strategy Modeling

Reread/Read Ahead   Read aloud the first paragraph on Student Worktext page 94. Then model using the Reread/Read Ahead Strategy. You might say:

Christy thinks, "He might as well open an account with us." What does she mean by this? At first I'm not sure, so I reread the sentences that come before. I find out that he comes to the car wash every Sunday. Now I get it. Christy thinks that he might as well open an account because he is such a regular customer.

Tell students that they can also try reading ahead if they come to something they find confusing. For example, if they were confused by the sentence "Then, one day, something funny happened," reading ahead would explain what funny thing Christy is thinking of.

🔺 Learning Styles

Interpersonal/Group Learning   Have students work in groups to complete the **More Word Work** exercises on Student Worktext page 93. Ask them to take turns reading each word aloud and telling where it should be split into syllables. Then have them write the word on the blank and draw a line between the syllables. If students disagree about where a word should be divided, have them check with you or with another group.

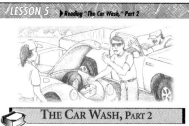

LESSON 5 ▸ Reading "The Car Wash," Part 2

THE CAR WASH, PART 2

Lots of people came into the gas station and the car wash. Some of them were cute boys. But in my book, none of them held a candle to Mr. Cool Blue Eyes, as I called him. I kept looking out for him each Sunday. And each Sunday, he showed up. "He might as well open an account with us," I thought. Then, one day, something funny happened. I had finished drying the car and was squeezing the water out of my drying rags. Cool as ever, Mr. Blue Eyes strolled up, carrying his claim check. He took his keys and went to turn on the car. All the motor did was crank and crank. It just didn't catch. His face turned red as he kept trying to get the motor to go. I didn't move. I just held on to my drying rags and spray bottle, waiting to see what would happen next.

He got out of the car and popped open the hood. He looked over at me. "I don't know what's wrong," he said lamely. "I think my battery is dead."

"Do you have any jumper cables?" I asked. "I think we could find another car here to help give you a **jump**. By the way, my name is Christy." I couldn't believe I said that!

"I'm Joe," he said. "Thanks, Christy, but I don't have any. We'll have to find some." He was looking right at me.

I was thinking, "Christy, wake up. Get hold of yourself!" I **floundered for words.** "I think we've got some in back . . ."

I ran quickly behind the station to find Dad. But I really wasn't thinking about the jumper cables. I was thinking, "His name is Joe!"

Dad drove his truck around to Joe's car. I saw Dad prop open the hood of the truck. He took out a set of jumper cables from behind the cab. Meanwhile, Joe pulled the back seat out of the car. Its battery was under there. Next, Dad strung the cables between the car and the truck, clamping the ends to both batteries. He safely kept the cables from getting crossed. Dad throttled up his truck and asked Joe to do the same. It worked. Joe's motor growled and sputtered, but soon it began to run.

Student page 94

Joe got out of the car. "How much money will it be for the jump?" he asked Dad.

"It's free, **buddy**," Dad said. "We would do the same for anyone." He jumped into the cab of his truck and drove around to the back of the station. That left me and Joe by ourselves again. He looked at me with those eyes.

✏️ **What do you think will happen next in the story? Write what you think on the lines below. Then read on to find out how the story ends.**

Answers will vary.

I was standing there in front of Joe. Inside me, chaos took control. He didn't seem to know what to say next. There was no sound other than the car wash and the traffic. Then he said, "Thanks, Christy." He put the seat back in his car, got in, and checked around for traffic. He turned on his right blinker signal, getting ready to pull out of the driveway.

I wished he would not drive off. I wished he would just talk a little longer to me. Well, he did not drive off. He just sat there for a bit. Then he got out of the car again. We both just looked at each other. "Christy," he said, "I have to tell you something. You have been giving my car a lot of special cleaning each time I come in here. I know it gets really muddy. I just want to say thanks for all your work."

This was surprising news. I didn't know he was keeping track of the fact that I was the one to dry his car each week. "Well, I have to say your car is one of the muddiest, dustiest ones I've ever worked on. I've wanted to know, how in the world does it get that way every week?"

Joe's face turned red. He was struggling to say something. "I have something else to tell you, Christy. The first time I came in here, I had driven on a muddy road after a rain. You were the one who dried my car. After that . . . well, I thought about you. So I went out each week and drove in the mud. Sometimes I just squished it all over the car. That way, I could bring the car in to be washed. I did it so I could see you, Christy!"

Those blue eyes were locked to mine. He didn't look away.

"No way!" I said. I looked away, surprised. But just as quickly, I looked back and smiled at him. I was so surprised—and happy. I thought about telling him how I had made a point of grabbing his car to dry each week. But I kept quiet. I smiled up at him, thinking again how cute he was. I thought, "In time, maybe I'll get around to telling that part of the story."

Student page 95

After Reading "The Car Wash," Part 2

Personal Response: What Do You Think?

Ask students whether they would have been as shy as Christy and Joe. Have them complete the questions under **What Do You Think?** on Student Worktext page 96 and then ask them to share their responses with the class.

Think About the Story: Reading Comprehension

Have students complete the remaining items on Student Worktext pages 96 and 97. Monitor their comprehension and, if necessary, have students reread the story individually or in groups and then check their responses.

Reading Comprehension Skill: Cause and Effect

Remind students that in fiction stories, one event often causes another event to happen. Point out that thinking about causes and effects can help readers understand and keep track of story events. Explain:

◆ A cause is an event that makes another event happen.

◆ An effect is what happens as a result.

◆ Sometimes clue words *because of* or *as a result* signal a cause-effect relationship. Sometimes readers have to figure out causes and effects on their own.

Guide students to recognize causes and effects by answering these questions about the story:

◆ Why didn't Joe's car start?

◆ Why did Joe's face turn red when he couldn't get his motor started?

◆ What caused Joe to sit in his car after Christy's dad got it started for him?

◆ When Joe tells Christy that he got his car dirty on purpose, what effect does that have on Christy?

 **Application**

In the Community Engage students in a discussion of the ways community organizations can raise money, such as holding car washes and rummage sales, selling things door to door, and so on. Ask students to describe any experiences they have had and share their opinions about which fundraisers are most effective and why.

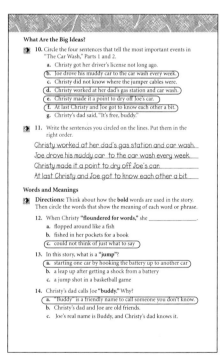

Student page 96

Student page 97

Reinforce & Extend

◆ SPELLING: Words that begin with *scr, str, spr, squ, shr,* or *thr*

1. stroll	**3.** string	**5.** street	**7.** squish	**9.** thrash
2. scrap	**4.** thrift	**6.** spring	**8.** strong	**10.** shrill

Write *thread* and *strap* on the board. Remind students that they have learned that the consonant blends *thr* and *shr* each stand for two sounds, while the blends *scr, str, spr* and *squ* each stand for three sounds. Then have students number a sheet of paper 1–10. Dictate the words above one at a time, pausing for students to write them. Next write the words on the board and have students check their work, making corrections as needed.

Reading and Writing Practice Activity 79 provides additional practice spelling words that begin with *scr, spr, str, squ, shr* or *thr.*

◆ LANGUAGE: Main Verbs and Helping Verbs

Write these sentences on the board:

Joe will take his car to the car wash.

Christy has cleaned his car before.

Underline the main verb and circle the helping verb in the first sentence. Read the sentence aloud and tell students that there are two verbs in the sentence that work together as a team. Ask if a volunteer can name the two verbs. (*will, take*) Tell students that *will* is a helping verb and *take* is a main verb. Then ask another volunteer if they know which verb in the second sentence is the main verb (*cleaned*). Underline *cleaned*. Then circle *has* and point out that it is the helping verb in the sentence. Explain:

- ◆ Main verbs tell the main action that a subject does in a sentence.
- ◆ *Do, does, did, have, has,* and *will* are helping verbs that are used to ask questions, to form negative sentences, or to show different times, or tenses.
- ◆ *Can, may, should, could,* and *would* are helping verbs that work with a main verb to bring special meaning to the verb.

Have student pairs write down the following sentences: *Joe will ask for a jump. Christy's dad can help him.* Have them circle the helping verbs and underline the main verbs.

Reading and Writing Practice Activity 80 provides additional practice identifying main verbs and helping verbs.

◆ LITERARY APPRECIATION: Narrative Voice

Tell students that every story has a voice—a point of view from which the story is told. Explain:

- ◆ The person who tells a story is called the *narrator.*
- ◆ Some stories are told by a character in the story, who refers to himself or herself as *I.* Stories told with this voice are told in the first-person.
- ◆ Some stories are told by an outside observer who refers to all of the characters using *he, she,* or *they.* Stories told with this voice are told in the third-person.

Ask students who is telling "The Car Wash," and how they know. (Christy is telling the story; she refers to herself as *I.*) Have students find examples in the story that show it is being told by Christy. If necessary, point out that the narrator's use of the pronouns *I, me,* and *my* are all clues to the narrative voice. Then ask pairs of students to go back to three or four previous fiction selections they have read in the Student Worktext and decide whether each is told from the first-person or the third-person point of view. Ask partners to share their conclusions with the class.

 # Lesson at a Glance

Preview: This lesson presents the first part of a story about a young woman who has to decide whether she should leave high school to pursue her passion for making music videos.

Objectives
- to read a fiction story
- to read words that contain the vowel diphthong /oi/ spelled *oy* or *oi*
- to learn a strategy for making decisions

- to locate information in an encyclopedia
- to identify present- and past-tense verbs
- to write a journal entry

Student Worktext Pages 98–103

Story Words

country, important, love, magazine, producer

◉ **Reading and Writing Practice Activities 81–87**

Before Reading "Video Dreams"

Letters and Sounds

Vowel Diphthong /oi/ Spelled *oy*, *oi*; Phonogram *oy*

Write the word *boy* on the board and say it aloud. Circle the letters *oy*. Explain that the letters *oy* stand for the vowel sound in *boy*. Tell students that once they can read *boy*, they can read other words that contain the letters *oy*. Write the words *soy, joy, toy,* and *employ* on the board. Ask volunteers to read the words aloud. Help students see how to divide *employ* into syllables. (em | ploy)

Write the word *point* on the board, say it aloud, and circle the letters *oi*. Explain that these letters can also stand for the /oi/ sound. Write *coin, choice, voice* and *loiter* on the board. Ask volunteers to read the words aloud. Then have students complete Student Worktext page 98.

◉ **Reading and Writing Practice** Activity 81: Decoding Words with /oi/ Spelled *oy* or *oi*.

Story Words

Read aloud these words: *country, important, love, magazine, producer.* Tell students that these words are important in the next story. Then write the words on the board and point to each one as you say it aloud a second time. Next, have students follow the ❏ *Read* ❏ *Say* ❏ *Write* sequence by completing **Story Words** on Student Worktext page 99. Have students add the words to their Word Bank at the back of the Student Worktext. To introduce the words in context, write these sentences on the board:

- Do you like <u>country</u> music?
- Who is the most <u>important</u> person in your life?
- This <u>magazine</u> is all about race cars.
- A <u>producer</u> plans and pays for films.
- All my friends <u>love</u> hip hop.

Have students make a word card for *country*. Ask a volunteer to read the first sentence aloud. Then have students copy the sentence onto the back of the word card. Follow the same procedure for the remaining words. To assess students' ability to read each new word, listen as individual students read the sentences on the board aloud.

◉ **Reading and Writing Practice** Activity 82: Reading Story Words.

More Word Work

Have students work in pairs to complete **More Word Work** on Student Worktext page 99.

◉ **Reading and Writing Practice** Activity 83: Adding *-ly*

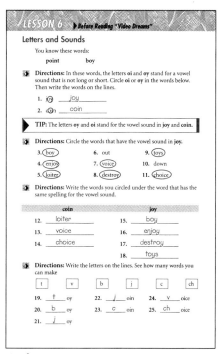

Student page 98

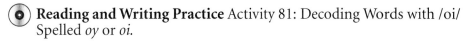

Student page 99

Reading "Video Dreams"

Preview and Predict

- ◆ Ask students to imagine their dream job. Have them discuss their choices in groups.
- ◆ Then tell students they are going to read a story about a young woman named Tina who has her eyes set on her dream job.
- ◆ Have a volunteer read the title of the story aloud. Ask students to predict what Tina's dream job might be.

Strategy Modeling

Set a Purpose Remind students that they can get more enjoyment out of reading if they set a purpose for reading. To set a purpose is to decide why they are reading and ask themselves what they want to get out of or learn from reading. Point out that when reading a nonfiction story, the purpose for reading might be to discover particular information. When reading a fiction story, the purpose for reading is probably to find out what will happen to various characters in the story. Model the Set a Purpose strategy. You might say:

I am guessing from the title that Tina's dream job involves making videos. I want to read the story to find out if I'm right, and if so, what kind of videos she makes.

Have students read pages 100–101 to find out what happens to Tina in the story.

VIDEO DREAMS

Tina Zappetini kicked open her locker and threw her books into it. "I can't wait to get out of this school," she said. "Boy, I feel like quitting right now! School's hard. And that math stuff makes no sense at all! What's the point? What's so important about math anyway?"

Tina found school harder and **harder to stomach.** Math was her biggest struggle. What she loved was making music videos. Many nights she stayed up late messing around with her video cam. She could edit the film on her computer to get just the effects she wanted. She would play a sound track over and over. She would edit the pictures until they fit the music just right. Her style was to put in a little bit of chaos. Her videos had an **edge.** "Just like me," Tina said to herself as she slammed her locker shut.

After school, Tina escaped to her car. She drove to the gas station, filled up, and checked the oil. She picked out and paid for two of the latest music magazines. Then she drove to the coin car wash. She turned off the motor and dropped coins in the slot. She squeezed the trigger on the sprayer. She sprayed her car. Hip-hop music was blasting. Tina eyed the spraying streams of water. It gave her an idea . . .

At home Tina hung her backpack full of books on her bed. She flopped down and flipped through both new magazines. She got out her sketch pad. Streams of spraying water danced through her brain. She wanted to make a video that had jets of water spraying through it. Lost in thought and sketching madly, she forgot about her math homework. Like many nights, the books might just stay in the backpack.

Student page 100

▲● Learning Styles

Visual/Spatial Invite students to describe their favorite music videos. Some students may want to act out or perform some of the moves in the videos they like best. If possible, view one or two music videos and discuss the elements that make them fun to watch and listen to.

Focus on ESL/LEP

Explain and discuss the following terms from the story:

- ◆ What's the point?
- ◆ messing around with
- ◆ had an edge
- ◆ in a flash
- ◆ submit (send in)

After a while, she logged on to the Internet. She wanted to download some music into her computer. "Water music," Tina thought. A sign flashed on the screen:

THE WHOLE COUNTRY WILL HAVE A CHANCE TO CHAT LIVE WITH
SONNY JONES, TOP MUSIC VIDEO PRODUCER, AT 8:00 P.M. TONIGHT.

"Sonny Jones!" thought Tina happily. "He's one of the most important producers in the country! This is SO important! I'm there!"

 What do you predict will happen in the live chat room with Sonny Jones? Write what you think on the lines below.

Answers will vary.

Promptly at 8:00 P.M., Tina logged on to the music video chat room. Sonny Jones had just come on line. He was answering questions. Tina eagerly typed in:

Sonny, I love your videos. You are the best producer around. I love making music videos. I have stacks of CDs I've mixed with videos. People say they like my work. I'm still in high school, but I would quit school in a flash if I could get a job doing what you do. Do you have any job openings at your company?

Sonny wrote back:

I worked for a long time to get to the place where I am now. For you and other young people, I would say, make the choice to stay in school. From what I have seen, I would say it is important for you to finish high school. I'm not going to say what's right or wrong for you. But if you finish school, more choices will be open to you. My company, Video Jam, is running a workshop for kids who are into making music videos. Why don't you think about applying for it? You'll need to submit a sample video. A few of this country's young people will be picked to join the workshop. If you are picked, it could lead to a chance to move into the world of music videos. Check out the Video Jam Web page to find out how to apply.

Tina didn't like the part about finishing school. But she loved the thought of going to a workshop run by Sonny Jones. She went to the Video Jam Web site. She printed out the application for the workshop and the rules for how to apply. Then she looked over at the backpack on her bed. Sighing, she tossed away the magazines and took out her math book. ▶

Student page 101

After Reading "Video Dreams"

Personal Response: You Be the Judge

Take an informal poll of whether students think Sonny gave Tina good advice. Have volunteers read aloud the questions under **You Be the Judge** on Student Worktext page 102. Then have pairs of students discuss and write their responses.

Think About the Story: Reading Comprehension

Ask students to complete the remaining items on Student Worktext pages 102 and 103 individually. Then have them check their answers in groups. Assign groups to report different sections. If their responses indicate some difficulty understanding story words or events, have them reread the story aloud in pairs and answer the questions again.

Critical Thinking Skill: Make Decisions

Point out that making decisions is an important life skill. Discuss with students various kinds of decisions people make in their daily lives, such as which career to choose, which school to go to, and so on. Also discuss how to go about making wise decisions:

- Gather all the information necessary to make a good decision.
- Take time to consider all sides of the issue.
- List the positive and negative effects that go along with each choice.
- Try to use reason over emotions such as anger or fear.
- Get the advice of someone who has special knowledge of the situation or experience making the same kind of decision.

Ask pairs of students to work together. Have them reread Student Worktext page 101. Then have them use this information, in addition to what they know, to decide whether it would be wiser for Tina to quit school or finish school before pursuing her dream career. Ask students to list the positive and negative effects of each decision, and remind them to weigh all the available information to arrive at a good decision.

Look Ahead

Tell students that they will be reading more about Tina in the next story. Ask students to form small groups and use the question at the bottom of Student Worktext page 103 to help them predict what will happen to Tina next.

Student page 102

Student page 103

Reinforce & Extend

◀▶ STUDY SKILL: Using an Encyclopedia

Ask students where they could look if they wanted to find out more about video filmmaking. Point out that one place they could look is in an encyclopedia. Explain:

- An encyclopedia is a set of books, or volumes, organized in alphabetical order by topic.
- An encyclopedia contains articles that give general information about a wide variety of topics.
- To find information on a topic, choose the right volume using alphabetical order. Then use the guide words to find the article you want.

Model using an encyclopedia to look up *videos* or *filmmaking*. Point out the list of related topics at the end of the article you find. Then have pairs of students practice using an encyclopedia by looking up careers or topics that interest them.

⊙ **Reading and Writing Practice** Activity 84 provides additional practice using an encyclopedia.

◀▶ LANGUAGE: Present Tense and Past Tense Verbs

Write these sentences on the board:

Tina makes music videos.

She filmed ten videos last year.

Ask volunteers to underline the verb in each sentence. (makes, filmed) Point out that *makes* is a present-tense verb and *filmed* is a past-tense verb. Explain:

- Present-tense verbs name an action that happens now, one that is always true, or one that is repeated.
- Past-tense verbs name an action that happened in the past. Many past-tense verbs end in *ed*.

Have pairs of students work together to write three sentences about things they do every weekend and three sentences about things they did last Saturday. Then have them underline present-tense verbs and circle past-tense verbs.

⊙ **Reading and Writing Practice** Activity 85 provides additional practice identifying and using present-tense and past-tense verbs.

◀▶ WRITING: A Journal Entry

Ask students what Tina could do to keep track of the different video projects she begins, or to record the important events that are happening in her life, such as her correspondence with Sonny Jones. Point out that one thing she could do is keep a daily journal. Ask students if any of them have kept journals, and if so, to describe their experiences. Explain:

- A journal is a book for writing down thoughts and memories. People keep journals for various reasons, such as to keep track of their daily activities in order to remember them later, to write down their personal thoughts, or to try out ideas for stories.
- Sometimes people write in their journals every day. Or, they may write in their journals only when they have something they want to write about. Each time a person writes in a journal, we say he or she is creating a journal entry.

⊙ **Reading and Writing Practice** Duplicate and distribute Activities 86–87, the Writing Model of a journal entry, and help students identify the date, place, opening, and body of the entry. Then have students write their own journal entries in response to one of these prompts:

- Imagine you are Tina. Write a journal entry about your "electronic chat" with Sonny Jones. Tell how you feel about his advice.
- Write a journal entry about your dreams for the future. Tell why they are important.
- Write about something exciting or important that has happened to you in the past few days.

Lesson at a Glance

Preview: This lesson presents the sequel to "Video Dreams." In this story, Tina makes a sample music video to enter in a national music video competition.

Objectives
- to read a fiction story
- to read and spell words that contain the r-controlled vowel /ôr/ spelled *or, ore,* and *our*
- to understand the difference between fantasy and realism
- to identify and use pronouns
- to identify the theme of a fiction story

Student Worktext Pages 104–109

Story Words
window, between, extra, never

Reading and Writing Practice Activities 88–91

Before Reading "Rain Dance"

Letters and Sounds

r-Controlled Vowel: /ôr/ Spelled *or, ore, our;* Phonogram *our*

Write the word *for* on the board, say it aloud, and circle the letters *or.* Point out that when a vowel is followed by *r,* the vowel has a sound that is neither long nor short. Write the words *fort, dorm,* and *cord* on the board. Ask volunteers to read them aloud. Then write the word *more* on the board. Circle the letters *ore.* Point out that these letters can also stand for the /ôr/ sound. Write *sore* and *before* on the board and ask volunteers to read the words. Finally, write the word *four* on the board and follow a similar procedure. Circle the letters *our.* Ask volunteers to read words *pour* and *your.* Then have students complete Student Worktext page 104.

Reading and Writing Practice Activity 88: Decoding Words with /ôr/ Spelled *or, ore,* or *our.*

Story Words

Read aloud these words: *window, between, extra, never.* Tell students that these words are important in the next story. Then write the words on the board and point to each one as you say it aloud a second time. Next, have students follow the ❑ *Read* ❑ *Say* ❑ *Write* sequence by completing **Story Words** on Student Worktext page 105. Have students add the words to their Word Bank at the back of the Student Worktext. To introduce the words in context, write these sentences on the board:

- I opened the <u>window</u>.
- My car is <u>between</u> two trucks.
- Do you want <u>extra</u> cheese on that burger?
- I <u>never</u> win things—do you?

Have students make a word card for *window.* Ask a volunteer to read the first sentence aloud. Then have students copy the sentence onto the back of the word card. Follow the same procedure for the remaining words. To assess students' ability to read each new word, listen as individual students read the sentences on the board aloud.

Reading and Writing Practice Activity 89: Reading Story Words.

More Word Work

Have students complete **More Word Work** on Student Worktext page 105.

 ## Learning Styles

Auditory/Verbal Have pairs of students work together on **More Word Work** on Student Worktext page 105. Ask students to take turns reading words aloud while the other decides how the word should be divided into syllables.

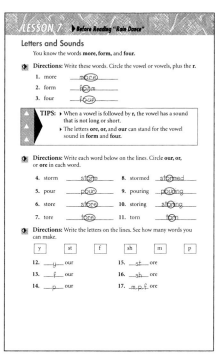

Student page 104

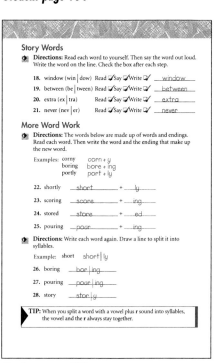

Student page 105

Reading "Rain Dance"

◆ *Preview and Predict*

- Ask volunteers to sum up what they remember from "Video Dreams."
- Tell students that they will be reading another story about Tina.
- Have students read the title on Student Worktext page 106 and preview the illustration on page 107.
- Then model the Use Context Clues strategy as described below.

◆ *Strategy Modeling*

Use Context Clues   Remind students that context clues can help them figure out the meaning of a word they don't know, or figure out which meaning of a word is being used in a sentence. Have students read the first paragraph of the story silently. Then have them locate the word *tight*. Ask a volunteer to tell how context clues can help them figure out its meaning in this sentence. If necessary, model using context clues to determine meaning. You might say:

> *The word* tight *can mean "close-fitting." But this meaning doesn't make sense here. The whole sentence is, "Many were tight, but not one looked great to her." I think that here,* tight *means "pretty good" or "fairly well done," but not excellent.*

Have other volunteers use context clues to figure out the meaning of the words *hot, slick,* and *beat* in the second paragraph. Remind students to use context clues as they continue to read.

Focus on ESL/LEP

Explain and discuss the following terms from the story:

- the band looked so lame ("so silly")
- hit on an idea
- Dude!
- the news sunk in

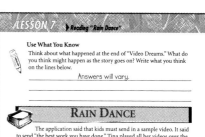

Use What You Know

Think about what happened at the end of "Video Dreams." What do you think might happen as the story goes on? Write what you think on the lines below.

Answers will vary.

RAIN DANCE

The application said that kids must send in a sample video. It said to send "the best work you have done." Tina played all her videos over the next few days. Many were tight, but not one looked great to her. **"I'll shoot a new one,"** she thought. "But what should it be like?"

She remembered her idea for a water video. Could that work? What if there was a hot band . . . dressed slick . . . a bright sheen-like rain coming down all over them . . . heavy beat. Flashing light between the beats. That would be extra cool. It was the kind of chaos Tina liked. She got on the phone and called her friend Fuzz.

Fuzz had a band called the Mud Pups. They were pretty good, too. Fuzz and Tina were old friends. It didn't take much to talk Fuzz into giving the idea a try. "Fuzz and the Mud Pups will win, no matter how the contest comes out," Tina said. "It won't cost you a dime. And lots of people will see your band. At least Sonny Jones will. And he is the greatest music video producer in the country."

Setting up took the longest time. At last everything was set. Tina sprayed the band with a water hose and then turned a bright green light on them as they faked playing. The band had never looked so **lame.** They also looked like they were in a fish tank. It wasn't quite what Tina was after.

"Why don't I send a shower of water drops on your heads while you really play?" Tina said.

"Right. And shock us into the next world," Fuzz said. "No way."

Then Tina hit on an idea. She would make two videos. One would just be of water streaming off a big glass window. The other would be of the Mud Pups really playing. On her computer, she would mix the pictures. She could make it look like the band was under the stream of water.

The idea worked! Her school let her use a big picture window for the water video. After she mixed the sound and the videos, the Mud Pups looked like they were inside a waterfall! The water in front of them made them gleam. The music seemed like it came out of them in waves.

Student page 106

Tina added some odd things to the picture. She put in a big yellow fish between the band and the water. She added some extra flashes of light on the beat. "I love this!" she thought as she worked. "And I bet Sonny Jones will love it, too. He has never seen anything like this."

Will Sonny like the video? Will Tina finish high school? Write what you think on the lines below. Then keep reading to find out.

Answers will vary.

Weeks passed. As it turned out, Tina did what Sonny had said to do. She stayed in school. She forced herself to pass math. She never did learn to like math, but it didn't matter. She was a high school grad!

One morning, shortly after school ended, Tina got a letter. It was from Video Jam! She tore it open so fast she ripped the edge. She could not believe what she was reading. Sonny Jones liked the video! She was not picked for the workshop, but that was OK. Sonny was coming through her town in about three weeks. He would be between videos, and he had some extra time. He wanted to meet Tina and see her way of working. And there was more good news.

She called Fuzz on the phone. "Dude! He loved my video!" she cried. She could not wait to tell him the next part. "He wants to meet me. And he wants to meet you, too. You and the Mud Pups."

"No way!" Fuzz said. "How in the world . . ."

"Sonny Jones liked your band," Tina said. "He's coming through here in three weeks and he wants to hear you live!"

There was real chaos, then, as the news sunk in. It was the kind of chaos Tina loved.

Student page 107

After Reading "Rain Dance"

Personal Response: What Do You Think?

Ask a volunteer to read aloud the questions under **What Do You Think?** on Student Workext page 108. Have students work in pairs to discuss and then write their responses. Then call on volunteers to read their responses aloud.

Think About the Story: Reading Comprehension

Have pairs of students complete the remaining items on Student Worktext pages 108 and 109. Check their responses and have pairs reread the story or parts of the story as necessary.

Reading Comprehension Skill: Fantasy versus Realism

Remind students that fiction stories are stories that come from a writer's imagination. All of the events and characters in a fiction story are made up by the author. Explain:

- Some fiction stories are *realistic*, or true to life. They tell about settings, characters, and events that could exist in real life.

- Other fiction stories contain events or characters that could not exist in real life. Such stories are called *fantasies*.

Ask students to think of some music videos they have seen. Have volunteers describe parts of the videos that were realistic and parts that were fantastic. Write their responses on the board. Then have students tell whether "Rain Dance" is a realistic story or a fantasy. (realistic) Ask them to describe things about it that are realistic. Next, ask students to name some fantasy stories they have read. You might prompt them by suggesting that they think about science fiction stories, fairy tales, and stories about superheroes.

 **Application**

At Home Point out that mixing videos and music on her computer is a job Tina can do at home. Have students learn about other jobs that can be done from the home, such as transcribing audiotapes for doctors and attorneys. Students can search on the Internet for home-based job or business opportunities and report their findings to the group.

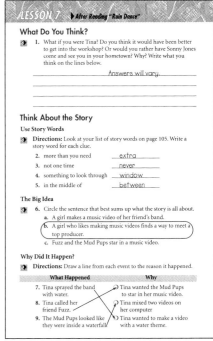

Student page 108

Student page 109

Reinforce & Extend

◈ SPELLING: *r*-Controlled Vowel: /ôr/ Spelled *or, ore,* or *our*

1. morning	**3.** boring	**5.** tore	**7.** more	**9.** your
2. before	**4.** shortly	**6.** four	**8.** storm	**10.** score

Write *for, store,* and *pour* on the board. Remind students that they have learned that the letters *or, ore,* and *our* can stand for the /ôr/ sound in each word. Then have students number a sheet of paper 1–10. Dictate the words above one at a time, pausing for students to write them. You will want to read the words *four* and *your* in an example sentence so students do not confuse them with *for* and *you're*. Next write the words on the board and have students check their work, making corrections as needed.

◉ **Reading and Writing Practice** Activity 90 provides additional practice spelling words with /ôr/ spelled *or, ore,* or *our*.

◈ LANGUAGE: Pronouns

Write these sentences on the board:

Tina sends a video to Sonny Jones.
She sends a video to him.

Underline *she* and circle *him*. Point out that these words are called pronouns. Explain:

- Pronouns are words that can be used in place of nouns.
- Subject pronouns (*I, you, we, he, she, it, they*) can take the place of the subject of a sentence.
- Object pronouns (*me, you, us, him, her, it, them*) can follow the verb in a sentence, or follow words such as *to, for, by,* and *about.*

Have pairs of students review the first paragraph on Student Worktext page 106 and underline all the subject pronouns and circle all the object pronouns they find.

◉ **Reading and Writing Practice** Activity 91 provides additional practice identifying and using pronouns.

◈ LITERARY APPRECIATION: Theme

Point out that the overall message a writer gives readers through a piece of writing is called *a theme.* Ask students what they think the theme, or message, of "Rain Dance" might be. (Possible response: You should follow your dreams. If you try hard enough, you will succeed.)

Then have students review another story they have read in class and tell what they think the theme of the story is.

To reinforce the concept of theme, have students discuss movies they have seen that communicate a strong message about right and wrong, the importance of following dreams, or another idea.

 # Lesson at a Glance

Preview: This lesson presents a brief chronological history of fashion fads from the 1960s through the 1990s.

Objectives

◆ to read a nonfiction selection and interpret information in a time line
◆ to read and spell words that contain the /ûr/ sound spelled *er*, *ur*, or *ir*

◆ to identify the author's purpose
◆ to identify possessive pronouns
◆ to write a summary

Student Worktext Pages 110–115
Story Words
children, polyester, decade, bottom, designer

◉ **Reading and Writing Practice Activities 92–98**

Before Reading "Fashion Time Line"

Letters and Sounds

r-Controlled Vowel: /ûr/ Spelled *er*, *ir*, *ur*; Phonogram *urn*

Remind students that they know the words *her*, *turn*, and *first*. Write the words on the board and circle *er*, *ir*, or *ur*. Point out that each of these letter pairs can stand for the /ûr/ sound in words like *her*, *turn*, and *first*. Write these words on the board and ask volunteers to read them: *burn*, *fern*, *herd*, *bird*, *burst*, *twirl*. Then have students complete Student Worktext page 110.

◉ **Reading and Writing Practice** Activity 92: Decoding Words with /ûr/ Spelled *er*, *ir*, or *ur*.

Story Words

Read aloud these words: *children, polyester, decade, bottom, designer*. Tell students that these words are important in the next story. Then write the words on the board and point to each one as you say it aloud a second time. Next, have students follow the ❑ *Read* ❑ *Say* ❑ *Write* sequence by completing **Story Words** on Student Worktext page 111. Have students add the words to their Word Bank at the back of the Student Worktext. To introduce the words in context, write these sentences on the board:

◆ How many <u>children</u> are in your family?
◆ Do you like <u>polyester</u> shirts?
◆ There are ten years in a <u>decade</u>.
◆ A new kind of shoe has springs in the <u>bottom</u> of it.
◆ A fashion <u>designer</u> has a fun job.

Have students make a word card for *children*. Ask a volunteer to read the first sentence aloud. Then have students copy the sentence onto the back of the word card. Follow the same procedure for the remaining words. To assess students' ability to read each new word, listen as individual students read the sentences on the board aloud.

◉ **Reading and Writing Practice** Activity 93: Reading Story Words.

More Word Work

Have students work in pairs to complete **More Word Work** on Student Worktext page 111.

◉ **Reading and Writing Practice** Activity 94: Reading and Writing Words with *er*.

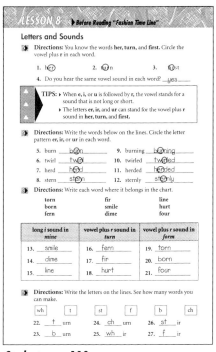

Student page 110

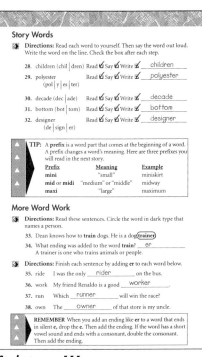

Student page 111

Reading "Fashion Time Line"

◆ Preview and Predict

- Tell students that next they will read a selection that is different from the other things they have read.
- Have a volunteer read the title on Student Worktext page 112. Then have students read the other words in dark type silently and preview the pictures.
- Ask volunteers to describe what seems different about this selection. (It is not in paragraphs. There is a quiz. Then there is a list of fashion fads.)
- Ask students if they expect to read a fiction story, or true information.

Tell students that this time line shows different fashions popular in the last 30 to 40 years. Have a volunteer tell when the time line begins (1960s) and when it ends (1990s). Explain that the first part of the selection presents a kind of quiz. In it, they will guess when each style listed was popular. Then they can check their answers using the time line. Make sure students understand that the quiz is just for fun—they will not be scored on their responses.

◆ Strategy Modeling

Make a Prediction Model the Make a Prediction strategy. You might say:

Based on the title, the subtitles, and the pictures, I expect to read about what people wore in the 1960s through the 1990s. I predict that there will be information about both women's and men's fashions.

Have students predict what information they will find, and then read the selection to check whether their predictions are true.

Focus on ESL/LEP

Have students acquiring English work with native English speakers as they read this selection. Have the native English speaker draw simple sketches of some of the fashion fads listed in the time line, such as bell bottoms, hip huggers, go go boots, and leggings. The English-speaking partner can clarify other fashions by pointing out examples of flannel, fleece, and hip-hop styles classmates are wearing.

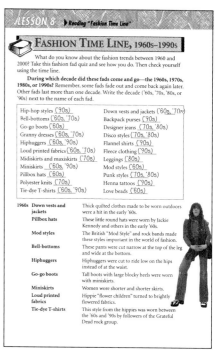

Student page 112

Student page 113

After Reading "Fashion Time Line"

Personal Response: You Be the Judge

Assign groups of students different decades from the 1960s through the 1990s. Have them imagine they are fashion designers who want to bring back styles from that decade. Have each group prepare reasons why their decade had the best fashions and why other decades had more "fashion mistakes." Then invite groups to present their opinions and reasons to the class. Finally, ask students to write their own responses to the questions under **You Be the Judge** on Student Worktext page 114.

Think About the Story: Reading Comprehension

Ask students to complete the remaining items on Student Worktext pages 114 and 115 individually. Monitor their responses and have students return to the reading if their answers indicate that they did not understand the information in the selection.

Reading Comprehension Skill: Author's Purpose

Remind students that writers have various reasons, or purposes, for writing stories. Point out that an author's purpose for writing will affect the way he or she writes. Explain:

- The purpose for writing a fiction story may be to entertain readers.
- The purpose for writing a news story or an encyclopedia article is to inform.
- The purpose for writing a political speech or a letter to the editor of a newspaper may be to persuade someone to do or feel something.

Ask students what they think the author's main purpose was for writing "Fashion Time Line." (To give information). Discuss what things make it easy for readers to get the information. (Possible responses: It is organized by time. The subtitles and pictures help.) Ask students whether or not they think the author also wanted to entertain readers. (Possible response: Yes, because there are sometimes funny comments like "What were those fashion designers thinking?")

 **Application**

Career Connection Encourage interested students to research careers in the fashion industry either on the Internet or at their local library. Ask them to report the information they discover to the class.

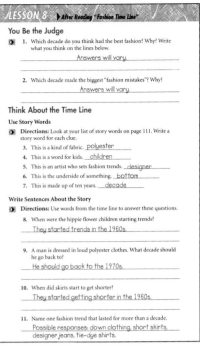

Student page 114

Student page 115

Reinforce & Extend

◆ SPELLING: *r*-Controlled Vowel: /ûr/ Spelled *er, ir,* or *ur*

1. super	**3.** stir	**5.** shirt	**7.** flower	**9.** her
2. hurt	**4.** purse	**6.** flirt	**8.** curl	**10.** skirt

Write *fern, first,* and *burn* on the board. Remind students that they have learned that the letters *er, ir,* and *ur* can stand for the /ûr/ sound. Then have students number a sheet of paper 1–10. Dictate the words above one at a time, pausing for students to write them. Next write the words on the board and have students check their work, making corrections as needed.

◉ **Reading and Writing Practice** Activity 95 provides additional practice spelling words with /ûr/ spelled *er, ir,* or *ur.*

◆ LANGUAGE: Possessive Pronouns

Write these sentences on the board:

Men's ties were wide in the 1970s.

Madonna's skirts were short in the 1980s.

Read the first sentence aloud and then replace *Men's* with *Their.* Read the second sentence aloud and ask a volunteer to name a word like *their* that could complete the sentence about Madonna. Replace *Madonna's* with *Her.* Point out that *their* and *her* are possessive pronouns. Explain:

- ◆ Pronouns are words that take the place of nouns in a sentence.
- ◆ Possessive pronouns take the place of possessive nouns such as *men's* and *Madonna's.*
- ◆ Possessive pronouns that come before a noun are *my, your, our, their, his, her,* and *its.*
- ◆ Possessive pronouns that stand alone are *mine, yours, ours, his, hers, theirs,* and *its.*

Assign pairs of students a possessive noun and have them use it to write a sentence. Have pairs of students exchange sentences and replace the possessive nouns in their sentences with the correct possessive pronoun. Then have students read both sentences aloud.

◉ **Reading and Writing Practice** Activity 96 provides additional practice identifying and using possessive pronouns.

◆ WRITING: A Summary

Ask students if they know what a summary is. If necessary, explain that a summary is a retelling of a story or an event. When writing a summary of a story, they should use their own words and not the words of the author. Explain:

- ◆ A written summary retells the most important events.
- ◆ A summary does not include details—just the big ideas.
- ◆ A summary does not include opinions.
- ◆ A summary is much shorter than the original piece of writing.

◉ **Reading and Writing Practice** Duplicate and distribute Activities 97–98, the Writing Model of a summary. Point out that it is a summary of "Video Dreams," a story students read earlier in Chapter 3. Have students read the summary and tell whether it sums up the most important parts of "Video Dreams." Next, have students write their own summaries in response to one of the following prompts:

- ◆ Write a summary of "Rain Dance."
- ◆ Choose one decade: 1960s, 1970s, 1980s, or 1990s. Write a summary of the fashion trends that were popular then. Use the time line to help you.

Lesson at a Glance

Preview: Kikai is a Hawaiian teenager who loves the waves. But while his friends and uncles surf the big waves, Kikai is often content to sit back and watch the waves. He gets teased, both for being small and for being a "chicken." Kikai makes friends with a surfer named Lani, whose jealous boyfriend makes things even more difficult for Kikai. One day, Kikai observes that the resort his mom works at is surrounded by land that has become loose and unstable. This could mean trouble in a rainstorm. When the island is hit by a terrible rainstorm, Kikai knows he must warn the resort owner and protect the guests from the mudslides that might occur. Kikai puts himself into the middle of the action, and proves his bravery both to himself and to those around him.

Objectives
◆ to complete a chapter book successfully
◆ to practice the word study and phonics skills learned in Chapter 2
◆ to practice reading the high-frequency and content words learned in Chapter 2
◆ to build reading fluency

Before Reading "Catch a Wave"

Introduce the Small Book

Use Prior Knowledge   Display a copy of the small book for Chapter 2, *Catch a Wave,* and tell students that next they will have an opportunity to read a chapter book. Explain that the book uses only words and letter sounds they have learned in Chapter 2, and that they will be reading the chapter book for fun. Explain:

◆ This book is about a boy who loves the surf, but gets teased for being small and for watching the big waves instead of riding them.

◆ Although people tease him, Kikai does not let what other people say prevent him from doing things he knows are right.

Invite students to share what they know about surfing from their own experience, or from watching TV or movies.

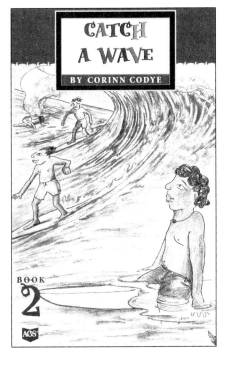

Preview and Predict

Distribute copies of *Catch a Wave.* Read aloud the introduction on the back cover. Have each student turn to the table of contents and read the chapter titles. Have students silently read the first three pages of the book. Guide them in making predictions about what might happen. Ask:

◆ Do you think Kikai will face problems because of his size?
◆ Why do you think Kikai does not surf the big wave that comes along?

Before students begin reading, you may want to introduce these geographical place names which appear in the story: Napili Bay, Kahana, Honoloa, and Maui. Also make sure students know the word *tourist,* ("a person who visits another place on vacation").

Read Independently

Students who have successfully read and understood the stories in Chapter 2 should be able to read *Catch a Wave* independently. You might periodically check their story comprehension by having them pause after completing each chapter and discuss the story. Discussion prompts for each chapter appear on the next two pages.

Read Strategically

Students who have struggled with the reading selections in Chapter 2, or who have been slow to master the phonics and word study skills presented in Chapter 2, may benefit from reading the book in groups of 3–5, pausing often to discuss events and use reading strategies to clear up confusion. The following procedure will help ensure that all students have a successful and positive reading experience.

- Read the first three pages aloud as students follow along. Call on students to summarize the main events. Then have students read to the end of Chapter 1 silently.

- Model using a reading strategy so that students can see how the strategy helps readers clear up confusion. You might say: *At first I did not understand why Kikai's uncles were upset that he did not surf the big wave. As I read ahead, I saw that they want their whole family to be good at surfing. It is a matter of family pride to them.*

- Model setting a purpose for reading the next set of pages. (Example: *to find out whether Kikai will start surfing the big waves*) Call on students to set their own purposes for reading. Have students read silently and pause at a designated stopping point. Each time you pause, call on students to explain how they used reading strategies as they read. Suggestions for specific questions you might ask appear on this page and the following page.

Reading "Catch a Wave"

◆ Comprehension Questions

Chapter 1
- How would you describe Kikai?
- What does Kikai like to do the most?
- How do Kikai's uncles treat him? Why?
- Do you think Kikai and Lani will become friends? Why or why not?

Chapter 2
- How does Kikai feel about his uncles' offer to help him surf? Why?
- How does Kikai do during the surfing lesson?
- What does Kikai see happening to the tourist? What does he do about it?
- What do Kikai and his uncles argue about at the end of the day?

Read Strategically Ask students whether anything in Chapter 1 or 2 confused them, and if so, what they did to clear up their confusion. Call on several students to give an oral summary of the main events in Chapters 1 and 2. Ask students to predict what might happen next.

Chapter 3
- Why does Kikai think about giving up surfing?
- What keeps Kikai from surfing the really big wave?
- Who is "the grommet"? How does the grommet react when Kikai tries to help him?
- What does Jimmi say to Kikai about the grommet? How does this make Kikai feel?

Chapter 4
- What does Kikai notice about the land where workers are digging?
- What does Kikai think could happen if it rains?
- Why does Elvin pick a fight with Kikai?
- Who helps Kikai out of the fight? What does he say to Kikai afterwards?

Read Strategically Ask a volunteer to summarize the main events in Chapters 3 and 4. Call on another student to tell how he or she used the Reread/Read Ahead or the Clarify strategy to clear up confusion. Discuss students' predictions for the next part of the story, and help each student set a purpose for reading Chapters 5 and 6.

Chapter 5

- What does Kikai worry about when the rain starts?
- What does Kikai do out in the ocean by himself? How does he feel?
- Why doesn't Kikai tell the other surfers about what he did?
- How does Elvin treat Kikai's warning? What do you think Kikai will do next?

Chapter 6

- What accident does Kikai run into? How does he help?
- What do Kikai, Lani, and Mimi decide to do?
- What do you think will happen next?

Read Strategically Ask each student to describe how he or she used one of these reading strategies: Use Prior Knowledge; Make a Prediction; Summarize; Clarify; Use Context Clues, Reread/Read Ahead. Then have students give an oral summary of Chapters 5 and 6, predict what might happen next, and set a purpose for reading the rest of the book.

Chapter 7

- What does Kikai tell Elvin and his boss, Lou Palapala? How do they react?
- What is the plan of action to get people to safety?
- What happens to the tourists as they try to cross the ditch?
- How does Kikai help one of the men? Do you think Kikai will be able to rescue the man's wife?

Chapter 8

- What happens when Elvin's car hits the tree?
- How does Kikai rescue the woman?
- How does Lou treat Kikai after the rescue? How do his uncles treat him? How does Lani treat him?
- How do you think Kikai feels after the mudslide is over? How can you tell?

Read Strategically Have students summarize the main events in Chapters 7 and 8. Then discuss with students whether their predictions turned out to be correct. Encourage students to compare their predictions with actual story events.

After Reading "Catch a Wave"

Personal Response

Ask students whether they liked *Catch a Wave,* and why or why not. Invite several volunteers to tell what they liked about the story. If some students did not like it, encourage them to give specific reasons why.

Critical Response

Prompt students to think critically about the story by asking questions such as these:

- How did the book's setting influence the events that happened?
- Which characters did you like? Which ones did you dislike? Why?
- Which part of the book was most exciting? Why?
- Do you think Kikai showed bravery? If so, how?

Extension Activities

Students can work on the activities below independently, in pairs, or in small groups.

Reading

Students who are interested in finding out more about Hawaii can look for books about Hawaii in the library. They can also use the Internet to look up sites such as the Hawaii Visitors Bureau at www.visit.hawaii.org. (This site even has a place to read information for school reports.) Students interested specifically in Maui can look up Maui Visitors Bureau at www.visitmaui.com/aloha.html.

Students interested in reading more about surfing can look at a few magazines about the topic. Some suggestions are:

- *Surfer Magazine*
- *The Surfer's Journal*
- *ZigZag*

Writing

Have interested students write a short (1–3 page) sequel to *Catch a Wave.* Students can write about what happens the next day when Kikai goes to school, or goes out to surf. You might prompt their ideas with questions such as:

- How do people act around Kikai after the rescue?
- Did the newspapers or TV stations cover this story?
- How does Kikai act now? Has anything changed for him?

Students who have ever surfed or spent time by the ocean may want to write a descriptive paragraph describing what either experience is like.

Kikai is a character who stands up for himself in the face of obstacles. Students can write about a similar experience, or a time when they stood up for themselves in some way.

Research

Students might find answers to the following questions, using resources such as the Internet, the telephone book, or the classified section of a local newspaper:

- Where could you go to learn more about Hawaii? about tourism in Hawaii?
- Are there any local Hawaiian cultural groups in your community?
- Where are some places you could go to learn about surfing? Are there any spots near you to learn how to surf? If not, what's the closest place you could go?

Chapter 2 Review

The Chapter Review on Student Worktext pages 117–124 will help students review and practice the skills presented in Chapter 2. The review is divided into four parts, A–D.

Suggestions to help students complete the Chapter Review:

- ◆ Make sure students understand that the Chapter Review is not a test. You may have students work in pairs and then compare responses, or you may work through the review as a class.
- ◆ Read the instructions for each part aloud.
- ◆ Have students complete one part of the review at a time. Pause to go over the answers and have students mark corrections using a second color.

Chapter Test

Reproducible blackline masters of the Chapter 2 Test can be found on pages 148–151 of this book. Use the test to assess students' comprehension of the skills taught in the chapter.

Additional Practice

Reading and Writing Practice Activities 50–98 can be used to reinforce the skills taught in Chapter 2.

Part A

Part A reviews the phonics skills taught in the chapter. Read aloud the summaries presented in the tip boxes before each exercise. Then have students complete the items. If students show difficulty understanding and using the new letters and sounds, review individual lessons or assign the corresponding Reading and Writing Practice Activities: 50, 57, 63, 70, 77, 81, 88, 92.

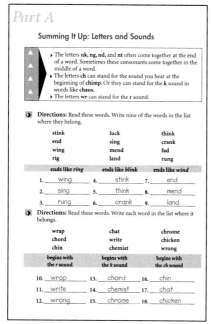

Student page 117

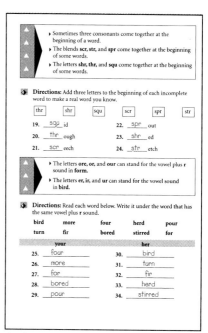

Student page 118

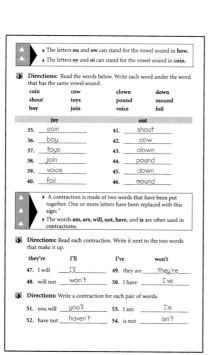

Student page 119

Part B

Part B reviews the word study and structural analysis skills taught in the chapter. Read aloud the summaries presented in the tip boxes before each exercise. Then have students complete the items. You may want to review the skills by looking back at individual lessons, presenting new examples on the board, or assigning the corresponding Reading and Writing Activities: 52, 65, 72, 83, 94.

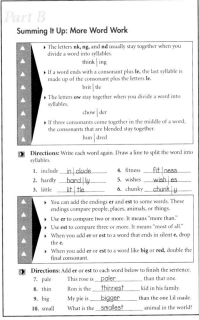

Student page 120

Part C

Part C reviews the story words and skills learned in the chapter. Students are asked to recognize story words and their meanings, to identify the number of syllables in story words. Have students review the story words in the Word Bank at the back of their Student Worktext or refer to the stories in the chapter to help them complete the review. For additional practice with word recognition, assign the corresponding Reading and Writing Practice Activities: 51, 58, 64, 71, 78, 82, 89, 93.

▸ You can add **ly** to some words.
▸ The ending **ly** means "in a way that is."
▸ You can add **er** to some words. The ending **er** means "one who."
▸ When you add **er** to a word that ends in silent **e**, drop the e.

Directions: Add **er** or **ly** to each word below. Then use the new word to finish the sentence.

11. paint + er   painter   I'd like to be a painter.
12. run + er   runner   The runner was fast.
13. slow + ly   slowly   We walked slowly.
14. win + er   winner   Will the winner please stand?
15. lose + er   loser   The loser wasn't sad at all.

Part C

Story Words

Directions: Write the word from the list that matches each clue.

| license | signal | motor | extra |
| special | stomach | producer | designer |

1. a job that has to do with fashion   designer
2. a job that has to do with making films   producer
3. one not like any other   special
4. part of your body on the inside   stomach
5. a paper needed to drive a car   license
6. what makes a car run   motor
7. more than what's needed   extra
8. what a stop light is   signal

Student page 121

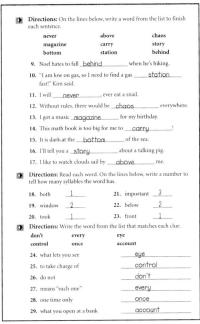

Directions: On the lines below, write a word from the list to finish each sentence.

never	above	chaos
magazine	carry	story
bottom	station	behind

9. Noel hates to fall behind when he's hiking.
10. "I am low on gas, so I need to find a gas station fast!" Kim said.
11. I will never, ever eat a snail.
12. Without rules, there would be chaos everywhere.
13. I got a music magazine for my birthday.
14. This math book is too big for me to carry!
15. It is dark at the bottom of the sea.
16. I'll tell you a story about a talking pig.
17. I like to watch clouds sail by above me.

Directions: Read each word. On the lines below, write a number to tell how many syllables the word has.

18. both   1
19. window   2
20. took   1
21. important   3
22. below   2
23. front   1

Directions: Write the word from the list that matches each clue.

| don't | every | eye |
| control | once | account |

24. what lets you see   eye
25. to take charge of   control
26. do not   don't
27. means "each one"   every
28. one time only   once
29. what you open at a bank   account

Student page 122

96 *Chapter 2 Review*

Part D

Part D reviews the content of the stories in the chapter. Students are asked to identify story characters, settings, and events, or to recall the main ideas in nonfiction selections. If students are having difficulty remembering story details, have them reread the stories they have trouble recalling and work in pairs or as a class to complete Part D again.

Directions: On the lines below, write a word from the list to finish each sentence.

saw	children	between	wash
country	polyester	love	decade

30. A __decade__ is made up of ten years.

31. There are three __children__ in our family.

32. I use soap and hot water to __wash__ my car.

33. Will smelled the cake before he __saw__ what shape it was.

34. The fresh __country__ air makes me sneeze.

35. The number two comes __between__ one and three.

36. In the 1970s people wore lots of __polyester__.

37. I __love__ figs, but my dad hates them.

Part D

Think About the Stories

Who Did What?

Directions: This list has the names of people who were in the stories in Chapter 2. Write a name to answer each question.

Tina	Jay	Joe	Sonny Jones
Brodie	Christy	Haksu	Fuzz

1. Who let a friend drive his van? __Jay__

2. Who liked making music videos? __Tina__

3. Who had a muddy car? __Joe__

4. Who worked at a car wash? __Christy__

5. Who was a driving teacher? __Brodie__

6. Who has a band? __Fuzz__

7. Who was a big-time producer? __Sonny Jones__

8. Who got a van? __Haksu__

Student page 123

Fiction or Nonfiction?

Directions: Write **fiction** next to stories that were made up by the writer. Write **nonfiction** next to the stories that tell about real life.

9. "The Driver's License" __fiction__

10. "Getting on the Road" __nonfiction__

11. "The Car Wash" __fiction__

12. "Video Dreams" __fiction__

13. "Fashion Time Line" __nonfiction__

Where Did It Happen?

Directions: This list has the names of some places where stories took place. Write each place name next to the story it goes with.

the DMV	a high school
an on-line chat room	Jay's house

14. "Video Dreams" __an on-line chat room__ __a high school__

15. "The Driver's License" __the DMV__ __Jay's house__

Think About Details

Directions: Each detail below comes from a story in Chapter 2. Write the details next to the stories they go with.

a lift gate	a dusty car	music videos
an eye test	go-go boots	

16. "The Driver's License" __a lift gate__

17. "Getting on the Road" __an eye test__

18. "The Car Wash" __a dusty car__

19. "Rain Dance" __music videos__

20. "Fashion Time Line" __go-go boots__

Student page 124

Chapter 3 Planning Guide

Skills and Learning Objectives

	Student Pages	Phonics and Phonograms	Word Study	Reading Strategy
Lesson 1 Twin Trouble	126–131	/är/ Spelled *ar, are*		Make a Prediction
Lesson 2 Sisters First	132–137	/âr/ Spelled *air, are,* (*are*)		Use Context Clues
Lesson 3 A Good Trade	138–143	/ir/ Spelled *eer, ear,* (*ear*)		Access Prior Knowledge (Use What You Know)
Lesson 4 The Poetry Slam	144–149	/f/ Spelled *gh, ph;* /j/ Spelled *dge, ge, gi, gy*		Summarize
Lesson 5 Poetry Slams—Words in Action	150–155	/aw/ Spelled *aw* (*aw*)		Reread/Read Ahead
Lesson 6 Stage Struck	156–161	/s/ Spelled *ce, ci* (*ace*)	Open VCV vs. Closed VCV	Set a Purpose
Lesson 7 X Games!	162–167	Prefixes *un-, re-*		Clarify
Lesson 8 X Games Stars	168–173	Suffixes *-ly, -ful*	Dividing Words with Prefixes and Suffixes	Summarize (Nonfiction)

Independent Reading

The Riddle of Buckman's Castle by Lorraine Sintetos
Lesson Plan: Teacher's Guide pages 132–135

Assessment and Review

Chapter 3 Summary of Skills and Strategies:
Student Worktext page 174

Chapter 3 Review:
Student Worktext pages 175–182

Chapter 3 Test:
Teacher's Guide pages 152–155

Level B Test:
Teacher's Guide pages 156–157

Reading Comprehension/ Critical Thinking	Spelling	Study Skill	Language	Writing	Literary Appreciation	Learning Styles	Focus on LEP/ESL or LD	Application	Reading and Writing Practice Activities
Note Sequence	103		103	103		101		102	99–104
Author's Purpose	107		107	107		105		106	105–110
Solve Problems	111		111	111		109		110	111–116
Draw Conclusions		115	115		115	113		114	117–120
Summarize (Nonfiction)		119	119	119			117	118	121–126
Categorize		123	123	123		121		122	127–132
Compare/Contrast		127	127		127	125	125	126	133–137
Distinguishing Fact from Opinion	131		131		131		129	130	138–142

Common Reading Errors	
If the Student . . .	**Then . . .**
◆ has difficulty learning and remembering blends	→ ◆ model the blending principle; provide additional practice with initial, medial, and final blends.
◆ struggles with literal story comprehension	→ ◆ ask questions such as *Who is in the story? Where did this happen? Why did it happen?* Have the student pause frequently to summarize.
◆ is slow to acquire sight words	→ ◆ reinforce or reteach the 5 steps to learning a word; provide extra practice with story words; encourage frequent review of words in the Word Bank.
◆ fails to construct overall meaning from text	→ ◆ reteach the lesson on Main Idea; discuss story ideas frequently while reading; encourage the student to construct oral summaries of passage or stories.
◆ is unable to increase the rate of reading with fewer errors	→ ◆ encourage the student to practice reading and rereading familiar text to build fluency.

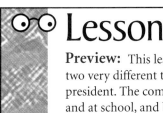 # Lesson at a Glance

Preview: This lesson presents a fiction story about two very different twin sisters who both run for class president. The competition causes conflict at home and at school, and both girls are surprised by the election's outcome.

Objectives
◆ to read a fiction story
◆ to read and spell words that contain /är/ spelled *ar* or *are*

◆ to note sequence in fiction
◆ to identify and use adjectives and articles
◆ to write an invitation

Student Worktext Pages 126–131
Story Words
president, council, election, student

◉ **Reading and Writing Practice Activities 99–104**

Before Reading "Twin Trouble"

Letters and Sounds
r-Controlled Vowel: /är/ Spelled *ar* or *are*

Remind students that they have learned the word *part*. Write it on the board and circle the letters *ar*. Explain that when *a* is followed by *r*, it has a vowel sound that is neither long nor short. Replace the *t* in *part* with *k* and read the new word aloud. Replace the initial *p* with *d* and then with *sh* and have students read the new words.

Next, write the word *are* on the board. Read it aloud and have students repeat it. Point out that in this word, the letters are stand for the same vowel-plus-*r* sound in *park*. Then have students complete Student Worktext page 126.

◉ **Reading and Writing Practice** Activity 99: Decoding Words with /är/ Spelled *ar* or *are*.

Story Words

Read aloud these words: *president, council, election, student.* Tell students that these words are important in the next story. Then write the words on the board and point to each one as you say it aloud a second time. Next, have students follow the ❏ *Read* ❏ *Say* ❏ *Write* sequence by completing **Story Words** on Student Worktext page 127. Have students add the words to their Word Bank at the back of the Student Worktext. To introduce the words in context, write these sentences on the board:

◆ We will vote on our next <u>president</u>.
◆ The town <u>council</u> held a meeting.
◆ They are still counting votes from the <u>election</u>.
◆ Jane is a good <u>student</u>.

Have students make a word card for *president*. Ask a volunteer to read the first sentence aloud. Then have students copy the sentence onto the back of the word card. Follow the same procedure for the remaining words. To assess students' ability to read each new word, listen as individual students read the sentences on the board aloud.

◉ **Reading and Writing Practice** Activity 100: Reading Story Words.

More Word Work

Have students work in pairs to complete **More Word Work** on Student Worktext page 127.

LESSON 1 ▶ *Before Reading "Twin Trouble"*

Letters and Sounds

▸ **Directions:** You know the words **car** and **part**. Write these words on the lines. Circle the letters **ar**.

1. car   c(ar)
2. part   p(ar)t

If you can read these words, you can read many words with **ar**. Try reading these words.

    mart   charm   dart   start

▸ **Directions:** The letters **ar** stand for the same sound in each word. Write the words below on the lines. Circle the letter pattern **ar** in each word.

3. farm   f(ar)m   7. farmer   f(ar)mer
4. dart   d(ar)t   8. darting   d(ar)ting
5. park   p(ar)k   9. parking   p(ar)king
6. harm   h(ar)m   10. harmed   h(ar)med

> ▲ **TIPS:** ▸ When **a** is followed by **r**, the **a** stands for a sound that is not long or short.
> ▸ The letters **ar** stand for the **ar** sound in **part**.

▸ **Directions:** Try reading these longer words. Circle the **ar** in each word.

11. h(ar)mless   14. b(ar)ter
12. f(ar)ther   15. sh(ar)ply
13. p(ar)tner   16. sh(ar)klike
17. Which word above means "someone you work closely with"? __partner__
18. Which word means "like a shark"? __sharklike__
19. Which word tells about something that can't hurt you? __harmless__

Student page 126

Story Words

▸ **Directions:** Read each word to yourself. Then say the word out loud. Write the word on the line. Check the box after each step.

20. president   Read ☑ Say ☑ Write ☑   __president__
   (pres | i | dent)
21. council (coun | cil)   Read ☑ Say ☑ Write ☑   __council__
22. election (e | lec | tion)   Read ☑ Say ☑ Write ☑   __election__
23. student (stu | dent)   Read ☑ Say ☑ Write ☑   __student__

More Word Work

▸ **Directions:** Add the ending **ly** or **er** to the words below.

24. charm   __charmer__   27. burn   __burner__
25. part   __partly__   28. paint   __painter__
26. work   __worker__   29. sharp   __sharply__

▸ **Directions:** Now use a word you wrote to finish each sentence.

30. We need to call a __worker__ to fix the dryer.
31. Turn on the __burner__ on the stove.
32. My dad is a __painter__ who uses tall ladders.
33. He turned __sharply__ and missed the rock.
34. My little sister is a __charmer__ with a great smile.
35. I am __partly__ to blame for the mess.

Student page 127

Reading "Twin Trouble"

◆ Preview and Predict

- ◆ Tell students that they are about to read a story about two twin sisters, Val and Vicki. Have a volunteer read the title on Student Worktext page 128 aloud. Then point out Val and Vicki in the picture on page 129.
- ◆ Explain that the sisters have both decided to run for class president. Ask students who have knowledge of student government to tell what the student council is, tell what a class president does, and describe the process of student elections.
- ◆ Read aloud and discuss with students the question under **Use What You Know** on Student Worktext page 128. Have students write their own answers to the question.

◆ Strategy Modeling

Make a Prediction Remind students that to make a prediction about a story is to make a guess about what might happen based on clues in the text and illustrations. Explain that making a prediction, and checking it as they read, can help readers keep track of story events. Model making a prediction. You might say:

From my preview of the story, I know that two twin sisters, Val and Vicki, are both planning to run for class president. Based on the title "Twin Trouble" and my real-life experiences, I'll bet that this causes jealousy between the sisters. I predict that one sister will try to steal the election from the other. I will read the story to find out if this happens and, if so, how it happens.

Invite students to make their own predictions about the story. Then have them read Student Worktext pages 128–129 to see if their predictions are correct.

▲ Learning Styles

Body/Kinesthetic To develop story background, have students pretend they are running for class president. Encourage them to design and create their own campaign signs with slogans like those in the story. Supply materials such as posterboard and markers. Then invite them to hold up their signs and call out their slogans as though campaigning.

Student page 128

Student page 129

After Reading "Twin Trouble"

Personal Response: What Do You Think?

Have pairs of students work together to answer the question under **What Do You Think?** on Student Worktext page 130. Then invite pairs to share their suggestions with the class.

Think About the Story: Reading Comprehension

Have students complete the remaining items on Student Worktext pages 130 and 131 independently or in pairs. Check their responses to help you assess their comprehension of the story. If students' responses indicate that they did not understand the story, reread the story in small groups.

Reading Comprehension Skill: Note Sequence

Tell students that story events happen in a certain sequence, or order, and that thinking about the order of events can help them understand and remember stories. Explain:

- Story events happen in an order that makes sense. They happen the way events happen in real life.
- Sometimes clue words such as *first, next, then,* or *tonight* help show the order of events.

Ask students to reread the first two paragraphs of the story. Then, write the following events on the board and have students put them in the correct order:

- Vicki smiles.
- Val says she will run for class president.
- Their mother says, "I hope you win."

Ask students how they know what order to put the events in.

Next, ask each student to copy three sentences from the story on a sheet of paper and put them out of order. Ask them to switch papers with a partner, and write 1, 2, or 3 next to each sentence to show when it happened. Students might also add a time-order word to each sentence.

Application

At Home Ask students to interview family members about their experiences with elections. If an election will be held soon, students might ask family members who they plan to vote for and why. Or, they might ask family members to talk about a particularly memorable election.

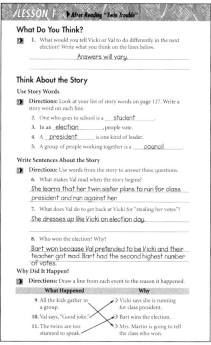

Student page 130

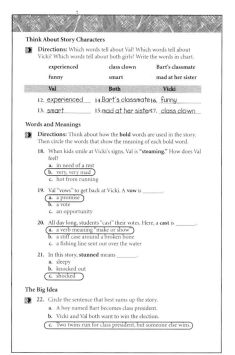

Student page 131

Reinforce & Extend

◆ SPELLING: *r*-Controlled Vowel: /är/ Spelled *ar* or *are*

1. car	**3.** farm	**5.** shark	**7.** charm	**9.** parking
2. are	**4.** yarn	**6.** market	**8.** darken	**10.** farther

Write *start* and *are* on the board. Remind students that they have learned that the letters *ar* and *are* can stand for the /är/ sound in *start*. Then have students number a sheet of paper 1–10. Dictate the words above one at a time, pausing for students to write them. Finally, write the words on the board and have students check their work, making corrections as needed.

◉ **Reading and Writing Practice** Activity 101 provides additional practice spelling words with /är/ spelled *ar* or *are*.

◆ LANGUAGE: Adjectives and Articles

Write this sentence on the board:

She puts on a red skirt, a white shirt, and black sneakers.

Ask volunteers to circle the nouns in the sentence. (*skirt, shirt, sneakers*) Then ask students which word describes the skirt (*red*), which word describes the shirt (*white*), and which word describes the sneakers (*black*). Tell students that *red, white,* and *black* are *adjectives*—words that tells more about a noun. Ask students how many skirts the sentence tells about and how they know. (one, because *a* refers to one) Point out that *a* is a special kind of adjective called an article. Explain:

- ◆ An *adjective* describes, or tells about, a noun.
- ◆ *A, an,* and *the* are special adjectives called *articles;* an article also comes before a noun.
- ◆ Use *a* before a word that begins with a consonant sound; use *an* before a word that begins with a vowel sound.
- ◆ An article (*a, an,* or *the*) comes before other adjectives in a sentence.

Have students work in pairs to use adjectives and articles to write sentences about objects in the class.

◉ **Reading and Writing Practice** Activity 102 provides additional practice with adjectives and articles.

◆ WRITING: An Invitation

Motivate students to plan an end-of-term party to which they will invite friends or family. Ask students what information they will need to include on the invitation. Explain:

- ◆ An invitation includes the date, day, time, and place of the event.
- ◆ An invitation often includes information about what will happen at the event.
- ◆ An invitation may tell people what they should or should not bring.
- ◆ An invitation to a party often includes an R.S.V.P. line which includes a name and phone number to call if the person invited decides to go to the party.

◉ **Reading and Writing Practice** Duplicate and distribute Activities 103–104. Point out the Writing Model of an invitation, and help students identify the key information (date, time, place, and so on). Then have pairs of students write their own invitations to the class party.

 # Lesson at a Glance

Preview: This lesson presents a nonfiction selection about Venus and Serena Williams, two sisters who play professional tennis.

Objectives

- to read a nonfiction selection
- to read and spell words that contain /âr/ spelled *air* or *are*
- to identify an author's purpose
- to recognize and use adverbs
- to write a two-paragraph report

Student Worktext Pages 132–137

Story Words

won, often, championship, doubles, competition, semi-final

 Reading and Writing Practice Activities 105–110

Before Reading "Sisters First"

Letters and Sounds

r-Controlled Vowel: /âr/ Spelled *air* or *are*; Phonogram *are*

Write the words *hair* and *dare* on the board and read them aloud. Underline the letters *air* or *are* in each word and explain that these letters can stand for the /âr/ sound in *hair*. Next, replace the *d* in *dare* with *c* and have students read the new word. Repeat the process several times, using the letters *r*, *sh*, and *st*. Explain that many words end in *are* and that these letters usually stand for the /âr/ sound. Then have students complete Student Worktext page 132.

 Reading and Writing Practice Activity 105: Decoding Words with /âr/ Spelled *air* or *are*.

Story Words

Read aloud these words: *won, often, championship, doubles, competition, semi-final.* Tell students that these words are important in the next story. Then write the words on the board and point to each one as you say it aloud a second time. Next, have students follow the ❑ *Read* ❑ *Say* ❑ *Write* sequence by completing **Story Words** on Student Worktext page 133. Have students add the words to their Word Bank at the back of the Student Worktext. To introduce the words in context, write these sentences on the board:

- We all cheered when our team team <u>won</u> the game.
- I <u>often</u> eat my lunch outside
- The two best teams played for the <u>championship</u>.
- In a <u>doubles</u> game, there are two players on each side.
- Swimmers from all over the state came for the <u>competition</u>.
- The winner of the <u>semi-final</u> game will go on to the championship game.

Have students make a word card for *won*. Ask a volunteer to read the first sentence aloud. Then have students copy the sentence onto the back of the word card. Follow the same procedure for the remaining words. To assess students' ability to read each new word, listen as individual students read the sentences on the board aloud.

 Reading and Writing Practice Activity 106: Reading Story Words.

More Word Work

Have students work in pairs to complete More Word Work on Student Worktext page 133. Before they begin, point out that many words with *r*- controlled vowels sound the same but are spelled differently, like *stair* and *stare*. Point out that sentence context can help them figure out which meaning is the right one.

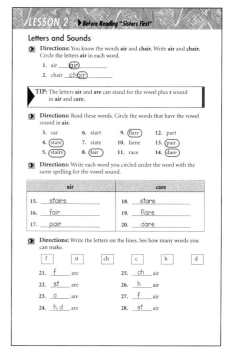

Student page 132

Student page 133

Reading "Sisters First"

◆ Preview and Predict

- Tell students that they are about to read about two real-life sisters, Venus and Serena Williams. Ask if any students have heard of these sisters, and if so, invite students to tell what they know about them. If necessary, explain that the sisters are both professional tennis players. Point out Venus and Serena in the picture on Student Worktext page 134. Then have a volunteer read the title aloud.
- Ask students to share what they know about tennis, including important tournaments such as Wimbledon and the U.S. Open.
- Next, explain that Venus and Serena played against each other in the 2000 Wimbledon championship. Then read aloud the questions under **Use What You Know** on Student Worktext page 134. Have students discuss the questions and then write their answers.

◆ Strategy Modeling

Use Context Clues Remind students that if they come to a word or term they are unfamiliar with as they read, they can use the meaning of nearby words and phrases to help them. Have students read the first paragraph on page 134. Ask them whether here, the word *match* means "a little stick used to light a flame" or "a kind of contest," and how they know. (The whole paragraph is about tennis, so here, *match* must mean "contest.") Then model using context clues to figure out the meaning of *strive* in the first paragraph. You might say:

I haven't seen the word strive *before and I'm not sure what it means. The text says, "One player serves with grace. The other returns the ball with force." I think that* strive *means "try hard." That meaning makes sense in this sentence.*

Encourage students to use context clues as they continue to read.

▲■ Learning Styles

Logical/Mathematical Invite students to use a K-W-L chart to aid them in reading and understanding the selection. To do this, they should create a three-column chart with the headings *What I **Know**, What I **Want** to Know,* and *What I **Learned**.* Encourage them to fill in the first two columns before reading, and to fill in the third column after reading.

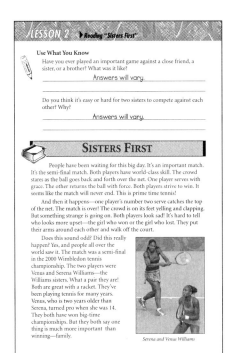

Student page 134

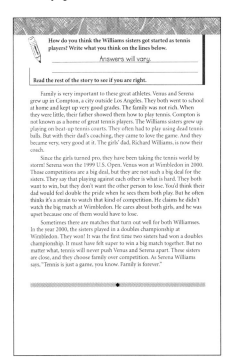

Student page 135

After Reading "Sisters First"

Personal Response: You Be the Judge

Have pairs of students work together to answer the question under **You Be the Judge** on Student Worktext page 136. Then invite pairs to share their responses with the class.

Think About the Story: Reading Comprehension

Have students complete the remaining items on Student Worktext pages 136 and 137 independently or in pairs. Check their responses to help you assess their comprehension of the selection. If students' responses indicate that they did not understand parts of the selection, reread those sections with students and invite them to paraphrase the content.

Reading Comprehension Skill: Author's Purpose

Remind students that authors write stories with a certain purpose in mind. To review what students have learned so far, ask volunteers to give examples of writing that is meant to entertain (fiction stories, mysteries), to give information (news stories, reference books), and to teach something (textbooks, how-to books). List their responses on the board. Then explain that sometimes writers can have more than one purpose in mind. For example, a magazine article about recycling might be written to give information, and also to try to persuade people to recycle. Ask students what they think the purpose or purposes of "Sisters First" might be. If necessary, model determining the purpose. You might say:

"Sisters First" contains information about the Williams sisters and their tennis careers. I think one purpose is to give information. I think a second purpose is to send a message about the importance of family. I think this because of the title, "Sisters First," because both sisters say family is more important than winning, and because of what Serena says at the end: "Tennis is just a game, you know. Family is forever."

Application

Career Connection   Help students brainstorm a list of careers related to sports. You might create one or more word webs to keep track of students' responses. Guide students to mention several sports that are played professionally as well as other sports-related jobs such as referees, coaches, trainers, agents, and jobs in sports medicine, management, promotions, writing, and broadcasting. Encourage interested students to find out more about these careers in books, magazines, encyclopedias, or on the Internet.

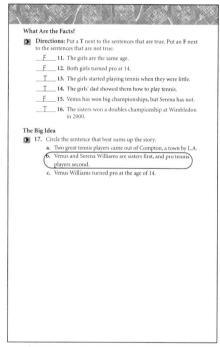

Student page 136

Student page 137

Reinforce & Extend

◆ SPELLING: r-Controlled Vowel: /âr/ Spelled *air* or *are*

1. air	**3.** unfair	**5.** stairway	**7.** share	**9.** glare
2. cares	**4.** dare	**6.** scare	**8.** chair	**10.** square

Write *pair* and *rare* on the board. Remind students that they have learned that the letters *air* and *are* can stand for the /âr/ sound in *rare*. Then have students number a sheet of paper 1–10. Dictate the words above one at a time, pausing for students to write them. Finally, write the words on the board and have students check their work, making corrections as needed.

Reading and Writing Practice Activity 107 provides additional practice spelling words with /âr/ spelled *air* or *are*.

◆ LANGUAGE: Adverbs

Write this sentence on the board:

Venus runs quickly across the tennis court.

Ask a volunteer to circle the verb in the sentence. (*runs*) Then ask students which word tells how Venus runs. (*quickly*) Tell students *quickly* is an adverb—a word that tells more about a verb. Explain:

- An *adverb* describes the action of a verb.
- Adverbs can tell how, when, or where about an action, or can give other information.
- Many adverbs are formed by adding *–ly* to adjectives. They often tell how; for example, *quickly, boldly, happily, sadly.*
- Some adverbs do not end in *–ly.* They often tell when or where; for example, *tomorrow, tonight, outside, inside.*

Help students brainstorm a list of adverbs. Then have students work in pairs to use these or other adverbs to write sentences about a sports event or a music performance.

Reading and Writing Practice Activity 108 provides additional practice with adverbs.

◆ WRITING: A Two-Paragraph Report

Write these sentences on the board:

Martha is a great tennis player.

She is also a great person.

Ask students to imagine that Martha is a real tennis star they know of. Have students tell some reasons that Martha is a great player and a great person. List their responses on the board. Work with students to use the information they provided to write a two-paragraph report about Martha, with each sentence on the board functioning as a topic sentence for one of the paragraphs. Then explain:

- Each paragraph in a two-paragraph report should include a *topic sentence* that tells the main idea of the paragraph.
- Each paragraph should also include three to five sentences that *support,* or explain, the topic sentence.

Reading and Writing Practice Duplicate and distribute Activities 109–110. Point out the Writing Model of a two-paragraph report, and help students identify the topic sentences and the supporting sentences. Then have students write their own two-paragraph report in response to one of these prompts:

- Write about a sports, music, or movie star. Explain who the star is and what makes the person a star.
- Write about an unusual place. Name the place and explain what makes it interesting or unusual.

Lesson at a Glance

Preview: This lesson presents a story about a young man named Ramon who is having problems maintaining his beloved old car—a classic that seems to need constant repair. He solves his problem when he meets a mechanic named Steve, who needs help of a different kind.

Objectives
◆ to read a fiction selection
◆ to read and spell words with /ir/ spelled *eer* or *ear*

◆ to recognize and develop problem-solving techniques
◆ to identify and use prepositions
◆ to write a business letter

Student Worktext Pages 138–143

Story Words
second, mechanic, errand

Reading and Writing Practice Activities 111–116

Before Reading "A Good Trade"

Letters and Sounds

r-Controlled Vowel: /ir/ Spelled *eer* or *ear*; Phonogram *ear*

Remind students that they know the word *year*. Write it on the board and circle the letters *ear*. Explain that the letters *ear* can stand for the /ir/ sound they hear in *year*. Write *hear* and *clear* next to *year*. Ask a volunteer to read the words aloud. Tell students that many words end in the letters *ear*, and that if they can read such words as *hear* and *clear*, they will be able to read other words with this pattern of letters.

Write the word *cheer* on the board, read it aloud, and have students repeat it. Circle the letters *eer* and tell students that these letters can also stand for the /ir/ sound. Write the word *steer* below *cheer* and ask a volunteer to read it aloud. Then have students complete Student Worktext page 138.

Reading and Writing Practice Activity 111: Decoding Words with /ir/ Spelled *eer* or *ear*.

Story Words

Read aloud these words: *second, mechanic, errand*. Tell students that these words are important in the next story. Then write the words on the board and point to each one as you say it aloud a second time. Next, have students follow the ❏ *Read* ❏ *Say* ❏ *Write* sequence by completing **Story Words** on Student Worktext page 139. Have students add the words to their Word Bank at the back of the Student Worktext. To introduce the words in context, write these sentences on the board:

◆ I will have a <u>second</u> hot dog.
◆ My <u>mechanic</u> fixed the brakes on my car.
◆ I have to go to town to run an <u>errand</u>.

Have students make a word card for *second*. Ask a volunteer to read the first sentence aloud. Then have students copy the sentence onto the back of the word card. Follow the same procedure for the remaining words. To assess students' ability to read each new word, listen as individual students read the sentences on the board aloud.

Reading and Writing Practice Activity 112: Reading Story Words.

More Word Work

Have students work in pairs to complete **More Word Work** on Student Worktext page 139.

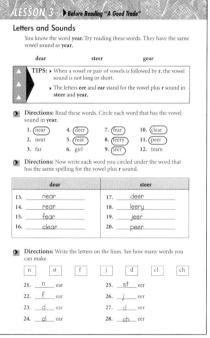

Student page 138

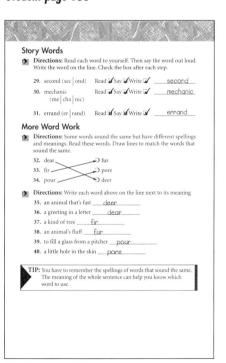

Student page 139

Reading "A Good Trade"

◆ Preview and Predict

- ◆ Tell students that they are about to read a story about a young man named Ramon and his old classic car. Have a volunteer read the title on Student Worktext page 140 aloud. Point out Ramon and his car in the illustration on page 141.
- ◆ Explain that Ramon is having some problems with his old car. Then have a volunteer read aloud the first question under **Use What You Know** on Student Worktext page 140. List students' responses on the board. Then invite students to write answers to the second question in their Student Worktext.
- ◆ Next, have students read the first paragraph on page 140 and then predict what Ramon might do about his car problems.

◆ Strategy Modeling

Access Prior Knowledge Tell students that readers use what they know about a topic to help them make sense of what they read. For this reason, it is helpful if they think, talk, or write about a topic before reading.

Ask students to think of what they know about cars and problems that old cars can have. Then model accessing prior knowledge to prepare for reading. You might say:

I know a little about old cars because my family has one. I know that the older a car gets, the more things go wrong with it. An old car often needs a lot of repairs. Some things that can go wrong are oil leaking, the clutch wearing out, the brakes needing to be replaced, and the battery dying.

Have students read Student Worktext pages 140 and 141 to find out what happens to Ramon and his old car. Tell them to use what they know about cars to help them as they read.

▲ Learning Styles

Interpersonal/Group Learning Have students work in small groups to read the story. Have groups begin by discussing together the questions under **Use What You Know** on Student Worktext page 140. Group members should then trade off reading each paragraph of the story aloud. If a word, sentence, or idea is confusing to any group member, the other group members should offer help. Then groups can discuss the story and answer the **What Do You Think?** questions on page 142 together.

Student page 140

Student page 141

After Reading "A Good Trade"

Personal Response: What Do You Think?

Have students work independently to answer the questions under **What Do You Think?** on Student Worktext page 142. Then invite students to share their responses with the class. If students have opposing views on the last question, invite them to debate the question, using reasons to support their opinions.

Think About the Story: Reading Comprehension

Have students complete the remaining items on Student Worktext pages 142 and 143 independently or in pairs. Check their responses to help you assess their comprehension of the selection. If students' responses indicate that they did not understand the story, reread the story in small groups.

Reading Comprehension Skill: Problem Solving

Ask students to sum up the problems Ramon had, and talk about how he solved them. Then share this problem-solving strategy:

- ◆ Name the problem.
- ◆ Talk about different ways the problem could be solved.
- ◆ Pick the one idea that seems to be the best.
- ◆ Make a list of steps to help you follow through with that idea and reach a solution.

Then have small groups use the steps above to come up with solutions to these problems:

- ◆ A friend from school calls you and wants to hang out tonight. You want to spend time with your friend, but you have lots of homework to do. What do you do?
- ◆ Your next-door neighbor has a pet dog for sale. You really want the dog, but you have no money. What solution would work for everyone?

Invite the groups to role-play the scenarios to show how they solved the problems. Encourage students to discuss and compare the solutions.

 **Application**

In the Community If possible, invite a mechanic from the community to speak with students about proper automobile maintenance, including do-it-yourself tips that can save drivers time and money.

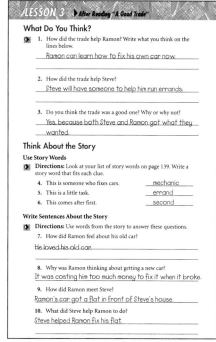

Student page 142

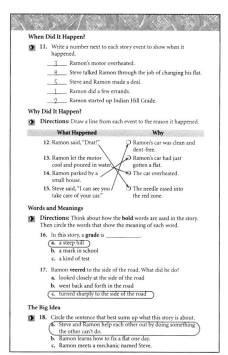

Student page 143

Reinforce & Extend

◆ SPELLING: *r*-Controlled Vowel: /ir/ Spelled *eer* or *ear*

1. rear	**3.** peered	**5.** clear	**7.** fear	**9.** steering
2. near	**4.** gear	**6.** jeer	**8.** veered	**10.** dearly

Write *cheer* and *hear* on the board. Remind students that they have learned that the letters *eer* and *ear* can stand for the /ir/ sound in *hear*. Then have students number a sheet of paper 1–10. Dictate the words above one at a time, pausing for students to write them. Finally, write the words on the board and have students check their work, making corrections as needed.

⊙ **Reading and Writing Practice** Activity 113 provides additional practice spelling words with /ir/ spelled *eer* or *ear*.

◆ LANGUAGE: Prepositions

Write these sentences on the board:

Ramon zoomed onto the highway.

The brakes in his car needed repair.

Ask students to identify the words in the first sentence that tell where Ramon zoomed. (*onto the highway*) Then have students identify the words in the second sentence that tell which brakes needed repair. (*in his car*) Underline both of these phrases and explain that they are called *prepositional phrases*. Have volunteers circle the noun in each phrase. (*highway, car*) Then draw a box around *onto* and *in* and tell students that these words are called prepositions. Explain:

- ◆ A *preposition* is a word that relates a noun to another word or words in a sentence.
- ◆ A *prepositional phrase* contains at least a preposition and a noun. It may contain other words that modify the noun, such as articles or adjectives.
- ◆ Some common prepositions are *to, in, on, under, from, across, beside, between,* and *behind.*

Write the above prepositions on the board. Then encourage pairs of students to play a guessing game. To play, the first partner uses prepositional phrases to describe the location of an object without naming it; for example, *It is **on** the table **beside** the door.* The second partner must guess the object.

⊙ **Reading and Writing Practice** Activity 114 provides additional practice with prepositions.

◆ WRITING: A Business Letter

Remind students that in the story they just read, Ramon is always having to take his car to the mechanic for repairs. Ask students how Ramon could let his mechanic know if the mechanic didn't seem to repair his car properly. If necessary, point out that one way would be to write his mechanic a letter explaining the problem. Remind students that there are two basic kinds of letters, a friendly letter and a business letter, and that today they will learn about business letters. Explain:

- ◆ A business letter is a formal letter written from a person to a business, from a business to a person, or from one business to another business.
- ◆ A business letter usually has these parts: the sender's address; the date; the recipient's address; a greeting such as "Dear Mr. Jones:" or "To whom it may concern:"; the body, or main part, of the letter; a closing such as "Sincerely,"; and the writer's signature.

⊙ **Reading and Writing Practice** Duplicate and distribute Activities 115–116, the Writing Model of a business letter, and help students identify the sender's address, date, recipient's addresses, greeting, body, closing, and signature. Then have students write their own business letters. You might offer these prompts:

- ◆ You are applying for a job. Write a letter explaining what job you are applying for, why you are interested in it, and why you think you would be good for the job.
- ◆ You ordered a product from a catalog but are not happy with what you received. Write a letter saying that you want to return the product for a refund and explain why.

Lesson 3 **111**

 # Lesson at a Glance

Preview: This lesson presents a story about a teenager named Philip who tries to impress a girl from his school by entering a poetry contest. Philip panics when he realizes he has never written a poem, but by drawing on what he knows and loves, he manages to write a poem that both the audience and the girl appreciate.

Objectives
- to read a fiction selection
- to read words with /f/ spelled *gh* or *ph*, and /j/ spelled *dge*, *ge*, *gi*, or *gy*
- to draw conclusions
- to organize information graphically (list, chart, time line)
- to capitalize proper nouns and words that begin sentences
- to appreciate poetry

Student Worktext Pages 144–149

Story Words
river, example, poetry, audience, perform, performance, practice

◉ **Reading and Writing Practice Activities 117–120**

Before Reading "The Poetry Slam"

Letters and Sounds

/f/ Spelled *gh* or *ph*; /j/ Spelled *dge*, *ge*, *gi*, or *gy*

Write the words *phone* and *enough* on the board. Read the words aloud and have students repeat them. Underline the letters *ph* and *gh*, and explain that these letter combinations can stand for the /f/ sound. Then write *photograph* and *laugh* on the board and guide students to read these words aloud.

Next, remind students that they have learned the word *large*. Then write the words *large*, *lodge*, *ginger*, and *gym* on the board. Have students read the words aloud. Explain that the letter *g* can stand for the /j/ sound when followed by *e*, *i*, or *y*, and that *dge* is a common way to spell the /j/ sound at the end of a word. Then have students complete Student Worktext page 144.

Note: You may wish to read aloud the sample words on page 144. Some of the words contain letter patterns students may not be familiar with.

◉ **Reading and Writing Practice** Activity 117: Decoding Words with /f/ Spelled *gh* or *ph*, and /j/ Spelled *dge*, *ge*, *gi*, or *gy*.

Story Words

Read aloud these words: *river, example, poetry, audience, perform, performance, practice*. Tell students that these words are important in the next story. Then write the words on the board and point to each one as you say it aloud a second time. Next, have students follow the ❑ *Read* ❑ *Say* ❑ *Write* sequence by completing **Story Words** on Student Worktext page 145. Have students add the words to their Word Bank at the back of the Student Worktext. To introduce the words in context, write these sentences on the board:

- We swam in the <u>river</u>.
- This is a great <u>example</u> of a book report.
- My dad gave me a book of <u>poetry</u>.
- The <u>audience</u> clapped at the end of the play.
- I will <u>perform</u> a song on the trumpet.
- The actors put on a great <u>performance</u>.
- I will <u>practice</u> this move until I get it right.

Have students make a word card for *river*. Ask a volunteer to read the first sentence aloud. Then have students copy the sentence onto the back of the word card. Follow the same procedure for the remaining words. To assess students' ability to read each new word, listen as individual students read the sentences on the board aloud.

◉ **Reading and Writing Practice** Activity 118: Reading Story Words.

More Word Work

Have students work in pairs to complete **More Word Work** on Student Worktext page 145.

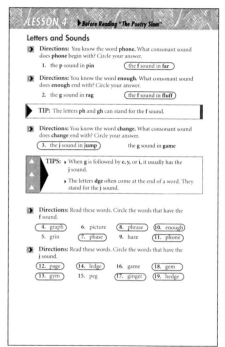

Student page 144

Student page 145

Reading "The Poetry Slam"

◆ *Preview and Predict*

- ◆ Tell students that they are about to read a story about a teenager named Philip, his friend George, and a girl from their school named Ginger. Point out Philip and Ginger in the picture on Student Worktext page 147.
- ◆ Explain that Philip wants to impress Ginger, but his friend George doesn't think he is Ginger's type. Then read aloud the questions under **Use What You Know** on Student Worktext page 146 and have students discuss them.
- ◆ Tell students that Ginger writes poetry. Then have them predict what Philip will do to try to impress her.

◆ *Strategy Modeling*

Summarize Tell students that to summarize a story is to sum up the most important events in their own words. Explain:

- ◆ A summary includes the most important ideas or events in a piece of writing.
- ◆ A summary does not include details. It does not include opinions.
- ◆ While reading, it can help to pause at certain points and sum up what has happened so far. Summarizing while reading helps readers understand and remember what they read.

Model summarizing. Read the first two paragraphs on Student Worktext page 146 aloud, and then give an oral summary such as the following:

Philip and his friend George go looking for Ginger in Philip's red sports car. Philip hopes Ginger will be impressed when she sees his car. He has tried talking to her before, but she has never paid attention to him.

Have students read the rest of Student Worktext pages 146–147 to find out what happens with Philip and Ginger. Tell them to pause at the end of page 146 to sum up the important events before reading the ending on page 147.

◆ Learning Styles

Visual/Spatial Have students copy each word from **More Word Work** on Student Worktext page 145 containing the /j/ or /f/ sound on graph paper, writing one letter in each square. Then have students use a colored pencil or highlighter to circle the letters that stand for the /j/ or /f/ sound in each word.

Student page 146

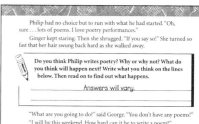

Student page 147

After Reading "The Poetry Slam"

Personal Response: What Do You Think?

Ask a volunteer to summarize the events in "The Poetry Slam." Then have students work in small groups to answer the questions at the top of Student Worktext page 148.

Think About the Story: Reading Comprehension

Have students complete the remaining items on Student Worktext pages 148 and 149 independently or in pairs. Check their responses to help you assess their comprehension of the story. If students' responses indicate that they did not understand the story, reread it in small groups.

Reading Comprehension Skill: Draw Conclusions

Remind students that writers do not always tell their readers everything directly. Readers therefore have to *draw conclusions,* or figure some things out on their own. Explain:

- Readers can use clues in a story to draw conclusions.
- Readers can use what they know to make a logical guess about something, such as how characters feel or why characters do certain things.

Guide students to draw conclusions in response to these questions:

- How does Ginger feel about Philip at the beginning of the story? How do you know?
- How does Ginger feel about Philip at the end of the story? How can you tell?

If necessary, model using story clues and prior knowledge to draw a conclusion:

At the end of the story, Ginger tells Philip that she would like a ride home sometime. From what I know about people, she would not say this unless she was becoming more interested in getting to know him. She must have been impressed by his poem, and is starting to like him.

🏔 Application

Career Connection   Remind students that in "The Poetry Slam," the characters attend an event where people read poetry they have written. Tell students that many people write for a living. Mention and discuss various kinds of writing, including literature, journalism, screenwriting, copywriting, technical writing, and writing for education. Ask if any students are interested in writing as a career, and what kinds of writing appeal to them. You might invite a writer from the community to speak to the class about writing careers.

LESSON 4 ▶ After Reading "The Poetry Slam"

What Do You Think?

1. What do you think Philip learned in the story? Write what you think on the lines below.
   He learned that he can write poems, too.

2. What do you think Ginger learned?
   Ginger learned that people aren't always what they seem to be.

Think About the Story

Use Story Words

Directions: Look at your list of story words on page 145. Write a story word to fit each clue.

3. what you do to get better at a skill ___ practice
4. a kind of writing ___ poetry
5. people who go to a play ___ audience
6. to act or dance for people ___ perform
7. one thing that shows what others of its kind are like ___ example
8. a show ___ performance

Write Sentences About the Story

Directions: Use words from the story to answer these questions.

9. What does Philip do first to try to impress Ginger?
   He tries to impress her with his car.
10. What does Philip say he can do that he really can't do?
    He says he can write poems.
11. How do Ginger's feelings change at the end of the story?
    She likes Philip better after she hears his poem.

Student page 148

Why Did It Happen?

Draw a line to match each story event with the reason it happened.

What Happened	Why
12. Ginger wants a ride in Philip's car.	He decides to write about what he knows.
13. Ginger gives Philip a hard look.	She doesn't believe that Philip writes poetry.
14. Philip writes a poem about cars.	She sees there is more to Philip than she thought.

When Did It Happen?

15. Write a number from 1 to 4 in front of each event to show when it happened.
   __1__ Philip says, "I'll see you at the River Mill Coffeehouse."
   __2__ Philip signs up for the poetry competition.
   __4__ Ginger asks Philip if she can have a ride home sometime.
   __3__ Philip reads his poem at the competition.

What Are the Big Ideas?

16. What points do you think the writer of this story wanted to make? Circle two sentences.
   a. Write about what you know and love.
   b. Poets and mechanics aren't right for each other.
   c. A great-looking car won't impress anyone.
   d. People are not always as they seem.

What Do You Think?

17. Philip wrote about something he loved and knew well—his car. What are some things you know and love that you might write a poem about? Write some ideas here.
   Answers will vary.

Student page 149

Reinforce & Extend

◈ STUDY SKILL: Organizing Information Graphically: List, Chart, Time Line

Ask students if they have ever made or used a list, a chart, or a time line. Explain:

- ◆ A list is a simple way of remembering a lot of single items, such as things to pack on a trip or things to buy at the store.
- ◆ A chart is used to organize more complicated information, like who is bringing what to a big event or who is working on the different parts of a project.
- ◆ A time line is used to organize dates so it is easy to see when events happened.

Work with students to create a simple example of each kind of graphic organizer (for example, a to-do list; a chart showing students' favorite TV shows on different days of the week at different times; a time line showing important events in your career). Then have students create a time line of their own lives, showing where they lived and went to school at different times.

◉ **Reading and Writing Practice** Activity 119 provides additional practice organizing information graphically.

◈ LANGUAGE: Capitalization

Write these sentences on the board (Capitalization is purposefully incorrect):

that weekend, philip went with george to the river mill coffeehouse.

just after the first poet performed, he saw ginger come in and sit down.

Read the first sentence aloud. Then ask students what is wrong with it. If necessary, point out that neither the first word in the sentence nor the proper nouns are capitalized. Remind students that a proper noun names a particular person, place, or thing.

Call on a volunteer to tell which words should be capitalized. (*That, Philip, George, River Mill Coffeehouse*) Then have students copy the second sentence, using proper capitalization.

◉ **Reading and Writing Practice** Activity 120 provides additional practice with capitalization.

◈ LITERARY APPRECIATION: Poetry

Ask students what kind of writing Ginger and Philip create in the story. (poetry) Invite students to describe how poetry is different from other kinds of writing. If necessary, explain that poetry is a form of writing that uses words in new and unusual ways to express a writer's feelings, beliefs, or observations. Explain:

- ◆ A poem usually is written in lines. Often the lines are grouped together to form stanzas.
- ◆ The lines in many poems rhyme. However, the lines in a poem do not have to rhyme.
- ◆ A poem may tell a story, but often poems are written to describe something in an interesting way, or to share feelings and thoughts.
- ◆ Poets often play with words and language in their poems. For example, they may use words that have a musical effect, or words that create a strong rhythm.

To give students the chance to appreciate poetry, choose several poems to read aloud to students. Then inform students that later they will have the opportunity to write their own poems.

 # Lesson at a Glance

Preview: This lesson presents a selection about poetry slams—popular poetry contests held in many cities. The selection also contains a poem written by Chicago poet Marc Smith, the founder of poetry slams.

Objectives
♦ to read a nonfiction selection and a poem
♦ to read words with vowel variant /aw/ spelled *aw*
♦ to summarize nonfiction

♦ to interpret graphic aids (diagram, map)
♦ to use proper end punctuation
♦ to write a poem

Student Worktext Pages 150–155

Story Words
nation, national, popular, dramatic

◉ **Reading and Writing Practice Activities 121–126**

Before Reading "Poetry Slams—Words in Action"

Letters and Sounds
Vowel Variant /aw/ Spelled *aw*; Phonogram *aw*

Write the words *dawn* and *crawl* on the board. Read the words aloud and have students repeat them. Underline the letters *aw* in each word, and explain that this letter combination usually stands for the /aw/ sound.

Next, write the word *law* on the board. Ask students to read the word. Replace the letter *l* with *r* and have students read the new word. Then add *d* to *raw* to form *draw* and have students read this word. Tell students that many words end in *aw*, and that if they are able to read the words *law, raw,* and *draw,* they will be able to read other words with this pattern of letters. Then have students complete Student Worktext page 150.

◉ **Reading and Writing Practice** Activity 121: Decoding Words with /aw/ Spelled *aw*.

Story Words

Read aloud these words: *nation, national, popular, dramatic.* Tell students that these words are important in the next story. Then write the words on the board and point to each one as you say it aloud a second time. Next, have students follow the ❏ *Read* ❏ *Say* ❏ *Write* sequence by completing **Story Words** on Student Worktext page 151. Have students add the words to their Word Bank at the back of the Student Worktext. To introduce the words in context, write these sentences on the board:

♦ People all over the <u>nation</u> watched the game on TV.

♦ The <u>national</u> election will be held next week.

♦ Basketball is a <u>popular</u> sport.

♦ We loved his <u>dramatic</u> performance.

Have students make a word card for *nation.* Ask a volunteer to read the first sentence aloud. Then have students copy the sentence onto the back of the word card. Follow the same procedure for the remaining words. To assess students' ability to read each new word, listen as individual students read the sentences on the board aloud.

◉ **Reading and Writing Practice** Activity 122: Reading Story Words.

More Word Work

Have students complete **More Word Work** on Student Worktext page 151.

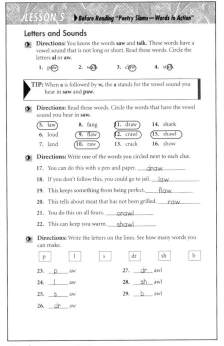

Student page 150

Student page 151

Reading "Poetry Slams—Words in Action"

◆ Preview and Predict

- ◆ Ask a volunteer to read aloud the title on Student Worktext page 152. Remind students that they have read a fiction story called "The Poetry Slam" and ask them to recall what a poetry slam is. If necessary, remind students that a poetry slam is a poetry contest in which poets read their poems and the audience judges them.
- ◆ Tell students that they will now read a nonfiction selection that tells about the history of poetry slams in this country. Then read aloud the questions under **Use What You Know** on Student Worktext page 152 and invite students to write answers in their Student Worktext.
- ◆ Finally, invite students to preview the selection by reading the first paragraph on page 152, and looking at the poem on page 153. Ask students what they would like to learn from the selection.

◆ Strategy Modeling

Reread/Read Ahead Ask students what they can do if they come to something that confuses them while they are reading. Remind students that they can often clear up their confusion by rereading to find a detail they might have missed. Explain that readers can also try reading ahead to see if what comes next clears up their confusion. Read the first paragraph on Student Worktext page 152 aloud. Then model the Reread/Read Ahead strategy:

I'm confused by the sentence "Performance poets from all over began to be drawn to the Green Mill's Uptown Poetry Slam." This is the first mention of Green Mill's Uptown Poetry Slam; I'm unsure of what that is. If I reread the whole paragraph, I understand that a new kind of poetry performance started at a Chicago club called the Green Mill. By reading ahead, I learn that a poetry slam is a kind of poetry competition. So, now I understand that the Uptown Poetry Slam was the name of the new poetry competition at the Green Mill.

Have students continue reading the selection to find out more about poetry slams. Remind them to try rereading or reading ahead to clear up any confusion.

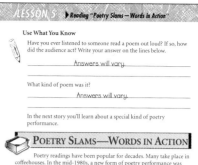

Student page 152

Student page 153

Focus on ESL/LEP

Explain and discuss the following terms used in the story:

- ◆ poetry readings
- ◆ club ("nightclub")
- ◆ to be drawn to
- ◆ sonnet
- ◆ hip-hop

After Reading "Poetry Slams—Words in Action"

Personal Response: What Do You Think?

Discuss with students the question under **What Do You Think?** on Student Worktext page 154. Invite them to write their answers on the lines provided.

Think About the Story: Reading Comprehension

Have students complete the remaining items on Student Worktext pages 154 and 155 independently or in pairs. Check their responses to help you assess their comprehension of the selection. If students' responses indicate that they did not understand the selection, reread it in small groups.

Reading Comprehension Skill: Summarize

Ask students what they know about summarizing a story. If necessary, remind them that to *summarize* a story means to retell the important events or ideas. Then ask students what they would do to summarize a nonfiction selection. Explain:

◆ A summary of a nonfiction selection is much shorter than the original selection.

◆ A summary includes the main ideas, facts, or events, not specific details.

◆ A summary does not include any of the reader's ideas or opinions.

Guide students in listing the main facts and events in "Poetry Slams—Words in Action," not including the poem. Then have small groups use the list to write a three- to five-paragraph summary of the selection. After they have finished writing, have groups read their summaries aloud.

👥 Application

In the Community Guide students to use the Internet, a local events calendar, or entertainment listings (such as those found in a newspaper) to find out about upcoming poetry readings in your area. You might also suggest that students call local bookstores to ask if they plan to host upcoming readings. If any poetry readings are to be held soon, encourage students to attend the reading that most appeals to them. You might have students submit a written report, or present an oral report, about any reading they attend.

Student page 154

Student page 155

Reinforce & Extend

◈ STUDY SKILL: Using Graphic Aids: Diagram, Map

Display a local map and a single diagram of how to assemble something. Hold them up as examples and ask students to share any experiences they have had using diagrams or maps. Explain:

- A *diagram* is a drawing or outline that shows how something works (like a car or the human body), how to do something (like put together a toy or a piece of furniture), or what the relationship is between different parts of something (like a family tree).
- A *map* is a drawing or chart of a place that helps people get to a specific location or find their way around.

Work with students to create a simple example of each kind of graphic aid, such as a fire drill evacuation diagram, and a map of how to get from school to a local landmark.

◉ **Reading and Writing Practice** Activity 123 provides additional practice using graphic aids.

◈ LANGUAGE: End Punctuation

Write these sentences on the board:

Poetry readings have been popular for decades.

Where was the first poetry slam held?

What a great poem!

Pull the next one up.

Invite volunteers to circle the end mark in each sentence. Then remind students that there are four kinds of sentences: a statement, a question, an exclamation, and a command. Use the examples on the board to explain the following:

- A statement tells something. It ends with a period.
- A question asks something. It ends with a question mark.
- An exclamation shows surprise or emotion. It ends with an exclamation point.
- A command tells someone what to do. It ends with a period or an exclamation point.

Have students suggest other examples of each kind of sentence. Write their suggestions on the board, omitting the end marks. Have volunteers add the proper end marks to the sentences.

◉ **Reading and Writing Practice** Activity 124 provides additional practice with end punctuation.

◈ WRITING: A Poem

Remind students that they read the poem "Pull the Next One Up" at the end of "Poetry Slams—Words in Action." Encourage students to discuss the poem. Explain that writers often play with language in poems, sometimes using rhyme, sound words, and words that "paint pictures." Invite students to point out ways the poet plays with language in "Pull the Next One Up." (Sample answers: use of language to create a picture; repetition of "Tied to the next man's/woman's waist," "Pull the next … up," and "Up, Up") Tell students that they will now have the opportunity to write their own poem.

Reading and Writing Practice Duplicate and distribute Activities 125–126, the Writing Models of two poems, and help students identify the special features that make up each poem. Then have individual students or pairs of students write their own poems in response to one of these prompts, or about a topic of their choosing:

- Write a poem describing a beautiful day in spring, summer, fall, or winter.
- Write a poem about your favorite wild creature.
- Write a poem about your best friend.

Lesson at a Glance

Preview: This lesson presents a story about a teenager named Bruce who is at first not interested in taking part in a civic theater performance. When the director asks the teenagers in the group to write and perform their own one-act play, Bruce finds himself assuming a leadership role, which comes as a surprise even to him.

Objectives
- to read a fiction selection
- to read words with initial /s/ spelled *ce*, *cy*, or *ci* and final /s/ spelled *ce*

- to categorize
- to follow directions
- to use commas correctly
- to write a personal narrative

Student Worktext Pages 156–161
Story Words
leave, earth, theater, director

Reading and Writing Practice Activities 127–132

Before Reading "Stage Struck"

Letters and Sounds

Initial /s/ Spelled *ce*, *cy*, or *ci*; Final /s/ Spelled *ce*; Phonogram *ace*

Remind students that they know the words *city* and *place*. Write these words on the board, along with the words *cent* and *cycle*. Read all four words aloud and have students repeat them. Underline the letters *ci*, *cy*, or *ce* in each word, and explain that the letter *c* usually stands for the /s/ sound when it is followed by *i*, *e*, or *y*. Then write *center*, *circle*, and *ice* on the board and guide students to read these words aloud.

Next, erase the *pl* in *place* to form *ace*. Have students read the new word. Then add *r* to the beginning to form *race* and have students read this word. Repeat the process by adding *b* to form *brace*. Point out to students that many words end in the letters *ace*, and that if they can read such words as *place* and *race*, they will be able to read other words with this pattern of letters. Then have students complete Student Worktext page 156.

Reading and Writing Practice Activity 127: Decoding Words with Initial /s/ Spelled *ce*, *cy*, or *ci*; Final /s/ Spelled *ce*.

Story Words

Read aloud these words: *leave, earth, theater, director*. Tell students that these words are important in the next story. Then write the words on the board and point to each one as you say it aloud a second time. Next, have students follow the ❑ *Read* ❑ *Say* ❑ *Write* sequence by completing **Story Words** on Student Worktext page 157. Have students add the words to their Word Bank at the back of the Student Worktext. To introduce the words in context, write these sentences on the board:

- Please <u>leave</u> the cat alone.
- We need to take care of the <u>earth</u>.
- I like going to the <u>theater</u>.
- The <u>director</u> tells the actors what to do.

Have students make a word card for *leave*. Ask a volunteer to read the first sentence aloud. Then have students copy the sentence onto the back of the word card. Follow the same procedure for the remaining words. To assess students' ability to read each new word, listen as individual students read the sentences on the board aloud.

Reading and Writing Practice Activity 128: Reading Story Words.

More Word Work

Have students work in pairs to complete **More Word Work** on Student Worktext page 157.

LESSON 6 ▶ *Before Reading "Stage Struck"*

Letters and Sounds

Directions: You know the word **city**. Which words below begin with the same consonant sound as **city**? Circle the words.
1. cycle   2. silly   3. cute   4. center

Directions: You know the word **place**. Which words below end with the same consonant sound as **place**?
5. flick   6. ice   7. pass   8. miss

TIPS: ▶ In words like **cat** and **cute**, c stands for the k sound.
▶ When c is followed by e, i, or y at the beginning of a word, it usually stands for the s sound in **city**.
▶ When c is followed by e at the end of a word, it usually has the s sound in **place**.

Directions: Read each word. Circle the words in which c stands for the s sound.
9. once   12. rich   15. cement   17. cell
10. civil   13. mock   16. produce   18. camel
11. canter   14. force

Directions: Write each word you circled in the chart where it belongs.

Starts with the s sound	Ends with the s sound
19. civil	22. once
20. cement	23. force
21. cell	24. produce

Directions: Write the letters on the lines. See how many words you can make.

n	r	pl	tw	f

25. r ace   28. n ice
26. pl ace   29. r ice
27. f ace   30. tw ice

Student page 156

Story Words

Directions: Read each word to yourself. Then say the word out loud. Write the word on the line. Check the box after each step.

31. leave   Read ☑ Say ☑ Write ☑ leave
32. earth   Read ☑ Say ☑ Write ☑ earth
33. theater (the|a|ter)   Read ☑ Say ☑ Write ☑ theater
34. director (di|rec|tor) Read ☑ Say ☑ Write ☑ director

More Word Work

You have learned how to divide words that have two consonants in the middle into syllables.
▶ You divide some words in between the two consonants.
   mag|net   win|ning
▶ You divide some words after the two consonants.
   with|er   wish|es
How do you divide a word that has just one consonant in the middle? Here's how.
   o|pen   des|ert

35. Does the first syllable in **open** have a long or short vowel sound? long
36. Does the first syllable in **desert** have a long or short vowel sound? short

TIPS: ▶ If the first syllable has a long vowel sound, divide the word after the vowel.
▶ If the first syllable has a short vowel sound, divide the word after the consonant.
▶ If you're not sure if the vowel sound is long or short, try both sounds. See which one forms a word you know.

Directions: Write each word. Draw a line in between the syllables.
37. pilot pi|lot   41. station sta|tion
38. comet com|et   42. never nev|er
39. city cit|y   43. paper pa|per
40. motor mo|tor   44. second sec|ond

Student page 157

Reading "Stage Struck"

◆ Preview and Predict

- Tell students that they are about to read a story about a teenager named Bruce. Bruce's mom wants him to take part in a summer theater workshop, but Bruce does not like the idea. Point out Bruce and his mom in the illustration on Student Worktext page 158. Then have a volunteer read the title of the story on the same page.
- Invite students to talk about any experiences they have had with theater. Ask students whether they would share Bruce's attitude toward theater if they were in Bruce's situation, and why or why not.
- Finally, ask students to predict whether they think Bruce will change his mind about the theater workshop.

◆ Strategy Modeling

Set a Purpose Tell students that people read different kinds of materials for different reasons. Explain:

- People usually read stories for fun.
- People read other kinds of materials, such as newspapers or magazines, to find out what is happening in the world.
- People read textbooks to learn facts about certain subjects.

Point out that setting a purpose before beginning to read a story can help readers get the most out of their reading. Model setting a purpose. You might say:

I know from my preview of the story that Bruce does not want to take part in the theater workshop. My purpose for reading the story is to see whether Bruce enjoys the theater workshop after all, and if so, what causes his attitude to change.

Have students read Student Worktext pages 158 and 159 to find out what happens when Bruce attends the theater workshop. Point out to students that they will pause at the top of page 159 to answer a question about the story before reading on; they can use this question to help them set a purpose for reading the rest of the selection.

Learning Styles

Auditory/Verbal Have students read the story aloud in small groups. Group members should take turns reading aloud each paragraph. At the end of each page, suggest that one group member orally summarize the events on that page.

Student page 158

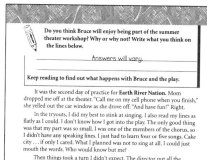

Student page 159

After Reading "Stage Struck"

Personal Response: What Do You Think?

Ask a volunteer to summarize the events in "Stage Struck." Then have students work in small groups to discuss and write answers to the questions under **What Do You Think?** on Student Worktext page 160.

Think About the Story: Reading Comprehension

Have students complete the remaining items on Student Worktext pages 160 and 161 independently or in pairs. Check their responses to help you assess their comprehension of the story. If students' responses indicate that they did not understand the story, reread it in small groups.

Critical Thinking Skill: Categorize

Write these terms from the story on the board: *theater, election, play, stage, council, performance, vice-president, director, act.* Ask students which words have to do with the theater. (theater, play, stage, performance, director, act) Put a check next to those words, write them in a separate list, and label it "theater words." Then put the remaining items in a list and ask students to suggest a title. (Possible response: student government) Point out that these lists show two categories, or groups, of words. Explain:

♦ *Categorizing,* or grouping similar things together, helps readers keep track of ideas.

♦ In order to put things into categories, think about what the items have in common.

Have students reread the last two paragraphs on Student Worktext page 158 and the first two paragraphs on page 159. Then have pairs do the following:

♦ Circle words for people in the last two paragraphs on page 158. (director, people, children, teenagers, grown-ups)

♦ Circle words in the first two paragraphs on page 159 that have to do with music. (singing, chorus, songs, sing)

♦ Add another related word to each category.

Help students write their two categories on the board. Once students have practiced identifying related ideas, have them think of two categories of their own and list several things that fit into each category. You can then collect all the lists from students and play a game in which you call out items in a list and teams try to name the category that the listed items belong to.

Application

Career Connection Have interested students find out about career opportunities in the theater. You might begin by brainstorming different jobs associated with the theater, such as actor, director, producer, stage hand, set designer, costume designer, and lighting and sound production.

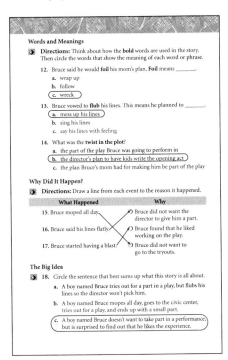

Student page 160

Student page 161

Reinforce & Extend

◆ STUDY SKILL: Following Directions

Tell students that following directions is an important skill. Discuss times when students may need to follow written directions, such as when taking a test, following a recipe, or putting something together. Then discuss these tips for following written directions:

- ◆ Read all the directions carefully.
- ◆ Gather any needed materials beforehand.
- ◆ Follow the steps in order.
- ◆ If you don't understand any part of the directions, ask for help.

Next, have pairs of students work together to write and then follow a simple set of directions. Each partner should write a set of numbered steps that can be carried out in the classroom, such as steps for folding a paper airplane, for finding an article in an encyclopedia, or for any other simple task. Then have partners exchange directions and follow each other's steps.

◉ **Reading and Writing Practice** Activity 129 provides additional practice following directions.

◆ LANGUAGE: Commas

Write these sentences on the board:

Children, teenagers, grown-ups, and even older people were in line to try out for the play.
The first performance was on Friday, December 8, 2000.

Call on volunteers to underline each type of person mentioned in the first sentence. Ask how many types of people are mentioned. (four) Then circle the commas in the first sentence. Explain that these are commas, and that one use for commas is to separate the items in a list. Then read the second sentence aloud and circle the commas. Explain that commas are also used when writing dates. Explain:

- ◆ If a sentence contains a list of three or more things, use a comma after each item in the list.
- ◆ Before the last item in the list, use a comma followed by the word *and*.
- ◆ Use commas to separate the day of the week from the month, and the date from the year.
- ◆ When reading a date aloud, pause when you come to a comma.

Write the following sentence on the board (commas are purposefully omitted):

The play had great costumes props and sound effects.

Ask volunteers to add commas to the sentence. Read the sentence aloud with students, noting how much easier it is to read with the commas in place. Next, write several dates on the board, omitting commas. Invite volunteers to add commas and read the dates aloud.

◉ **Reading and Writing Practice** Activity 130 provides additional practice with commas.

◆ WRITING: A Personal Narrative

Tell students that a *personal narrative* is a story about a real experience, told by the person who experienced it. Point out that if Bruce, the narrator in "Stage Struck," were a real person, "Stage Struck" would be a personal narrative. Explain:

- ◆ In a personal narrative, an author uses the words *I, me,* and *my*—the first person point of view.
- ◆ A personal narrative has a beginning, a middle, and an end.
- ◆ A personal narrative often includes an explanation of what the writer learned from the experience, or why the experience was important.

◉ **Reading and Writing Practice** Duplicate and distribute Activities 131–132, the Writing Model of a personal narrative, and identify its features. Then have students write their own personal narratives. They might write about an experience they have had in which they grew to like something they did not think they were going to like, or about an experience they have had with a theater performance, a civic group, or a community project.

Preview: This lesson presents a fiction story about two boys from a small Midwestern town who go to San Francisco to compete in the X Games. Though they are accomplished BMX stunt riders and big shots in their home town, the boys are stunned by the big city and grateful when a competitor takes them under his wing.

Objectives

- to read a fiction story
- to read words that contain the prefixes *un-* and *pre-*

- to learn test-taking strategies for multiple-choice tests
- to compare and contrast
- to practice using troublesome words
- to understand mood in literature

Student Worktext Pages 162–167

Story Words

bicycle, excitement, awesome

Reading and Writing Practice Activities 133–137

Before Reading "X Games!"

Letters and Sounds

Prefixes *un-* and *pre-*

Write the word *unhappy* on the board and circle *un*. Point out that the word *unhappy* has two parts, *un* and *happy*, and that *happy* is called the base word and *un* is a prefix. Explain that a prefix is a word part that can be added to the beginning of some base words to change their meaning. The prefix *un* means "not," so *unhappy* means "not happy." Write the words *unimportant, untried,* and *unsaid* on the board. Ask volunteers to read the words aloud and define them based on what they have learned about the prefix *un*.

Point out that the word *prefix* itself includes the prefix *pre*, meaning "before." Explain that *fix* can mean "to attach," so *prefix* means "to attach before." Write the words *preview, preread,* and *prejudge* on the board and ask volunteers to read the words aloud and define them. Point out that understanding the prefixes *un* and *pre* will help them read many other words that contain these prefixes. Then have students complete Student Worktext page 162.

Reading and Writing Practice Activity 133: Decoding Words with the Prefixes *un* and *pre*.

Story Words

Read aloud these words: *bicycle, excitement, awesome*. Tell students that these words are important in the next story. Then write the words on the board and point to each one as you say it aloud a second time. Next, have students follow the ❏ *Read* ❏ *Say* ❏ *Write* sequence by completing **Story Words** on Student Worktext page 163. Have students add the words to their Word Bank in the back of the Student Worktext. To introduce the words in context, write these sentences on the board:

- It is not safe to ride a <u>bicycle</u> in the street.
- The fans felt great <u>excitement</u> when their team won.
- The skater made an <u>awesome</u> flip.

Have students make a word card for *bicycle*. Ask a volunteer to read the first sentence aloud. Then have students copy the sentence onto the back of the word card. Follow the same procedure for the remaining words. To assess students' ability to read each new word, listen as individual students read the sentences on the board aloud.

Reading and Writing Practice Activity 134: Reading Story Words.

More Word Work

Have students complete **More Word Work** on Student Worktext page 163.

Reading and Writing Practice Activity 135: Reading and Writing Words with Prefixes or Endings.

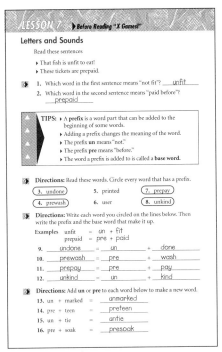

Student page 162

Student page 163

Reading "X Games!"

 Preview and Predict

- Have students read the title of the story on Student Worktext page 164.
- Engage students in a discussion of the X Games. If necessary, explain that the *X* in X Games stands for "extreme." Point out that the X Games include risky, exciting sports such as stunt bike riding, in-line skating, skateboarding, and other "extreme" sports, and that each year a competition is held in San Francisco, California, where some of the best and most daring athletes in the world perform.
- Tell students that they are going to read a story about two boys named Ryan and Colin who compete in the X Games in San Francisco.
- Have student pairs work together to answer the question under **Use What You Know** at the top of Student Worktext page 164.
- Once students have written their predictions about the things that Ryan and Colin might experience in the big city, have them read the first part of the story to see whether their predictions come true. Then have students answer the question at the top of page 165 before continuing.

Strategy Modeling

Clarify Remind students that experienced readers often need to stop to clarify points that confuse them before reading on. Have students read the first paragraph on Student Worktext page 164. Then model the Clarify strategy. You might say:

The fourth sentence says: "They were the winners of the day's doubles competition!" I'm a little confused by the idea of bicycle doubles, so I stop a minute to think about it. I know that there are doubles games in tennis in which two players play as a team. I guess bike doubles means that they do tricks at the same time, or maybe they do different tricks around each other, like pairs of skaters. Now I'll continue reading to see if that makes sense.

◼ Learning Styles

Body/Kinesthetic Display pictures of stunt cyclists or have a volunteer mime some of the stunts in front of the class. Elicit vocabulary students possess to describe the moves. Supplement their vocabulary as necessary with key words such as *twisting, double spin, sailing off ramps,* and so on.

Focus on ESL/LEP

For **More Word Work,** have students first draw a box around each prefix and suffix and then write the base word on the line.

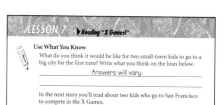

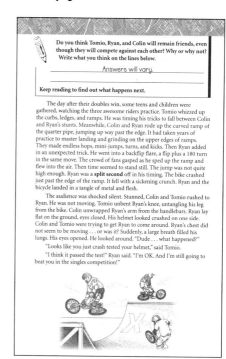

Student page 164

Student page 165

After Reading "X Games!"

Personal Response: What Do You Think?

Point out to students that bike helmets, like motorcycle helmets, must be replaced after even one crash. Then discuss the questions under **What Do You Think?** at the top of Student Worktext page 166 as a group. Encourage students to support their opinions with reasons. Then have individual students write their responses on the lines.

Think About the Story: Reading Comprehension

Ask students to complete the remaining items on Student Worktext pages 166 and 167 individually or in pairs.

Reading Comprehension Skill: Compare and Contrast

Remind students that thinking about how characters, events, or places in a story are alike and different can help them understand what they read. Explain:

- ◆ To compare two things is to tell how they are alike.
- ◆ To contrast two things is to tell how they are different.

Work with students to compare Ryan and Tomio. Record their responses in a chart:

Ryan	true for both	Tomio
◆ uncomfortable in the big city ◆ rides in doubles	◆ awesome stunt bike riders ◆ ride in singles competition	◆ used to the big city

Then have pairs of students create a similar chart that compares two sports they are familiar with, such as snow skiing and water skiing, basketball and hockey, or soccer and football.

👥 Application

In the Community Students may be interested in finding out where in their community they can get training and equipment to learn skateboarding, in-line skating, or stunt bike riding. They might also use resources such as the local newspaper or the Internet to find out about local competitions involving these sports.

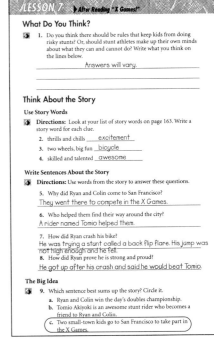

Student page 166

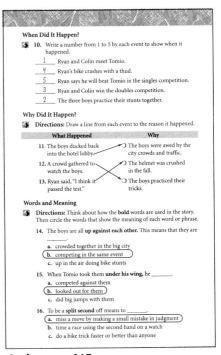

Student page 167

Reinforce & Extend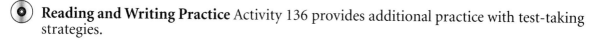

◆ STUDY SKILL: Test-Taking Strategies: Multiple-Choice Tests

Discuss with students the purposes for giving multiple-choice tests. Invite students to share their experiences taking multiple-choice tests. Point out that there are special skills involved in taking multiple-choice tests and that by learning these skills, they can do better on tests. Explain the following steps:

- ◆ Read the directions and make sure you understand them.
- ◆ Read each question carefully.
- ◆ Think about what you already know. Think about what the answer might be.
- ◆ Read each answer choice. Then choose the one that seems best.
- ◆ If there is enough time, go back and reread the questions and check your answer choices.

Model these strategies using the **Words and Meaning** exercises on Student Worktext page 167.

Reading and Writing Practice Activity 136 provides additional practice with test-taking strategies.

◆ LANGUAGE: Troublesome Words

Write the following sentences on the board and underline the problem words as indicated:

1. Ryan and Colin are over <u>there</u> by the ramp. <u>They're</u> going to ride <u>their</u> bikes.
2. <u>You're</u> going to hurt yourself if you don't wear <u>your</u> helmet.
3. <u>It's</u> important to wear a helmet. <u>Its</u> job is to protect your head.

Tell students that some words cause trouble for writers because they are easily confused. Read aloud the sentences by number 1. Ask volunteers to identify which of the underlined words is a contraction for "they are," which one names "at that place," and which one means "belonging to them." (*they're, there, their*) Write down each of these words and their definitions. Then read aloud sentence 2. Ask which word means "belonging to you" and which one means "you are." (*your, you're*) Again, write these words and their definitions on the board. Finally, read aloud sentence 3. Ask which word means "It is" and which means "belonging to it." (*it's, its*) Write the words and their definitions on the board.

Have pairs of students practice writing their own sentences using these words.

Reading and Writing Practice Activity 137 provides additional practice with troublesome words.

◆ LITERARY APPRECIATION: Mood

Ask students how they feel when they are in a good mood or a bad mood. (Possible responses: good mood—happy, positive, like laughing; bad mood—angry, sad, frustrated) Tell students that writers can create similar moods in stories through the words they use, the length of their sentences, and the things they choose to write about.

Read aloud the first paragraph on Student Worktext page 164. Ask volunteers for some words that the writer used that helped create a mood of excitement in this paragraph. (Possible responses: *deafening cheers, poetry on bikes, sailing off ramps, daredevil, death defying*) Then point out that in this paragraph the writer also used an exclamation: *They were the winners. . !*

Next, have students read the third-to-last paragraph on page 165 and ask students to describe the mood. (Possible response: tense, anxious, suspenseful) Have students discuss how the writer created this mood. (Possible responses: using words and phrases such as *shocked silent, stunned, rushed, His helmet looked crushed*; by not telling us right away if Ryan was okay; some short sentences like *He was not moving.*) Repeat this process using other passages from "X Games!" or other stories students have read.

Lesson at a Glance

Preview: This lesson presents a nonfiction selection that profiles several top Summer X Games stars and their most amazing feats.

Objectives
◆ to read a nonfiction story
◆ to read words that contain the suffixes -ly or -ful
◆ to change y to i when spelling words ending in -es or other suffixes
◆ to distinguish fact from opinion
◆ to write dates and addresses
◆ to identify and use similes

Student Worktext Pages 168–173

Story Words
feature, aggressive, vertical, medal

◉ **Reading and Writing Practice Activities 138–142**

Before Reading "X Games Stars"

Letters and Sounds

Suffixes -ly, -ful

Write this sentence frame on the board:

Moving slowly means moving in a way that is _____.

Ask a volunteer to complete the sentence, or supply the answer yourself. Write the word *slow* on the line. Then circle *slowly* and underline *in a way that is.* Point out that *slowly* is made up of two word parts, a base word plus the suffix *ly.* Explain that a suffix can be added to the end of a word to change the meaning of the word; the suffix *ly* usually means "in a way that is."

Next, introduce the suffix *ful* by writing these sentence frames on the board:

A careful person is full of _____. A joyful person is full of _____.

Ask volunteers to complete the sentences. Write in their responses. (care, joy) Point out that *ful* is a suffix that usually means "full of." Inform students that once they know the suffixes *ly* and *ful,* they can read many words that are formed with those suffixes. Then have students complete Student Worktext page 168.

◉ **Reading and Writing Practice** Activity 138: Reading Words with Suffixes -*ly* and -*ful.*

Story Words

Read aloud the words: *feature, aggressive, vertical, medal.* Tell students that these words are important in the next story. Then write the words on the board and point to each one as you say it aloud a second time. Next, have students follow the ❑ *Read* ❑ *Say* ❑ *Write* sequence by completing **Story Words** on Student Worktext page 169. Have students add the words to their Word Bank at the back of the Student Worktext. To introduce the words in context, write these sentences on the board:

◆ Action movies often <u>feature</u> car chases.

◆ You have to be <u>aggressive</u> to play football.

◆ A <u>vertical</u> jump is a jump made up into the air.

◆ The first place runner won a gold <u>medal</u>.

Have students make a word card for *feature.* Ask a volunteer to read the first sentence aloud. Then have students copy the sentence onto the back of the word card. Follow the same procedure for the remaining words. To assess students' ability to read each new word, listen as individual students read the sentences on the board aloud.

◉ **Reading and Writing Practice** Activity 139: Reading Story Words.

More Word Work

Have students complete **More Word Work** on Student Worktext page 169.

◉ **Reading and Writing Practice** Activity 140: Reading and Writing Words with -*ly* or -*ful.*

LESSON 8 ▶ Before Reading "X Games Stars"

Letters and Sounds

◉ **Directions:** Read these sentences.
▸ The old man turned around quickly.
▸ You should be careful with that tray!

◉ 1. Which word in the first sentence means "in a way that is quick"?
   quickly

2. Which word in the second sentence means "full of care"?
   careful

TIPS: ▸ A suffix is a word part that can be added to the end of a word.
▸ Adding a suffix changes the meaning of the word.
▸ The suffix ly means "in a way that is."
▸ The suffix ful means "full of."

◉ **Directions:** Read these words. Circle every word that has a suffix.
3. (slowly) 5. (joyful) 7. (shyly)
4. (powerful) 6. fly 8. cuddle

◉ **Directions:** Write each word you circled on the lines. Write the base word and the suffix that made it up.

Examples: kindly = kind + ly
          careful = care + ful

9. slowly = slow + ly
10. powerful = power + ful
11. joyful = joy + ful
12. shyly = shy + ly

◉ **Directions:** Add ly or ful to each word below. Write the new word on the line.
13. play + ful = playful
14. near + ly = nearly
15. cheer + ful = cheerful
16. dear + ly = dearly

Student page 168

Story Words

◉ **Directions:** Read each word to yourself. Then say the word out loud. Write the word on the line. Check the box after each step.

17. feature (fea | ture)   Read ✓ Say ✓ Write ✓ feature
18. aggressive   Read ✓ Say ✓ Write ✓ aggressive
    (ag | gres | sive)
19. vertical (ver | ti | cal)   Read ✓ Say ✓ Write ✓ vertical
20. medal (med | al)   Read ✓ Say ✓ Write ✓ medal

More Word Work

TIPS: ▸ Sometimes the base word changes when a suffix is added.
▸ When you add ful or ly to a word that ends in y, change the y to i. Then add the suffix.
   Examples: handy + ly = handily
            mercy + ful = merciful
▸ When you add ly to a word that ends in a consonant plus le, drop the e. Then add the ending.
   Example: gentle + ly = gently

◉ **Directions:** Add ly or ful to each word below.
21. dainty + ly = daintily
22. cheery + ly = cheerily
23. plenty + ful = plentiful
24. fancy + ful = fanciful

◉ **Directions:** Write a word with a suffix from the list above to finish each sentence.
25. The artist made fanciful drawings of flying pigs.
26. The queen stepped daintily over the puddle in her fancy heels.
27. The farmer smiled and waved cheerily as he went by.
28. Apples are plentiful in October.

Student page 169

Reading "X Games Stars"

◆ Preview and Predict

- ◆ Tell students they are going to read a true story about some daring young athletes who have made a national name for themselves by competing in the X Games. Invite volunteers to share what they already know about X Games stars such as Dave Mirra, Fabiola da Silva, Tony Hawk, or Andy Macdonald.
- ◆ Have students read the title on Student Worktext page 170. Then have them preview the subtitles and look at the photos.
- ◆ Ask students to predict which kinds of stars and events they will read about. List their responses on the board. Then have students read the story to see if their predictions come true.

◆ Strategy Modeling

Summarize Remind students that if they summarize, or sum up, key events and ideas while they read, they will understand more. If necessary, point out that to summarize means to tell the most important events or ideas in their own words. Have students read the first paragraph of Student Worktext page 170. Then model the Summarize strategy. You might say:

I don't have to remember everything I just read. I want to focus on the key points. This paragraph introduces the X Games, so I think it's important to say that the X Games have only been around since 1994 but they have fans all over the world. It is also important to note that there are X Games held in winter and summer, but I don't think I have to list all the events. That is too much detail. I should also say that this article tells about some stars of the Summer X Games.

Have pairs of students read the second paragraph on Student Worktext page 170. Pause and ask students to summarize the most important information. Then have students continue reading the selection on their own. Remind them to summarize each section before continuing.

Focus on LD

Have students read the story in a small group. After they finish each section, ask students to stop and cover up what they have read. Ask one or two students to orally summarize that section. If necessary, have students reread that section. Then continue reading and have other students take turns summarizing.

X GAMES STARS

The first national X Games were held in 1994. X is short for "extreme." Each year X Games champs thrill fans and TV audiences all over the earth. Events in the Summer X Games include aggressive in-line skating, bicycle stunt riding, freestyle motocross, skateboarding, skysurfing, sportclimbing, street luge, and wakeboarding. The Winter X Games feature snowboarding, ice climbing, snow mountain bike racing, free-skiing, and skiboarding. How are all these events alike? They are all dramatic displays of daring and skill. Here's the skinny on some top Summer X Games stars.

Bicycle Stunt Riding: Dave Mirra. Dave won his fifth gold medal in a row in BMX on the X Games skate park course in 2000. He has won the gold or silver every year since 1995 in the vertical, or "vert," ramp competition. He took first place in 1997–99. He was born in 1974 in Syracuse, New York. He has been competing since 1987. His nickname is "Miracle Boy," partly because of the crashes he has experienced. Many times doctors have told him he should have died, or that he would never ride again. His nickname also comes from the exciting tricks he pulls that no one else has done. Dave has won more X Games medals than any other athlete. He has won medals in every event in which he has competed. In 2000, tumbling like an asteroid in space, he made the world's first-ever double back flip in a contest in Raleigh, North Carolina!

Aggressive In-Line Skating: Yasutoko Brothers and Fabiola Da Silva

Eito and Takeshi Yasutoko. Japanese brothers Eito and Takeshi are nicknamed "Eight" and "Samurai." They were the first brother team in X Games history to take medals in the same event at the same time. This happened at the 2000 X Games in San Francisco. Takeshi, three years younger than Eito, is the youngest and smallest boy on the ramps.

Student page 170

Still, he sometimes wins against his brother in in-line vert contests. These two brothers are as fast as lightning on skates. They can make aggressive 900-degree flat spins and catching huge air look as easy as pie. Their father claims that Eito is a better skater because he can do tricks "switch." That is, he can lead with his left or his right foot.

Fabiola Da Silva. This 5'3", 108-pound star of women's aggressive in-line skating was born in 1979 in Sao Paulo, Brazil. She skates against both men and women in pro contests. She often aces both street and vertical ramp competitions. Nicknamed "Fabby," she now makes her home in California. Like other extreme skating stars, she is a legend in her own time.

Skateboarding: Tony Hawk and Andy Macdonald

Tony Hawk. Tony Hawk is one of the top examples of extreme skateboarding in the world. He has invented more than 80 tricks. Two great ones are the 720 and the stale fish. He has won five X Games gold medals in vertical and vertical doubles since 1995. At the 1999 X Games, he became the first and only person to land on the skateboard after spinning like a top. He made a full 900-degree turn in mid-air. That means he spun 2.5 times. This masterful trick took more than six years of practice. He also does stunt riding. He became an ESPN-TV announcer after retiring in 1999. Even so, he won the X Games doubles skateboarding competition in 2000 for the fourth year in a row, with co-star Andy Macdonald. He is also a husband and father.

Andy Macdonald. Andy was named the Overall World Cup Skateboarding Champion in 1999 at the end of the '99 X Games. He was also vert champion and second-place winner in street competition. He is always on the go, and he travels to all corners of the earth. He has done so well through the years that people think he can't lose. His nickname is "Mac" or "Andy Mac." He was born in Boston in 1973. He has been featured in every X Games since 1995, and remains stoked about his awesome wins. Andy is hopeful that the X Games will last. He wants young bicycle riders who are children now to grow up to compete in the sport.

Student page 171

After Reading "X Games Stars"

Personal Response: What Do You Think?

Ask several volunteers which X Games star they would most like to see and why. Then have students fill out their responses to the question under **What Do You Think?** on Student Worktext page 172.

Think About the Story: Reading Comprehension

Have students complete the remaining items on Student Worktext pages 172 and 173. Then have them check their responses in groups. Assign groups to report particular answers to the class. If reponses indicate that students had trouble understanding key information in the story, have groups reread the whole story or particular sections.

Reading Comprehension Skill: Distinguish Fact from Opinion

Write these sentences on the board:

Fabiola da Silva is 5' 3" tall.

Fabiola is fun to watch.

Ask students which sentence gives information that can be proven. (the first) Point out that the first sentence is a *fact*, while the second is an *opinion*, or something that someone believes but can't prove. Explain:

- ◆ A fact is a statement that can be proven true.
- ◆ An opinion is a statement of something someone believes or thinks. An opinion can't be proven.
- ◆ Being able to tell fact from opinion helps readers understand and evaluate what they read.

Say these statements aloud and ask students if each states a fact or an opinion.

- ◆ Tony Hawk is the most daring stunt rider in the world. (opinion)
- ◆ Andy Macdonald was born in Boston in 1973. (fact)
- ◆ Dave Mirra's nickname is "Miracle Boy." (fact)
- ◆ Eito Yasutoko makes skating look easy. (opinion)

Then have pairs of students write their own examples of facts and opinions about various athletes they know about.

Application

At Home Students may want to work with family members to create an inventory of sports equipment they have at home so that family members know what is available and where to find it. They might organize the inventory by sport.

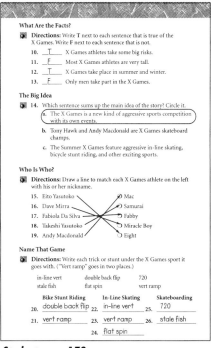

Student page 172

Student page 173

Reinforce & Extend

◆ SPELLING: Change *y* to *i* When Adding Endings

1. flies	**3.** skies	**5.** babies	**7.** cries	**9.** plentiful
2. happily	**4.** pennies	**6.** tries	**8.** driest	**10.** roomiest

Write *dry* on the board. Remind students that they have learned that when a word ends in *y*, they may need to change the *y* to an *i* before adding *es* or another ending. Then have students number a sheet of paper 1–10. Dictate the words above one at a time, pausing for students to write them. Next write the words on the board and have students check their work, making corrections as needed.

 Reading and Writing Practice Activity 141 provides additional practice changing *y* to *i* when adding endings.

◆ LANGUAGE: Writing Dates and Addresses

Ask volunteers what information they need to include when writing and sending a postcard. Point out that it's a good idea to include the date on the postcard so that the person receiving it knows when it was written. It's also important for the address to be easy to read so that it will arrive safely.

Draw an outline of a postcard on the board. Ask a volunteer for the current date. Write it on the board above where the message would be. Point out the use of capital letters, and the comma after the day of the month and before the year. Then write your own name and the address of the school in the address space. Point out the use of capital letters and the division of information into three lines.

Distribute postcards to the class (preferably ones with postage already included). Pair students up and have each student write down his or her partner's name and address on the postcard. Then have each student write the date at the top of the postcard, followed by a short note. Finally, have students mail the postcards and bring the ones they receive to class a few days later.

 Reading and Writing Practice Activity 142 provides additional practice writing dates and addresses.

◆ LITERARY APPRECIATION: Similes

Write these sentences on the board:

Dave Mirra tumbled like an asteroid in space.

The Yasutoko brothers are as fast as lightning

Circle Dave Mirra in the first sentence and ask volunteers what he is being compared to in the sentence. Underline *an asteroid in space.* Then ask students what the Yasutoko brothers are being compared to in the second sentence. (lightning) Point out that these two sentences are examples of similes. Explain:

- ◆ A simile compares two things that are very different.
- ◆ A simile helps readers form a mental picture of the thing being described.
- ◆ Similes use the words *like* or *as* to compare the two things.
- ◆ These are two ways that similes can be formed:

  _____ is like _____.

  _____ is as _____ as a _____.

Have students work in pairs to write similes about one of the following: a blazing red sunset; a perfect pass of a football; a dancer's graceful leap.

Lesson at a Glance

Preview: A new girl named Carlotta Twotrees arrives at a school in a small town. Tony is interested in Carlotta. He sends Mandy, his friend, to find out more about her. Mandy discovers that Carlotta's family lives in Buckman's Castle, a spooky old house at the edge of town. As they begin to investigate Carlotta, they stumble upon even more mysteries. Why is Carlotta so reluctant to talk about herself? Who does Carlotta talk to secretly on the phone? Who is the mysterious stranger who arrives at Buckman's Castle? Why are there coffins stacked in a nearby warehouse?

And what accounts for the screams and the strange lights that come out of the Buckman place at night? At last Mandy and Tony find out the big secret Carlotta has been hiding—her dad is directing a scary movie and using the house to shoot it in!

Objectives

- ◆ to complete a chapter book successfully
- ◆ to practice the word study and phonics skills learned in Chapter 3
- ◆ to practice reading the high-frequency and content words learned in Chapter 3
- ◆ to build reading fluency

Before Reading "The Riddle of Buckman's Castle"

Introduce the Small Book

Use Prior Knowledge Display a copy of the small book for Chapter 3, *The Riddle of Buckman's Castle,* and tell students that next they will have an opportunity to read a chapter book. Explain that the book uses only words and letter sounds they have learned in Chapter 3, and that they will be reading the chapter book for fun; they will not be expected to learn new words or skills. Explain:

- ◆ This mystery book is about two friends, Mandy and Tony, who are trying to discover the truth about a place called Buckman's Castle.

- ◆ A new girl named Carlotta has just moved into Buckman's Castle. She seems to hiding a big secret, and Tony and Mandy want to find out what it is.

Invite students to share simple descriptions of mystery stories they have read. Have them talk about how someone goes about figuring out a mystery.

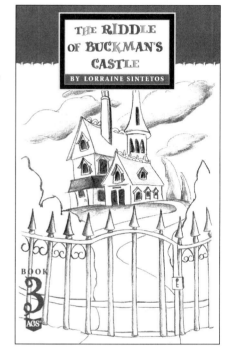

Preview and Predict

Distribute copies of *The Riddle of Buckman's Castle.* Read aloud the introduction on the back cover. Have students silently read the first four pages of the book. Guide them in making predictions about what might happen. Ask:

- ◆ Do you think Carlotta will like Tony?
- ◆ Do you think Carlotta will talk about herself to Mandy?
- ◆ Do you think Carlotta is hiding anything? If so, what?

Before students begin to read, you might discuss Sherlock Holmes. If necessary, tell students that he is a fictional detective created by a British writer named Arthur Conan Doyle, and that Sherlock Holmes is famous for solving tough mysteries.

Read Independently

Students who have successfully read and understood the stories in Chapter 3 should be able to read *The Riddle of Buckman's Castle* independently. You might periodically check their story comprehension by having them pause after completing each chapter to discuss the story. Discussion prompts for each chapter appear on the next two pages.

Read Strategically

Students who have struggled with the reading selections in Chapter 3, or who have been slow to master the phonics and word study skills presented in Chapter 3, may benefit from reading the book in groups of 3–5, pausing often to discuss events and to use reading strategies to clear up confusion. The following procedure will help ensure that all students have a successful and positive reading experience.

- Read the first three pages aloud as students follow along. Call on students to summarize the main events. Then have students read to the end of Chapter 1 silently.

- Model using a reading strategy so that students can see how the strategy helps readers clear up confusion. You might say: *At first I did not understand why Mandy was so surprised and uneasy when she learned that Carlotta lived in Buckman's Castle. When I read ahead, I learned that there are many creepy stories about that place.*

- Model setting a purpose for reading the next set of pages. (Example: *to find out more about Buckman's Castle*) Call on students to set their own purposes for reading. Have students read silently and pause at a designated stopping point. Each time you pause, call on students to explain how they used reading strategies as they read. Suggestions for specific questions you might ask appear on this page and the following page.

Reading "The Riddle of Buckman's Castle"

◆ Comprehension Questions

Chapter 1
- What is unusual about Carlotta?
- What are some of the stories about Buckman's Castle?
- How does Tony feel about Carlotta?
- Why do you think Carlotta interests Tony?

Chapter 2
- What does Tony tell Mandy about living near the Buckman place?
- Why does Tony want to switch their project to Buckman's Castle?
- What does Mrs. Denny tell Tony and Mandy about Buckman's Castle?
- What do you think Tony and Mandy will do next?

Read Strategically Ask students whether anything in Chapter 1 or 2 confused them, and if so, what they did to clear up their confusion. Call on several students to give an oral summary of the main events in Chapters 1 and 2. Ask students to predict what might happen as the story continues.

Chapter 3
- What has Juan Sanchez seen up at the Buckman house?
- Why does Tony think Carlotta needs a friend?
- Why do you think Carlotta does not want anyone to come into her house?

Chapter 4
- What strange things do Mandy and Tony see at the fair?
- Do you think it really was Carlotta who went into the tent? If so, what was she doing there?
- Do you think the old woman really is Carlotta? Why or why not?

Read Strategically Ask a volunteer to summarize the main events in Chapters 3 and 4. Call on another student to tell how he or she used the Reread/Read Ahead or the Clarify strategy to clear up confusion. Discuss students' predictions for the next part of the story, and help each student set a purpose for reading Chapters 5 and 6.

Chapter 5
- What is Tony's theory about Carlotta? What is Mandy's theory?
- What do Tony and Mandy overhear Carlotta talking about on the phone?
- What does Carlotta say about spare bodies?
- What do you think Carlotta was talking about?

Chapter 6
- What is the "errand" Tony has to run?
- What does Tony see inside the shed? How does he react?
- What do you think Tony will do next?

Chapter 7
- Who owns the Buckman place now?
- What does Mandy find out about the Buckmans? What does she find out about the Henrys?
- What do the cops tell Tony?
- What do you think Tony's next plan will be?

Read Strategically Ask each student to describe how he or she used one of these reading strategies: Use Prior Knowledge, Make a Prediction, Summarize, Clarify, Reread/Read Ahead, Use Context Clues. Then have students give an oral summary of Chapters 5, 6, and 7, predict what might happen next, and set a purpose for reading the rest of the book.

Chapter 8
- How does Mandy get Carlotta to let her inside the house?
- What are some of the strange things Mandy sees inside the Buckman place?
- What does Mandy find in Carlotta's closet? Why is this odd?
- What does Carlotta say when Mandy says she wishes they could hang out more often? Why do you think she says this?

Chapter 9
- How does Mandy feel about Carlotta after her visit?
- What does Tony want to do next?
- What do Carlotta and the stranger talk about? Who do you think the stranger is?
- Who do you think "Little Nicky" is?

Chapter 10
- Describe what Tony and Mandy see through the window.
- Who are the people in the house?
- How does Carlotta explain all the strange happenings? Who is her father?
- What actually happened to the Henrys?
- Were you surprised by the ending? Why or why not?

Read Strategically Have students summarize the main events in Chapters 8, 9, and 10. Then discuss with students whether their predictions about the mystery turned out to be correct. Encourage students to compare their predictions with actual story events.

After Reading "The Riddle of Buckman's Castle"

Personal Response

Ask students whether they liked *The Riddle of Buckman's Castle,* and why or why not. Invite several volunteers to tell what they liked about the story. If some students did not like it, encourage them to give specific reasons why.

Critical Response

Prompt students to think critically about the story by asking questions such as these:

- Which parts of the story seemed believable to you? Which parts seemed hard to believe?
- What do you think Tony and Mandy learned from their experience?
- Would you have predicted the ending? Why or why not?

Extension Activities

Students can work on the activities below independently, in pairs, or in small groups.

Reading

- Students who enjoyed this mystery story may want to search for other mystery books in the library. Tell students they can do a search by author using an electronic card catalog system. Some popular mystery authors include Ray Bradbury and Agatha Christie.
- Students can also do research on the Internet to find stories or information about old or historic houses in their communities.

Writing

- Students who are interested in creative writing can write their own short mystery story. Tell them to include clues that distract the reader.
- Students interested in ghost stories can collect stories from friends and family. Then they can create a collection of stories and write an introduction to their collection.

Research

Students might find answers to the following questions, using resources such as the Internet, the telephone book, or the classified section of a local newspaper:

- What are some historical or landmark homes in your town?
- How would you find information about the history of a home?
- Where could someone work if they were interested in a career in film?

Chapter 3 Review

The Chapter Review on Student Worktext pages 175–182 will help students review and practice the skills presented in Chapter 3. The review is divided into four parts, A–D.

Suggestions to help students complete the Chapter Review:

- Make sure students understand that the Chapter Review is not a test. You may have students work in pairs and then compare responses, or you may work through the review as a class.
- Read the instructions for each part aloud.
- Have students complete one part of the review at a time. Pause to go over the answers and have students mark corrections using a second color.

Chapter Test

Reproducible blackline masters of the Chapter 3 Test can be found on pages 152–155 of this book. Use the test to assess students' comprehension of the skills taught in the chapter.

Additional Practice

Reading and Writing Practice Activities 99–142 can be used to reinforce the skills taught in Chapter 3.

Level B Test

Reproducible blackline masters of the Level B Test can be found on pages 156–157 of this book. Use the test to assess students' comprehension of the skills taught in Level B.

Part A

Part A reviews the phonics skills taught in the chapter. Read aloud the summaries presented in the tip boxes before each exercise. Then have students complete the items. If students show difficulty understanding and using the new letters and sounds, review individual lessons or assign the corresponding Reading and Writing Practice Activities: 99, 105, 111, 117, 121, 127, 133, 138.

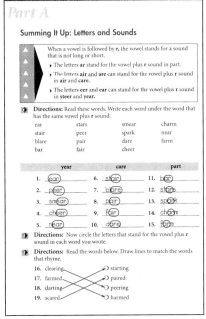

Student page 175

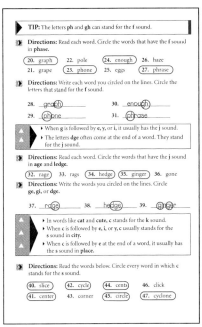

Student page 176

Part B

Part B reviews the word study and structural skills taught in the chapter. Read aloud the summaries presented in the tip boxes before each exercise. Then have students complete the items. You may want to review the skills by looking back at individual lessons, presenting new examples on the board, or assigning the corresponding Reading and Writing Practice Activities: 135, 140.

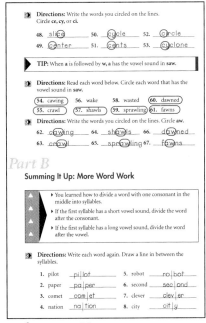

Student page 177

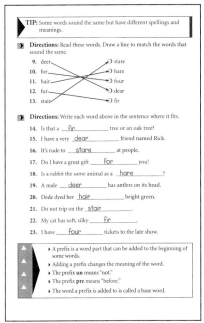

Student page 178

Part C

Part C reviews the story words and skills learned in the chapter. Students are asked to recognize story words and their meanings and to identify the number of syllables in story words. Have students review the story words in the Word Bank at the back of their Student Worktext or refer to the stories in the chapter to help them complete the review. For additional practice with word recognition, assign the corresponding Reading and Writing Practice Activities: 100, 106, 112, 118, 122, 128, 134, 139.

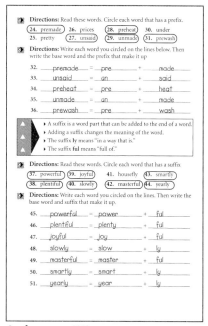

Directions: Read these words. Circle each word that has a prefix.

24. (premade) 26. prices 28. (preheat) 30. under
25. pretty 27. (unsaid) 29. (unmade) 31. (prewash)

Directions: Write each word you circled on the lines below. Then write the base word and the prefix that make it up

32. __premade__ = __pre__ + __made__
33. __unsaid__ = __un__ + __said__
34. __preheat__ = __pre__ + __heat__
35. __unmade__ = __un__ + __made__
36. __prewash__ = __pre__ + __wash__

> ▶ A suffix is a word part that can be added to the end of a word.
> ▶ Adding a suffix changes the meaning of the word.
> ▶ The suffix **ly** means "in a way that is."
> ▶ The suffix **ful** means "full of."

Directions: Read these words. Circle each word that has a suffix

37. (powerful) 39. (joyful) 41. housefly 43. (smartly)
38. (plentiful) 40. (slowly) 42. (masterful) 44. (yearly)

Directions: Write each word you circled on the lines. Then write the base word and suffix that make it up.

45. __powerful__ = __power__ + __ful__
46. __plentiful__ = __plenty__ + __ful__
47. __joyful__ = __joy__ + __ful__
48. __slowly__ = __slow__ + __ly__
49. __masterful__ = __master__ + __ful__
50. __smartly__ = __smart__ + __ly__
51. __yearly__ = __year__ + __ly__

Student page 179

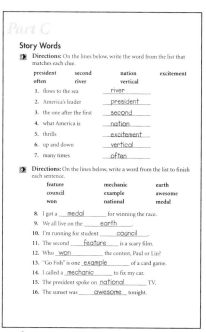

Part C

Story Words

Directions: On the lines below, write the word from the list that matches each clue.

| president | second | nation | excitement |
| often | river | vertical | |

1. flows to the sea — __river__
2. America's leader — __president__
3. the one after the first — __second__
4. what America is — __nation__
5. thrills — __excitement__
6. up and down — __vertical__
7. many times — __often__

Directions: On the lines below, write a word from the list to finish each sentence.

feature	mechanic	earth
council	example	awesome
won	national	medal

8. I got a __medal__ for winning the race.
9. We all live on the __earth__.
10. I'm running for student __council__.
11. The second __feature__ is a scary film.
12. Who __won__ the contest, Paul or Lin?
13. "Go Fish" is one __example__ of a card game.
14. I called a __mechanic__ to fix my car.
15. The president spoke on __national__ TV.
16. The sunset was __awesome__ tonight.

Student page 180

Directions: Read each word. On the lines below, write a number to tell how many syllables it has.

17. perform __2__   20. leave __1__
18. performance __3__   21. doubles __2__
19. popular __3__   22. aggressive __3__

Directions: On the lines below, write a word from the list to finish each sentence.

| election | bicycle | poetry | championship |
| student | errand | practice | director |

23. The __director__ of a play is like a boss.
24. A __bicycle__ is cheaper to own than a car.
25. Who will you vote for in the __election__?
26. Sean is a __student__ at Ben Franklin School.
27. I am reading my __poetry__ at the open mike performance.
28. Do I have to __practice__ playing my tuba?
29. The winner of the __championship__ gets a free trip to Texas!
30. I have one more __errand__ to do, and then I'll be home.

Directions: On the lines below, write a word from the list to finish each sentence.

| competition | semi-final | audience |
| dramatic | theater | |

31. We were in line outside the __theater__ before it opened, so we got great seats.
32. The __audience__ clapped loudly when Luke took the stage.
33. "Yell! Cry! Pound your fists! Be __dramatic__!" the director said.
34. The athlete who wins the __semi-final__ game will go on to the championship game.
35. The __competition__ was the strongest I had ever faced, and I barely won my race.

Student page 181

Part D

Part D reviews the content of the stories in the chapter. Students are asked to identify story characters, settings, and events, and to identify stories as fiction or nonfiction. If students are having difficulty remembering story details, have them reread the stories they have trouble recalling and work in pairs or as a class to complete Part D again.

Part D

Think About the Stories

Fiction or Nonfiction?

Directions: Write **fiction** next to the stories that were made up by the writer. Write **nonfiction** next to the stories that tell about real life.

1. "Twin Trouble" _fiction_
2. "Sisters First" _nonfiction_
3. "A Good Trade" _fiction_
4. "Stage Struck" _fiction_
5. "X Games Stars" _nonfiction_

Who Did What?

Directions: Answer each question with the name of a person from the stories in Chapter 3.

Vicki	Ramon	Bruce	Val
Venus	Steve	Serena	

6. Who are sisters in real life? _Venus_ and _Serena_
7. Who loves an old car that needs fixing all the time? _Ramon_
8. Who had been on student council for three years? _Val_
9. Who started poetry slams? _Steve_
10. Who was class clown? _Vicki_
11. Who didn't want to take part in a play? _Bruce_

Where Did It Happen?

Directions: Write each place name next to the story it goes with.

Wimbledon   a theater   San Francisco
Indian Hill Grade   the River Mill Coffeehouse

12. "Stage Struck" _a theater_
13. "A Good Trade" _Indian Hill Grade_
14. "Sisters First" _Wimbledon_
15. "The Poetry Slam" _the River Mill Coffeehouse_
16. "X Games Stars" _San Francisco_

Student page 182

◆ Reproducible Blackline Masters

◆ Individual Record Form
Level B

Name _____ Period _____ Date _____

Skill Level at Beginning _____

Student Worktext

Chapter 1	Before	During	After	
1 A Plan for Cash	_____/42	+ ✔ -	_____/17	**Chapter Review**
2 The Ad	_____/64	+ ✔ -	_____/15	_____ out of 142
3 Dog Trouble	_____/43	+ ✔ -	_____/18	**Chapter Test**
4 How to…Want Ad	_____/53	+ ✔ -	_____/19	_____ out of 50
5 Video Game 1	_____/57	+ ✔ -	_____/18	Small Book *Lost in the Mountains*
6 Video Game 2	_____/52	+ ✔ -	_____/16	
7 Teen Net Bosses	_____/53	+ ✔ -	_____/16	+ ✔ -
8 Young Inventors	_____/63	+ ✔ -	_____/22	

Chapter 2	Before	During	After	
1 Driver's License 1	_____/41	+ ✔ -	_____/20	**Chapter Review**
2 Driver's License 2	_____/52	+ ✔ -	_____/22	_____ out of 126
3 Getting on the Road	_____/27	+ ✔ -	_____/15	**Chapter Test**
4 Car Wash 1	_____/30	+ ✔ -	_____/17	_____ out of 50
5 Car Wash 2	_____/46	+ ✔ -	_____/14	Small Book *Catch a Wave*
6 Video Dreams	_____/37	+ ✔ -	_____/16	
7 Rain Dance	_____/28	+ ✔ -	_____/14	+ ✔ -
8 Fashion Time Line	_____/38	+ ✔ -	_____/26	

Chapter 3	Before	During	After	
1 Twin Trouble	_____/35	+ ✔ -	_____/22	**Chapter Review**
2 Sisters First	_____/43	+ ✔ -	_____/17	_____ out of 169
3 A Good Trade	_____/40	+ ✔ -	_____/18	**Chapter Test**
4 Poetry Slam	_____/31	+ ✔ -	_____/17	_____ out of 50
5 …Words in Action	_____/45	+ ✔ -	_____/17	Small Book *The Riddle of Buckman's Castle*
6 Stage Struck	_____/44	+ ✔ -	_____/18	+ ✔ -
7 X Games!	_____/34	+ ✔ -	_____/16	**Level B Test**
8 X Games Stars	_____/28	+ ✔ -	_____/26	_____ out of 20

Reading Skills for Life–B

◆ Individual Record Form
Level B

Name _____ Period _____ Date _____

Skill Level at Beginning _____

Reading and Writing Practice

Chapter 1	Phonics	Story Words	Word Work	Spelling	Study Skills	Lang. Arts	Writing
1 A Plan for Cash							
2 The Ad							+ ✔ -
3 Dog Trouble							
4 How to…Want Ad							+ ✔ -
5 Video Game 1							+ ✔ -
6 Video Game 2							+ ✔ -
7 Teen Net Bosses							
8 Young Inventors							+ ✔ -

Chapter 2	Phonics	Story Words	Word Work	Spelling	Study Skills	Lang. Arts	Writing
1 Driver's License 1							+ ✔ -
2 Driver's License 2							+ ✔ -
3 Getting on the Road							+ ✔ -
4 Car Wash 1							+ ✔ -
5 Car Wash 2							
6 Video Dreams							+ ✔ -
7 Rain Dance							
8 Fashion Time Line							+ ✔ -

Chapter 3	Phonics	Story Words	Word Work	Spelling	Study Skills	Lang. Arts	Writing
1 Twin Trouble							+ ✔ -
2 Sisters First							+ ✔ -
3 A Good Trade							+ ✔ -
4 Poetry Slam							
5 …Words in Action							+ ✔ -
6 Stage Struck							+ ✔ -
7 X Games!							
8 X Games Stars							

Reading Skills for Life–B

◆ Class Record Form
Reading Skills for Life

Chapter _____ Level _____

Student	Story	Before	During	After	Before	During	After	Before	During	After	Before	During	After	Before	During	After	Before	During	After	Before	During	After	Before	During	After	Chapter Review	Chapter Test
1																											
2																											
3																											
4																											
5																											
6																											
7																											
8																											
9																											
10																											
11																											
12																											
13																											
14																											
15																											
16																											
17																											
18																											
19																											
20																											

Chapter I Test

Letters and Sounds

◆ Read these words. Write each word in the list where it belongs.

head	mine	tune
joke	pane	clean
stuck	stack	still

short vowel sound	long vowel sound
1. _____	5. _____
2. _____	6. _____
3. _____	7. _____
4. _____	8. _____
	9. _____

◆ Read these words. Write each word in the list where it belongs.

float	stay	pie	blow
true	light	brain	flew

long *a* sound	long *i* sound	long *o* sound	long *u* sound
10. _____	12. _____	14. _____	16. _____
11. _____	13. _____	15. _____	17. _____

◆ Read these words. Then write each word where it belongs.

steam	stem	like

CVC	CVC*e*	CVVC
18. _____	19. _____	20. _____

Reading Skills for Life–B

Word Work

◆ Write each sentence again. Use **'s** to show that something belongs to a person, place, or thing.

1. The cake Pat made is great.

   _____

2. The dog Tim has is mean.

   _____

3. The clock Rich got does not work.

   _____

◆ Write each word again. Draw a line to split the word into syllables.

4. sentence _____   7. boring _____

5. witness _____   8. porter _____

6. patches _____

◆ Add **ed** to each word. Write the new word in the sentence.

9. fake   I _____ a pass.   10. trim   I _____ the grass.

Story Words

◆ Write each word next to its meaning.

mountain	video	computer	opportunity	company
paper	trouble	family	develop	invention

1. something new _____   6. mom, dad, kids _____

2. moving pictures _____   7. a chance to do something _____

3. big hill _____   8. a place to work _____

4. what you write on _____   9. gets you onto the Internet _____

5. bad news _____   10. means "work to make happen" _____

Read and Think

◆ This is part of "Dog Trouble," a story you read in Chapter 1. Read the passage. Then answer the questions.

Rick puts his ad up all over. He puts four ads up on four light poles. He tacks one up at the pet shop. He also slips one under Mr. Green's door. "That should be enough," he thinks. "Ads always work. Soon the phone will start to ring."

The ad works. Mr. Green does call! "Can you watch Beanie two days after school?" he asks. "I will do more than watch him," Rick thinks. "I will make him walk all that fat off." But he does not tell Mr. Green that.

"I can pick Beanie up at three," Rick says. His plan is to first get Beanie, and then pick up Rabbit. He will walk the dogs in Glade Park together. What a snap!

Beanie is a big and clumsy dog. But he is fast! Rick learns this the hard way. It is his first day walking the dogs together. Things start out OK, but Rabbit keeps nipping Beanie. Beanie is big enough to eat Rabbit in one bite. Lucky for Rick, Beanie does not do it. Then Beanie sees a cat. In a flash, he is off and running. The leash just snaps out of Rick's hand. Then Rabbit tugs on her leash, hard. She slips free, too.

"Rabbit, NO! Beanie, COME!" Rick yells again and again. But it is no use. The dogs race off together. Soon Rick does not see them at all. "What now?" Rick thinks. "It is all over for me. I am dead."

Write Sentences About the Story

◆ Use words from the story to answer these questions.

    1. How does Rick get a job walking Beanie?

    _____

    _____

    _____

    2. What bad thing happens at Glade Park?

    _____

    _____

    _____

When Did It Happen?

◆ **3.-7.** Write a from 1–5 number next to each sentence to show the order of events.

_____ Mr. Green calls Rick.

_____ Rabbit nips Beanie.

_____ Beanie and Rabbit run off.

_____ Rick takes the two dogs to Glade Park.

_____ Rick puts up his ads.

Why Did It Happen?

◆ Draw a line from each event to the reason it happened.

8. Rick thinks, "I am dead."   ◯ He spots a cat.

9. Beanie runs off.   ◯ He has lost the dogs.

10. Mr. Green calls Rick.   ◯ He saw Rick's ad.

Chapter 2 Test

Letters and Sounds

◆ Read these words. Write each word in the list where it belongs.

chore   wrap   chemist

chord   chapter   wreath

begins with the *r* sound	begins with the *k* sound	begins with the *ch* sound
1. _____	3. _____	5. _____
2. _____	4. _____	6. _____

◆ Read these words. Write each word under the word that has the same vowel plus **r** sound.

pour   stir   bored

turn   store   herd

four	fir
7. _____	10. _____
8. _____	11. _____
9. _____	12. _____

◆ Circle each word that has the vowel sound you hear in **join** or **pound.**

blow   spoil   spool

loop   stir   low

enjoy   count   clown

◆ Write the words you circled on the lines. Circle the letters that stand for the vowel sound.

vowel sound in *join*	vowel sound in *pound*
13. _____	15. _____
14. _____	16. _____

◆ Write each pair of words as a contraction.

17. have not   _____   19. you will   _____

18. they are   _____   20. I am   _____

Reading Skills for Life–B

Chapter 2 Test, page 2

Word Work

◆ Write each word again. Draw a line to split the word into syllables.

1. indent _____   4. slinky _____

2. partly _____   5. sashes _____

3. brittle _____   6. unless _____

◆ Add **er** or **est** to each word below to finish the sentence.

7. thin   This pen is _____ than that one.

8. lonely   That is the _____ road I know.

◆ Add **ly** to each word below. Write the new word on the line.

9. swift _____

10. lucky _____

Story Words

◆ Write each word next to its meaning.

| designer | signal | story | decade | above |
| license | station | children | country | behind |

1. a traffic light _____

2. what you need to drive a car _____

3. where a train stops _____

4. on top of _____

5. means "kids" _____

6. one who works in fashion _____

7. ten years _____

8. a tale told with words _____

9. open land _____

10. in back of _____

Read and Think

◆ This is part of "Video Dreams," a story you read in Chapter 2. Read the passage. Then answer the questions.

Tina Zappetini kicked open her locker and threw her books into it. "I can't wait to get out of this school," she said. "Boy, I feel like quitting right now! School's hard. And that math stuff makes no sense at all! What's the point? What's so important about math anyway?"

Tina found school harder and harder to stomach. Math was her biggest struggle. What she loved was making music videos. Many nights she stayed up late messing around with her video cam. She could edit the film on her computer to get just the effects she wanted. She would play a sound track over and over. She would edit the pictures until they fit the music just right. Her style was to put in a little bit of chaos. Her videos had an edge. "Just like me," Tina said to herself as she slammed her locker shut.

After school, Tina escaped to her car. She drove to the gas station, filled up, and checked the oil. She picked out and paid for two of the latest music magazines. Then she drove to the coin car wash. She turned off the motor and dropped coins in the slot. She squeezed the trigger on the sprayer. Tina eyed the spraying streams of water. It gave her an idea . . .

At home Tina hung her backpack full of books on her bed. She flopped down and flipped through both new magazines. She got out her sketch pad. Streams of spraying water danced through her brain. She wanted to make a video that had jets of water spraying through it. Lost in thought and sketching madly, she forgot about her math homework. Like many nights, the books might just stay in the backpack.

Write Sentences About the Story

◆ Use words from the story to answer these questions.

1. How does Tina feel about school? Why?

_____

_____

2. What is one thing Tina does feel good about? How do you know?

_____

_____

When Did It Happen?

◆ **3.–6.** Write a number from 1–4 next to each sentence to show the order of events.

_____ Tina escapes to her car.

_____ Tina gets an idea for a music video.

_____ Tina sprays her car with water.

_____ Tina sketches her ideas.

What Can You Tell?

◆ Write a **T** next to the sentences that tell about Tina. Write an **F** next to the sentences that do not describe her.

7. _____ She thinks for herself.

8. _____ She thinks math is important.

9. _____ She has a good sense of art.

10. _____ She is at the top of her class at school.

Chapter 3 Test

Letters and Sounds

◆ Read these words. Write each word under the word that has the same vowel plus **r** sound.

stare   clear   cared

mart   part   peer

steer	hair	far
1. _____	3. _____	5. _____
2. _____	4. _____	6. _____

◆ Read these words. Write each word under the word that has the same beginning or ending sound.

ginger   cement   phone   enough

ledge   place   huge   gym

                  graph

begins like *gem*	begins like *city*	begins like *fake*
7. _____	9. _____	10. _____
8. _____		

ends like *age*	ends like *mice*	ends like *fluff*
11. _____	13. _____	14. _____
12. _____		15. _____

◆ Write each word next to the word it rhymes with.

your   lawn   stock

clear   mall

16. shawl   _____

17. talk   _____

18. fawn   _____

19. peer   _____

20. for   _____

Reading Skills for Life–B

Chapter 3 Test, page 2

Word Work

◆ Write each word again. Draw a line to split the word into syllables.

1. pilot _____ **4.** city _____

2. robot _____ **5.** comet _____

3. paper _____

◆ Write a word from the list to finish each sentence.

deer   fir   hair   dear   fur   hare

6. My dad has red _____.

7. A cat has soft _____.

8. My mom calls me _____ sometimes.

9. Is that a _____ tree or a pine?

10. A baby _____ is called a fawn.

11. A _____ is a kind of rabbit.

◆ Read these words. Circle each one that has a prefix or a suffix added to it.

housefly   prepaid   premade   yearly   pretty   joyful

◆ Use the words you circled to finish these sentences.

12. I felt _____ when my team won.

13. Our family picnic is a _____ event.

14. We _____ lunch and stored it in the cooler.

15. Juan _____ for the tickets.

Story Words

◆ Write each word next to its meaning.

mechanic   example   earth   popular   practice

1. do something until you get good at it   _____

2. the planet we live on   _____

3. word for something lots of people like   _____

4. one who fixes cars   _____

5. one thing that shows what others of its kind are like _____

Reading Skills for Life–B

◆ Write each word next to its meaning.

audience   election   medal   performance   student

6. something you might get for winning a race   _____

7. people who see a show   _____

8. kid in school   _____

9. a contest in which people vote   _____

10. what you could call a song and dance act   _____

Read and Think

◆   This part of "Stage Struck," a story you read in Chapter 3. Read the passage. Then answer the questions on the next page.

It was the second day of practice for Earth River Nation. Mom dropped me off at the theater. "Call me on my cell phone when you finish," she yelled out the car window as she drove off. "And have fun!" Right.

In tryouts, I did my best to stink at singing. I also read my lines as flatly as I could. I don't know how I got into the play. The only good thing was that my part was so small. I was one of the members of the chorus, so I didn't have any speaking lines. I just had to learn four or five songs. Cake city. . . if only I cared. What I planned was not to sing at all. I could just mouth the words. Who would know but me?

Then things took a turn I didn't expect. The director put all the teenagers in charge of writing and producing a one-act play. The idea was for the kids to write, direct, and perform this play as an opening act. This twist in the plot could wreck all my plans!

I was left with seven other kids my age. At first we just sat and looked at each other. I think we were all kind of stunned. After a few seconds of silence, something sort of snapped inside me. I must have gone insane. Suddenly, I started talking to the others. I was joking around and getting everyone's name. Even more awful, I started to take charge. I had ideas for how it all needed to go. I got everyone started on brainstorming ideas for the plot of the play.

By the end of the afternoon, we had the beginning written. It was going to be funny! We had lots of ideas for comic props and costumes. I ended up being cast as one of the main parts. And I was having a blast. How was I ever going to keep it from my mom that I was having fun?

Write Sentences About the Story

◆ Use words from the story to answer these questions.

1. Did Bruce want to be in the play at first? How do you know?

_____

_____

_____

2. What changed Bruce's feelings about being in the play?

_____

_____

_____

When Did It Happen?

◆ **3.–7.** Write a number form 1–5 next to each sentence to show the order of events.

_____ The director puts the teenagers in charge of a play.

_____ Bruce's mom drops him off at the theater.

_____ Bruce starts to joke around and get people's names.

_____ Bruce starts to have a blast.

_____ The kids just stared at each other.

Why Did It Happen?

◆ Draw a line from each event to the reason it happened.

8. Bruce tries to stink at singing.   ○ Bruce starts talking to the other kids.

9. Bruce says he will mouth the words.   ○ Bruce doesn't want to be part of the play.

10. Bruce says he must have been insane.   ○ Bruce has gotten a part in the chorus.

Reading Skills for Life–B

◆ Read this story. Then answer the questions.

Have you ever dreamed of being an artist? There are many kinds of jobs that have to do with the arts. If you like to write, for example, you could write stories or **plays**. You could write for magazines. You could write poetry, or you could write for a newspaper. Do you like the theater? There are lots of jobs both on the stage and behind the stage. **Stage hands** help out with props. Lighting designers have a different kind of job, but it's important, too. Directors must keep the whole show running — that's a big job. Performers are the ones the audience sees. But they are only part of the crew that makes a show happen.

Maybe you like fashion design or painting. Or, maybe producing music videos is the right job for you. Do you like music? Maybe you could play in a **band**, or write songs. If you like art, go for it!

1. What is this story mostly about? Circle the sentence that best sums up the main idea.
   a. A lighting designer has an important job.
   b. If you like writing, you could write poetry, plays, stories, or news features.
   c. There are many different kinds of jobs in the arts.

2. Why do you think the writer of this story wrote it?

   _____

   _____

   _____

3.–4. Which two of these statements do you think the writer would agree with? Circle them.
   a. Not many people can make a living in the arts.
   b. There are many paths in life to choose from.
   c. Follow your dreams.

◆ Think about how the **bold** words are used in the story. Then circle the answer that shows the meaning of each word or phrase.

5. In this story, a **play** is _____.
   a. a show on stage
   b. a set of moves in a ball game
   c. a game kids take part in

6. In this story, a **band** is _____.
   a. a rubber band
   b. a music group
   c. a tag on a bird's leg

7. **Stage hands** are _____.
   a. stages with hands painted on them
   b. hands joined together on a stage
   c. people who help out with props

◆ Read these words. Write the parts that make up each word.

8. spaceship _____ + _____

9. prepaid _____ + _____

10. unsafe _____ + _____

11. isn't _____ + _____

12. happily _____ + _____

13. sailboat _____ + _____

14. they're _____ + _____

◆ Find three pairs of rhyming words. Write the words on the lines.

    cheer   stirring   chowder
    powder   during   smear

15. _____ and 16. _____

17. _____ and 18. _____

19. _____ and 20. _____

◆ Test Answer Key

◆ Chapter 1 Test

Letters and Sounds

1. head
2. stuck
3. stack
4. still
   (in any order)

5. joke
6. mine
7. pane
8. tune
9. clean
   (In any order)

10. stay
11. brain
    (in any order)
12. light
13. pie
    (in any order)
18. stem
19. like
20. steam

14. float
15. blow
    (in any order)
16. true
17. flew
    (in any order)

Word Work

1. Pat's cake is great
2. Tim's dog is mean.
3. Rich's clock does not work.
4. sen|tence
5. wit|ness
6. patch|es
7. bor|ing

8. por|ter
9. faked
10. trimmed

Story Words

1. invention
2. video
3. mountain
4. paper
5. trouble

6. family
7. opportunity
8. company
9. computer
10. develop

Read and Think

1. Answers will vary. Sample answer: He puts his ad under Mr. Green's door and Mr. Green calls him.
2. Answers will vary. Sample answer: Beanie and Rabbit get free and run from Rick.
3.–7. Correct order: 2, 4, 5, 3, 1

Lines should connect to these phrases:

8. He has lost the dogs.
9. He spots a cat.
10. He saw Rick's ad.

◆ Chapter 2 Test

Letters and Sounds

1. wrap
2. wreath
   (in any order)
3. chord
4. chemist
   (in any order)
5. chore
6. chapter
   (in any order)

7. pour
8. bored
9. store
   (in any order)
10. turn
11. stir
12. herd
    (in any order)

These words should be circled: enjoy, spoil, count, clown

13. enjoy (oy should be circled)
14. spoil (oi should be circled)
    (in any order)
15. count (ou should be circled)
16. clown (ow should be circled)
    (in any order)
17. haven't
18. they're
19. you'll
20. I'm

Word Work

1. in|dent
2. part|ly
3. brit|tle
4. slink|y
5. sash|es
6. un|less
7. thinner
8. loneliest
9. swiftly
10. luckily

Story Words

11. signal
12. license
13. station
14. above
15. children
16. designer
17. decade
18. story
19. country
20. behind

Read and Think

1. Answers will vary. Sample answer: Tina does not like school. She says she feels like quitting. She doesn't think school is important.

2. Answers will vary. Sample answer: Tina loves making music videos. She stays up late making videos and using her computer to edit them.

3.–6. Correct order: 1, 3, 2, 4

7. T
8. F
9. T
10. F

◆ Chapter 3 Test

Letters and Sounds

1. clear
2. peer
   (in any order)
3. stare
4. cared
   (in any order)
5. mart
6. part
   (in any order)
7. ginger
8. gym
   (in any order)
9. cement
10. phone
11. ledge
12. huge
    (in any order)
14. graph
15. enough
    (in any order)
13. place
16. mall
17. stock
18. lawn
19. clear
20. your

Word Work

1. pi|lot
2. ro|bot
3. pa|per
4. cit|y
5. com|et
6. hair
7. fur
8. dear
9. fir
10. deer
11. hare

These words should be circled: yearly, prepaid, premade, joyful

12. joyful
13. yearly
14. premade
15. prepaid

Story Words

1. practice
2. earth
3. popular
4. mechanic
5. example
6. medal
7. audience
8. student
9. election
10. performance

Read and Think

1. Answers will vary. Sample answer: No. He tried to stink at singing and he read his lines flatly.

2. Answers will vary. Sample answer: He stared talking to the other kids his age and had fun working on the one-act play.

3.–7. Correct order: 2, 1, 4, 5, 3

Lines should connect to these phrases:

8. Bruce doesn't want to be part of the play.

9. Bruce has gotten a part in the chorus.

10. Bruce starts talking to the other kids.

◆ Level B Test

1. **c.** There are many different kinds of jobs in the arts. (circled)

2. Answers will vary. Sample answer: The writer wrote it to tell about jobs in the arts and to get people to think about getting a job in the arts.

3.–4. **b.** There are many paths in life to choose from. (circled)

   c. Follow your dreams. (circled)

5. **a.** a show on stage (circled)

6. **b.** a music group (circled)

7. **c.** people who help out with props (circled)

8. space + ship

9. pre + paid

10. un + safe

11. is + not

12. happy + ly

13. sail + boat

14. they + are

15. cheer   and   16. smear

17. powder and   18. chowder

19. during and   20. stirring

(Order of answers may vary.)